THE BOOK OF

Curious and Entertaining Information

THE BOOK OF

Curious and Entertaining Information

The Laṭā'if al-ma'ārif of Tha'ālibī

Translated with introduction and notes by

C. E. BOSWORTH

THE UNIVERSITY PRESS

EDINBURGH

EDINBURGH UNIVERSITY PRESS
22 George Square, Edinburgh 8
North America
Aldine Publishing Company
320 West Adams Street, Chicago
Australia and New Zealand
Hodder & Stoughton Limited
Africa, Oxford University Press
India, P. C. Manaktala & Sons
Far East, M. Graham Brash & Son
85224 012 0

L

ISBN
0852240120

Printed in Great Britain by
Robert Cunningham & Sons Limited, Alva

Preface.

The *Laṭā'if al-ma'ārif* was one of the first of Tha'ālibī's many works to appear complete in print, either in Europe or in the Orient (the *adab* work *Mu'nis al-waḥīd fi'l-muḥāḍarāt*, of which a text and German translation by G. Flügel appeared at Vienna in 1829, is not, as Flügel believed, by Tha'ālibī at all, but is part of the *Muḥāḍarāt al-udabā'* of ar-Rāghib al-Iṣfahānī, d. 502/1108). Excerpts from Tha'ālibī's works had earlier appeared in anthologies, but, in 1844, the Dutch scholar J. P. Valeton produced at Leiden an edition and Latin translation of Tha'ālibī's collection of striking passages from and aphorisms of well-known leaders and writers, the *Aḥāsin kalim an-nabī wa'ṣ-ṣaḥāba . . .* (see below, p. 16) under the title of *Specimen e litteris orientalibus exhibens Thaálibi syntagma.* Prints of Tha'ālibī's works began to appear from oriental presses, and then in 1867 another Dutchman, Paul de Jong, who was in charge of the Warnerian collection of oriental manuscripts at Leiden, produced his edition *Latá'ifo 'l-ma'árif auctore . . . at-Tha'álibí.*

De Jong used two manuscripts for this, an inferior Leiden one and a much better Gotha one, and for the completion of his critical text, had further recourse to manuscripts of two more of Tha'ālibī's works, the *Thimār al-qulūb* and the *Yatīmat ad-dahr* (see below, pp. 8-10). Like many Islamic authors, Tha'ālibī incorporated in his compositions passages from his other works, and in the *Laṭā'if* occur many items of information to be found in the *Thimār al-qulūb* (see below, pp. 8-9) and many verses also given in the *Yatīmat ad-dahr.* De Jong placed before his text a Latin *Praefatio* and a thirty-two page *Glossarium* of those words and terms occurring in the text which were lacking in Freytag's *Lexicon Arabicum* or were inadequately explained there (the publication of Lane's great *Lexicon* had begun only four years previously). Of course, de Jong had available to him only a limited range of printed and therefore easily accessible Arabic philological and lexicographical works, and the oriental scholarship of the succeeding century has rendered much of his glossary self-evident to the modern Arabist; but in its time it was a praiseworthy attempt to explain many hitherto puzzling and unusual terms. In *Journal Asiatique*, Ser. 6, Vol. x (July-Dec. 1867), 345-53, Ch. Defrémery contributed a long review-article of de Jong's work suggesting certain slight improvements to the text and making additions to the glossary (a further review by Defrémery in *Revue critique d'histoire et de littérature*, II/2 (1867), 278-82, was essentially the same as his *Journal Asiatique* one). The lexicographical material assembled by de Jong was later largely incorporated by Dozy in his *Supplément aux dictionnaires arabes* (Leiden 1881).

De Jong justly claimed that the reader of the *Laṭā'if* would find it 'utilissima et scitu dignissima' and the book has in fact been drawn upon by scholars interested in the general culture and civilisation of Islam, and in particular, of eastern Islam, including Goldziher, Mez and Barthold. However, no further edition of the text appeared until very recently when two Egyptian scholars, Ibrāhīm al-Abyārī and Ḥasan Kāmil aṣ-Ṣairafī, produced an excellent and well laid-out text, with a preface and indexes (Dār Iḥyā' al-Kutub al-'Arabiyya, Cairo 1960). They mention in their Introduction, p. 29, a new manuscript of the *Laṭā'if* in the Dār al-Kutub al-Miṣriyya, of unknown origin and provenance; this is presumably the one listed by Brockelmann in his *Geschichte der Arabischen Literatur*, I, 338, as given in the catalogue of the library, *Fihrist al-kutub al-'arabiyya* (Cairo 1345-8/1926-9), II, 72. They are extremely vague in their textual indications, but it seems that they have used basically the text of de Jong, and have made slight emendations in the light of the Cairo manuscript and in accordance with their perusal of parallel texts and citations. They have, however, added to their text what was hardly possible for de Jong to do in his time, sc. a copious and valuable commentary in the footnotes; these are almost exclusively parallel citations from other Arabic texts or else explanations of terms from the native dictionaries.

I have based my own translation on the text of Abyārī and Ṣairafī, but occasionally I have chosen the reading of de Jong where this seemed preferable. The places where the two editions have significantly different readings, affecting the translation, are given in the footnotes, with an indication of the reading followed in the translation. The pagination of the Arabic text, indicated by the symbol and a folio at the end of the line, thus: [57, in my translation, is that of Abyārī and Ṣairafī's edition.

In commenting on the text, I have utilised a certain amount of the information given by Abyārī and Ṣairafī, but I have also tried to give references, where relevant, to the works of European orientalists; and in certain places I have found that the results of recent studies in related fields such as the Persian field, as well as the Arabic one, have shed useful light. Furthermore, I have endeavoured to keep this annotation within bounds, for, as I worked on the text, it soon became apparent to me that the *Laṭā'if* could easily be used as the point of departure for a commentary on a truly immense sector of early Islamic culture and civilisation. If I have followed any principle, it has been the commonsense one to avoid comment on the obvious and to concentrate on the more recondite; but where some selectiveness is necessary, a choice of terms and passages for comment is inevitably somewhat arbitrary.

So far as I have been able to ascertain, this is the first translation of the *Laṭā'if* into a European, or for that matter, into any language. Of individual chapters, the indefatigable O. Rescher (Reşer) has translated the greater part of the tenth, geographical one as 'Ein Kapitel zur arabischen Städte- und Länderkunde (Abschnitt x aus eth-Tha'âlibî's laṭâ'if el-ma'ârif)' in his *Orientalistische Miszellen*, I (Istanbul 1925), 194–228; unfortunately, this book is not easy to find now, since only seventy copies of it were printed. Rescher is an Arabist of profound learning; his translation is very reliable, and I have found it of considerable help. On the other hand, his annotation of this very interesting chapter is fairly fragmentary, and I have tried to fill the gap here.

For the translator of a text, there are two extremes of approach: absolute literal fidelity in his translation, or else a free, more literary rendering. With such a language as Arabic, the translator who adopts the first extreme faces many difficulties; some Arabic expressions appear awkward and unusual, even grotesque, when literally Englished, and in any case, the concision of Arabic often necessitates a long English expression for a short Arabic one if the complete range of meaning is to be faithfully conveyed. The second extreme is often justified when the work in question is itself written in a style with clear literary pretensions; here, the translator can attempt to infuse something of the beauty or incisiveness of the original into his own translation.

With regard to the *Laṭā'if*, no particular claim can be made for attractiveness of style. Tha'ālibī himself was not a dazzling stylist of the stamp of such contemporaries of his as Abū Bakr al-Khwārazmī, Badī' az-Zamān al-Hamadhānī or Abū'l-Fatḥ al-Bustī, and, as will be explained in the Introduction, his aim in the *Laṭā'if* was a practical one, to give snippets of information and learning for certain classes of people requiring educational polish. I myself have consequently adopted for this translation an attitude which lies between the two extremes of approach, but where artistic effect seemed likely to conflict with accuracy of interpretation, I have plumped for the latter. It may well be that such a compromise will please no one, but I have nevertheless found it a useful working principle in dealing with a text of this sort.

Two final points are worth making. The first is that certain difficulties confront the translator of a work from the early 5th/11th century like the *Laṭā'if*. The literary Arabic used in this period was a post-classical one, and we have as yet no thorough knowledge of the language in this evolutionary period. J. Fück in his *'Arabīya, Untersuchungen zur arabischen Sprach- und Stilgeschichte* (Berlin 1950, French tr. Paris 1955) has made an attack on the problem in his general survey of the trends of the period, giving also an analysis of some of the linguistic changes of the time, although J. Blau has recently criticised Fück for not paying enough attention to Middle Arabic. At present, we need more studies of individual post-classical authors, their language and style. Certain major figures are, it is true, being examined – one thinks of the studies of Professors R. Blachère on Mutanabbī, Ch. Pellat on Jāḥiẓ and G. Lecomte on Ibn Qutaiba – but Tha'ālibī has attracted no one since Rescher did some work on certain of his texts earlier this century. Beyond some citations of authors from the *Yatīmat ad-dahr*, Fück himself makes very little use of the rich corpus of Tha'ālibī's works as examples of post-classical style and usage.

The second point follows from the first: that for the actual work of translating a post-classical text, *Hilfsmittel* are few. A European dictionary such as Lane's follows the purist attitude of native lexicographers like Ibn Duraid and Ibn Manẓūr, and to a slightly less extent Fīrūzābādī and Sayyid Murtaḍā, in not deigning to notice post-classical, *muwallad* words and usages; hence their dictionaries are not always helpful when dealing with an author like Tha'ālibī. Much more useful are works like Dozy's *Supplément* (although this has a bias towards the usage of the western rather than the eastern Islamic world) and the glossaries compiled by de Goeje from the various geographical works, almost all from the 4th/10th century, which he edited in the *Bibliotheca Geographorum Arabicorum* series; but even with these, the student of the later Arabic of the eastern Islamic world is inadequately provided for.

There remains the important and pleasurable task of acknowledging with thanks those who have helped me with this translation and the commentary. Foremost must come my colleague Dr M. A. Ghul, who has put his intimate knowledge of his own language at my disposal over many difficult passages of the text. In particular, he has given indispensable help over much of the early Arabic poetry with which the text of the *Laṭā'if* is plentifully sprinkled. The difficulties and ambiguities of such poetry are well known to scholars, and I would hesitate to claim that my rendering of all these verses is definitive. And of course, the final responsibility for the translation as a whole remains entirely with me. Others to whom I am grateful for information or references include Sir Gerard Clauson, Emeritus Professor James Robson and Mr R. Y. Ebied, and for help with matters botanical I am indebted to my wife and to my colleague Dr D. C. Weeks.

Contents.

Abbreviations xiii

Introduction

Tha'ālibī and the composition of the *Laṭā'if al-ma'ārif* 1

1. The author and his age 1
2. Tha'ālibī's literary work 7
3. The *Laṭā if al-ma'ārif* and its contents 16

The Laṭā'if al-ma'ārif

Exordium 35

CHAPTER ONE. *Concerning the first occurrences of various things and the first persons to do various things* 38

CHAPTER TWO. *Concerning the nicknames given to poets which were taken from their own poetry* 52

CHAPTER THREE. *Concerning the nicknames further given in Islamic times to great leaders and prominent figures* 56

CHAPTER FOUR. *Concerning the secretaries of former ages* 68

CHAPTER FIVE. *Concerning those with the longest family traditions of possessing certain qualities or of exercising certain functions, and concerning those who could trace back the longest unbroken lines of descent in regard to various functions or qualities* 72

CHAPTER SIX. *Concerning outstanding levels of achievement or character reached by various classes of people* 79

CHAPTER SEVEN. *Concerning curious coincidences and patterns in names and patronymics* 85

CHAPTER EIGHT. *Concerning diverse items of curious and striking information about the Prophet, Quraish and the rulers of the Arabs* 88

CHAPTER NINE. *Concerning interesting and entertaining pieces of information about various unusual happenings and strange coincidences* 104

CHAPTER TEN. *Concerning some examples of the specialities of the different lands, together with something about the excellences and imperfections of these places* 116

Addenda and Corrigenda 147
Bibliography of the principal works consulted 149

Indexes
1. Persons, dynasties, tribes 155
2. Places, rivers, battles 161
3. Products, specialities, etc. 162
4. Book titles 164

Abbreviations.

1. *Texts of the Laṭā'if al-ma'ārif*

AS	Text of Ibrāhīm al-Abyārī and Ḥasan Kāmil aṣ-Ṣairafī (Cairo 1960)
J	Text of Paul de Jong (Leiden 1867)

2. *Periodicals, series, reference works, etc.*

AJSL	*American Journal of Semitic Languages* (Chicago)
APAW	*Abhandlungen der Preussischen Akademie der Wissenschaften*, Phil.-Hist. Klasse (Berlin)
BGA	*Bibliotheca Geographorum Arabicorum* (Leiden)
BSO[A]S	*Bulletin of the School of Oriental [and African] Studies* (London)
EI	*Encyclopaedia of Islam* (Leiden)
GAL	Brockelmann, *Geschichte der Arabischen Literatur* (Leiden)
GMS	*E. J. W. Gibb Memorial Series* (London)
JA	*Journal Asiatique* (Paris)
JAOS	*Journal of the American Oriental Society* (New Haven, Conn.)
JRAS	*Journal of the Royal Asiatic Society* (London)
RAAD	*Revue de l'Académie Arabe de Damas* (Damascus)
RCAL	*Rendiconti de l'Accademia dei Lincei*, Classe di Scienze Morali, Storiche e Filologiche (Rome)
SBWAW	*Sitzungsberichte der Wiener Akademie der Wissenschaften*, Phil.-Hist. Kl. (Vienna)
SI	*Studia Islamica* (Paris)
WZKM	*Wiener Zeitschrift für die Kunde des Morgenlandes* (Vienna)
ZDMG	*Zeitschrift der Deutschen Morgenländischen Gesellschaft* (Leipzig, Berlin)

In citations from the Qur'ān, where two different numbers are given for a verse, the first is that of Flügel's text and the second that of the official Egyptian edition.

TO THE
MEMORY
OF MY
FATHER

Introduction.

Tha'ālibī and the composition of the *Laṭā'if al-ma'ārif*.

1. *The author and his age.*

Despite a great contemporary fame as a scholar and author, remarkably little is known about the life of Abū Manṣūr 'Abd al-Malik b. Muḥammad b. Ismā'īl ath-Tha'ālibī. In a brief article on him, the 7th/13th century biographer Ibn Khallikān gives the date of his birth at Nīshāpūr as 350/961 and the date of his death as 429/1038, and he says that he derived his *nisba* or by-name 'ath-Tha'ālibī' from the fact that he dealt in the furs of foxes (*tha'ālib*).[1] The date of 429/1038 for his death seems to be a firm one, for it is also given by al-Bākharzī, who lived a generation or so after Tha'ālibī and who wrote a continuation, the *Dumyat al-qaṣr*, to Tha'ālibī's *Yatīmat ad-dahr*. Bākharzī was born in Nīshāpūr and as a child was brought up by Tha'ālibī. His knowledge of our author was first-hand and must have been intimate; it is all the more regrettable that the information which he does give on him is extremely meagre.[2] Although Tha'ālibī was a prolific writer, there are few definite autobiographical indications to be found in his works; the contemporary historical sources of the last years of the Sāmānids and of the early years of the Ghaznavids, such as 'Utbī, Gardīzī and Abū'l-Faḍl Baihaqī, are silent about him; and the later compilers of biographical works confine themselves to laudatory generalities when dealing with him.

The obscurity surrounding the life of the man has even led certain western orientalists like Caetani and Brockelmann to deny the attribution to him of one of his most important and lengthy works, the *Ta'rīkh ghurar as-siyar* 'History of men with illustrious lives', a universal history of which the latter part is now lost. Brockelmann in his GAL, Suppl., I, 581-2, makes the author of

[1] *Wafayāt al-a'yān*, tr. de Slane (Paris 1842-71), II, 129-30.

[2] *Dumyat al-qaṣr* (Aleppo 1349/1930), 183-5; unfortunately, this is a very defective edition.

the *Ghurar as-siyar* one Abū Manṣūr 'Abd al-Malik b. Muḥammad b. Ismā'īl ath-Tha'ālibī al-Marghānī, but Franz Rosenthal has rightly rejected this name as an artificial construction from manuscript indications and has demonstrated from internal, stylistic correspondences that the author of the *Ghurar as-siyar* and of all the literary and philological works by Tha'ālibī must be one and the same person.[3]

[3] 'From Arabic books and manuscripts. III. The author of the Gurar as-siyar', JAOS, LXX (1950), 181-2.

Whilst we can cite no watertight dates for marking off the different divisions of Tha'ālibī's life, we can delineate these periods roughly and can characterise the geographical regions in which he lived and worked.

His home town of Nīshāpūr was the administrative capital of the eastern Persian province of Khurāsān, and in the 4th/10th and 5th/11th centuries it was one of the most flourishing cities, both economically and intellectually, of the eastern Islamic world.[4] Until 384/994, Khurāsān was in the hands of the ethnically Persian Sāmānid dynasty, whose Amīrs ruled from their capital Bukhārā over Transoxania and Khurāsān and exercised a loose sovereignty over the outlying regions of Khwārazm and what is now Afghanistan. Towards the end of the 4th/10th century, their empire was under pressure externally because of the attacks from the Central Asian steppes of the Turkish Qarakhanids and internally because of the revolts of ambitious military commanders in Khurāsān. The Amīr Nūḥ b. Manṣūr (366-87/977-97) attempted in 384/994 to salvage the situation in Khurāsān by calling in Sebüktigin, the Turkish slave governor of Ghazna in eastern Afghanistan and a nominal vassal of the Sāmānids. Sebüktigin and his son Maḥmūd quelled the revolts, but the Sāmānid empire was now seriously enfeebled. The dynasty toppled completely in 389/999 and the last Sāmānid was killed in 395/1005. Maḥmūd of Ghazna and the Qarakhanid Ilig Khan Naṣr partitioned the territories of the Sāmānids, the latter taking the lands north of the Oxus, and for the next forty years, until the rise of the Seljuqs, the fortunes of the eastern Iranian world lay essentially with the Ghaznavids and Qarakhanids.[5]

[4] For a demographic, social and economic survey of Nīshāpūr at this time, see Bosworth, *The Ghaznavids: their empire in Afghanistan and eastern Iran 994-1040* (Edinburgh 1963), 145-202.

[5] For all these events, see Barthold, *Turkestan down to the Mongol invasion* (London 1928), 252ff.

Tha'ālibī's lifetime was thus a politically troubled one, and his native province of Khurāsān suffered from the marchings and countermarchings of the rebellious Sāmānid generals and the Amīrs' troops, from the invasions of the Qarakhanids and, towards the end of his life, from the incursions of the Seljuq nomads. Agriculture was hard hit and severe famines took place. Despite all these, the land of Khurāsān and its people showed a remarkable resilience. It was in the Sāmānid dominions that the renaissance of New Persian language and literature developed, but Khurāsān was also the home of Sunnī Islamic orthodoxy in religion and law and a great centre for the cultivation of such Arab sciences as grammar, philology, poetry and belles-lettres. The contemporary geographer Abū 'Abdallāh al-Maqdisī, who travelled widely in the Sāmānid empire, stresses how 'the people who wear *ṭailasāns* (sc. the scholars and ulema)' are respected in eastern Persia, whereas in Shīrāz and western Persia in general, 'the people who wear *durrā'as* (sc. the officials and secretaries)' command the greatest prestige.[6] We do not know how interested Tha'ālibī was in the renaissance of New Persian, if indeed he was interested at all (the question is considered in more detail below, pp. 11-12); in his works he appears as a lover of traditional Arabic learning in all its aspects, and he seems to have used the Arabic language for all scholarly purposes. It is true that in the first part of the *Ghurar as-siyar* he deals with the ancient kings of Persia, but, by his time, this sector of human history had been definitely brought within the framework of Perso-Islamic civilisation and orthodoxy. Certainly, Tha'ālibī shows little of the boundless intellectual curiosity about other epochs and cultures which is so characteristic of his Khwārazmian contemporary Abū'r-Raiḥān al-Bīrūnī, the first direct interpreter to the Islamic world of Indian civilisation; the sections on India, China and the Turks in the *Ghurar as-siyar* are exiguous, and Tha'ālibī acknowledges a debt here to the work of another contemporary, the *Kitāb al-bad' wa't ta'rīkh* 'Book of the creation and of history' of al-Muṭahhar b. Ṭāhir al-Maqdisī al-Bustī.[7]

Tha'ālibī aimed rather at keeping high in the eastern Iranian world the standard of Arabic learning. The first half of his life fell within the period when the Amīrs were firmly in control at Bukhārā and Nīshāpūr and when learning and literature flourished under their enlightened patronage. During this period Tha'ālibī could have travelled freely within the Sāmānid dominions, visiting the various centres of learning and meeting fellow scholars. The fourth *qism* or section of the *Yatīmat ad-dahr* is devoted to the poets and writers of Khurāsān and Transoxania, with special subsections on those of Bukhārā, Khwārazm and Nīshāpūr. The whole section gives a rich and many-sided picture of the flourishing cultural state of the region, with not unimportant sidelights on social and political affairs. Tha'ālibī's praise of Bukhārā at this time has often been quoted: 'In the time of the Sāmānids, Bukhārā

[6] *Aḥsan at-taqāsīm*, ed. de Goeje (Leiden 1906), 440.

[7] ff. 273b-277a of the Istanbul ms. of the *Ghurar as-siyar*, Damad Ibrahim Paşa 916, cf. Zotenberg's preface to the part of the *Ghurar* which he edited and translated (Paris 1900), xxi-xxii. Al-Muṭahhar's information in turn probably goes back to the lost geographical work of the Sāmānid Vizier Jaihānī; cf. G. A. Reinaud, 'Mémoire géographique, historique et scientifique sur l'Inde . . . d'après les écrivains arabes, persans et chinois', *Mémoires de l'Institut, Académie des Inscriptions*, XVIII/2 (1849), 294-5.

was the meeting-place of all nobility, the centre of all authority, the place where the outstanding people of the age congregated, the rising-place of the stars of the learned scholars of all the earth and the place of pilgrimage for all the brilliant men of the time.'[8]

Contemporary with the fall of the Sāmānids at the end of the century came changes in the adjacent region of Khwārazm on the lower Oxus, a province connected culturally and economically with the provinces under direct Sāmānid rule, Transoxania and Khurāsān. In 385/995 the ancient line of Afrīghid Khwārazm-Shāhs of Kāth was overthrown by a local family of Gurgānj, the commercial rival of Kāth. This family, the Ma'mūnids, assumed the traditional title of Khwārazm-Shāhs and reigned for twenty-two years until they were overthrown by Maḥmūd of Ghazna (see below, p. 5).

Art and learning flourished at the Ma'mūnid court of Gurgānj. The Shāh Abū'l-'Abbās Ma'mūn b. Ma'mūn (390-407/1000-16) and his Vizier Abū'l-Ḥusain Aḥmad as-Suhailī were both scholars themselves and the friends of scholars. Around them gathered such men as the polymath al-Bīrūnī, the philosophers Ibn Sīnā and Abū Sahl al-Masīḥī, the mathematician Abū Naṣr al-'Arrāq and the physician Abū'l-Khair b. al-Khammār – and, it seems, Tha'ālibī himself, perhaps impelled to move thither by the prevailing disorders in Khurāsān. The brilliance of Abū'l-'Abbās Ma'mūn's court is said to have been such that Sultan Maḥmūd, himself desirous of adorning his court with the leading lights of the age, sent to the Khwārazm-Shāh a polite ultimatum demanding that these prominent scholars be despatched forthwith to Ghazna.[9]

Judging by frequent references to the Khwārazm-Shāh in several of his works, Tha'ālibī must have spent a good period of time at his court. Thus in the *Laṭā'if*, tr. below, p. 143, he states that Abū'l-'Abbās Ma'mūn requested him to improvise some verses about the excessive cold of the Khwārazmian winter. In a minor work, the *Bard al-akbād fī'l-a'dād* 'The cooling refreshment of hearts (literally, 'livers') concerning the use of the numerals', Tha'ālibī quotes some of the Shāh's maxims on government and ethics.[10] The fourth *bāb* or subsection of the fourth *qism* of the *Yatīmat ad-dahr* is devoted to the outstanding contemporary writers of Khwārazm, and contains examples of eulogies addressed to the Ma'mūnids and to their predecessors the Afrīghids. Indeed, a passage added to one of the manuscripts of the *Yatīmat ad-dahr*, seen by the Persian scholar 'Abbās Iqbāl (who edited Tha'ālibī's

[8] *Yatīmat ad-dahr* (Cairo 1375-7/1956-8), IV, 101, tr. Barbier de Meynard, JA, Ser. 5, Vol. III (1853), 291-2; cf. Browne, *Literary History of Persia* (London and Cambridge 1902-24), I, 365-6.

[9] An anecdote about this ultimatum occurs in Niẓāmī 'Arūḍī Samarquandī's *Chahār maqāla* (q. in Bosworth, *op. cit.*, 132), but is not confirmed in any of the specifically historical sources.

[10] In *Khams rasā'il* (Istanbul 1301/1884), 106, 118, tr. Rescher, 'Zahlensprüche in der arabischen Litteratur ("Berd al-akbâd fî'l-a'dâd" des Tha'âlibî)', in *Orientalistische Miszellen*, II (Istanbul 1926), 43, 61.

own continuation of this work, the *Tatimmat al-yatīma*), says that various hindrances prevented Tha'ālibī from carrying on the compilation of his anthology beyond the end of the third *qism* on the poets of Jibāl, Fārs, Gurgān and Ṭabaristān, until he arrived at the court of Abū'l-'Abbās Ma'mūn, who put him in charge of his library and encouraged him to write the fourth *qism*.[11] Since the date Muḥarram 402/August 1011 is mentioned in the *Yatīmat ad-dahr*, Tha'ālibī was probably in Khwārazm during the middle years at least of the Shāh's reign.

During these years, he dedicated to Abū'l-'Abbās Ma'mūn several of his works, including the *Nashr an-naẓm wa ḥall al-'aqd* 'Releasing of the poetic string and untying of the knot', a prose version of a well-known anthology, the *Mu'nis al-udabā'*; a collection of anecdotes and *bons mots*, the *Kitāb al-laṭā'if wa'ẓ-ẓarā'if fī madḥ al-ashyā' wa aḍdādihā* 'Book of curious and amusing stories concerning the praise of things and their opposites'; and the *Kitāb al-kināya wa't-ta'rīḍ* 'Book of hinting and allusion', a handbook on rhetoric with special reference to the use of euphemism, metaphor and figurative language. An early example of the 'Mirror for Princes' genre, the *Kitāb ādāb al-mulūk al-Khwārazm-shāhī* 'The book on the conduct of princes composed for the Khwārazm-Shāh', is dedicated to 'al-Amīr as-Sayyid al-Malik al-'Ādil Walī an-Ni'ma Abū'l-'Abbās Ma'mūn b. Ma'mūn Khwārazm-Shāh Maulā Amīr al-Mu'minīn'[12]; this is possibly identical with the *Sirāj al-mulūk* 'Lamp for princes', although the Khwārazm-Shāh to whom this last work is dedicated is not specifically named.[13]

In 408/1017 Maḥmūd of Ghazna's troops invaded Khwārazm, extinguished the line of the Ma'mūnids and added the province to the existing Ghaznavid territories of Khurāsān, Afghanistan and northern India.[14] This brutal act of aggression may have ended one of the pleasantest periods of Tha'ālibī's life, one spent in a congenial atmosphere of scholarship and encouragement. It did, however, mean that he was now drawn into the sphere of the Ghaznavids, who were creating a vast cosmopolitan empire in the Islamic east, the greatest known there since the decline of the Baghdad Caliphate. As a well-known author and scholar, Tha'ālibī could be sure of an audience of students and pupils, and the last two decades or so of his life were probably spent teaching in Nīshāpūr once more, interspersed with visits to the Sultan's court or to the circles which gathered around provincial governors and officials. Like the Ma'mūnids, the Ghaznavids were eager to act

[11] Iqbāl, introd. to the *Tatimmat al-yatīma* (Tehran 1353/1934), I, 5 n. 1. This added passage seems to be absent from all the printed editions of the *Yatīma*.

[12] f. 1b of Istanbul ms. Es'at Efendi 1808.

[13] D. Sourdel has recently pointed out that a further work, the *Tuḥfat al-wuzarā'* 'Presentation to Viziers', attributed in GAL to Tha'ālibī, must on internal evidence have been written for a later Khwārazm-Shāh, perhaps for 'Alā' ad-Dīn Muḥammad or his son Jalāl ad-Dīn Mingburnu, and he also surmises that this *Sirāj al-mulūk*, likewise written for an unnamed Shāh, may also be falsely attributed to Tha'ālibī *Le vizirat 'Abbāside de 749 à 936 (132 à 324 de l'Hégire)* (Damascus 1959-60), I, 13-14.

[14] Cf. Barthold, *Turkestan*, 275-9, and M. Nāẓim, *The life and times of Sulṭān Maḥmūd of Ghazna* (Cambridge 1931), 56-60.

as Maecenases, and their court nurtured a brilliant group of Persian and Arabic poets.[15] The *Ghurar as-siyar* was dedicated by Tha'ālibī to Maḥmūd of Ghazna's brother, the Amīr Abū'l-Muẓaffar Naṣr b. Sebüktigin, who until his death in 412/1021 was military governor of Khurāsān and Sīstān. According to 'Utbī, he gained a great reputation in Nīshāpūr from his charitable works, and it was presumably in Nīshāpūr that Tha'ālibī came under his patronage.[16] Also dedicated to the Amīr Naṣr was his *Kitāb al-mutashābih* 'Book of similarities in comparison', a work on paronomasia and other ornaments of style. In the *Laṭā'if*, tr. below, p. 136, he mentions a personal conversation with the Amīr, and the latter's words are further cited in others of Tha'ālibī's works; indeed, it is abundantly clear that Tha'ālibī was intimately connected with the Amīr Naṣr's court circle. The 9th/15th century Persian literary biographer Daulat Shāh even says that Maḥmūd of Ghazna once employed Tha'ālibī as a diplomatic envoy to the Caliphs of Baghdad, but there are strong grounds for denying the authenticity of the story of this mission.[17]

One of Tha'ālibī's best-known and most popular works, the *Thimār al-qulūb* (see below, pp. 8-9), was written for one of the notables of Nīshāpūr, Abū'l-Faḍl 'Ubaidallāh b. Aḥmad Mīkālī, member of the extremely influential local family of the Mīkālīs. These last had been established in Nīshāpūr since the early 4th/10th century and had a long tradition of attachment to learning and its exponents; in the past they had been patrons of the Arabic lexicographer and philologist Ibn Duraid. Mīkālīs filled both municipal and central government offices under the Sāmānids and Ghaznavids, and Abū'l-Faḍl 'Ubaidallāh was high in the favour of Mas'ūd of Ghazna.[18] The *Laṭā'if* itself is dedicated to the great Ghaznavid Vizier Aḥmad b. Ḥasan Maimandī, called *Shams al-Kufāt* 'Sun of the capable ones' for his secretarial and administrative expertise, and himself famous for his Arabic scholarship; whereas the previous, less-educated Vizier had changed the language of the administration in Ghazna from Arabic to Persian, one of Maimandī's first acts on taking over the office was to restore the primacy of Arabic. He had begun his career as an official for the Ghaznavids in Khurāsān, had been for a brief spell civil governor of Khurāsān, and then in 404/1013 became the Sultan's Vizier till his fall in 415/1024. He later became Vizier to Maḥmūd's son Mas'ūd, but died early in the new reign in 424/1032.[19] Clearly, the paths of Tha'ālibī and Maimandī could have crossed at several points, but exact information is lacking.

[15] This court culture is dealt with by Bosworth, *The Ghaznavids*, 129-41, and the individual poets are considered by J. Rypka, etc., *Iranische Literaturgeschichte* (Leipzig 1959), 170ff.

[16] 'Utbī, *at-Ta'rīkh al-Yamīnī*, with commentary of Manīnī (Cairo 1286/1869), II, 330-1; on the relations of Tha'ālibī with the Amīr Naṣr, see Zotenberg, *Ghurar as-siyar*, tr., Preface, v-vi.

[17] *Tadhkirat ash-shu'arā'*, ed. M. 'Abbāsī (Tehran 1337/1958), 40; cf. Zotenberg, *op. cit.*, x-xii, and Bosworth, 'The titulature of the early Ghaznavids,' *Oriens*, XV (1962), 218.

[18] See on Abū'l-Faḍl and his family, Bosworth, *The Ghaznavids*, 176-85.

[19] Cf. Nazim, EI[1] Art. 'Al-Maimandī'.

The last years of Tha'ālibī's life are wholly obscure. There is extant a work by him on *adab*, without a title, written for the library of another great Ghaznavid official, Abū Sahl Ḥamdūnī or Ḥamdawī, who acted as Vizier for Sultan Muḥammad b. Maḥmūd during his first brief Sultanate of 421/1030 and thereafter held high office under Mas'ūd[20]; this work probably therefore dates from the last years of Tha'ālibī's life. In the year of his death, 429/1038, the Seljuq Turkmen bands, from whose depredations the province of Khurāsān had for some years past been suffering, actually appeared in Nīshāpūr, and within two years of Tha'ālibī's death, Khurāsān passed finally from the control of the Ghaznavids into that of the Seljuqs.

[20] Cf. Bosworth, *op. cit.*, 71, 85-6.

2. *Tha'ālibī's literary work.*

Tha'ālibī early acquired a reputation as a profound scholar, and Ibn Khallikān in his biographical notice of him quotes a fine passage on his genius from the *Kitāb adh-dhakhīra fī maḥāsin ahl al-jazīra* 'Book of the treasure-house concerning the elegant aspects of the people of the [Iberian] peninsula' of Ibn Bassām of Santarem (d. 542/1147):

> In that age, he was the man who pastured his genius on the loftiest summits of knowledge; the great compiler of prose and verse; the chief author of his time, and the ablest also in the opinion of that epoch; his reputation spread abroad like a proverb which circulated far and wide; the camels [which bore travellers to see him were constantly] arriving, their breasts panting from the rapidity of their speed; his compilations rose over the horizon not only in the East but in the West, and they ascended [to the zenith of fame] as the stars ascend through the darkness; his works hold a place of high eminence, shining with refulgence even from their first appearance; the number of persons who learned them by heart or who collected them can neither be defined nor described, and it would be vain to essay, even in the finest and most harmonious style, to do full justice to the merits of his writings.

Because of his many-sided intellect, says Bākharzī, Tha'ālibī was called 'the Jāḥiẓ of Nīshāpūr'.[21]

[21] *Dumyat al-qaṣr*, 183.

He was undoubtedly a prolific writer. The 8th/14th century author Ṣalāḥ ad-Dīn Khalīl b. Aibak aṣ-Ṣafadī, compiler of the *Wāfī bi'l-wafāyāt*, a biographical dictionary continuing and completing the earlier one of Ibn Khallikān, is the only one of the writers mentioning Tha'ālibī who gives a comprehensive list of his works. To the eighty-six titles given by Ṣafadī, the latest editors of the *Laṭā'if*, Abyārī and Ṣairafī, have added seven more works known to be by Tha'ālibī.[22] It is certain that we have in Ṣafadī's list much duplication. Zotenberg noted Tha'ālibī's tendency towards repetition and his practice of utilising material from one work in another, and gave several examples of this last fact: 'Al-Tha'âlibî, malgré les ressources de sa facile mémoire, aime à se répéter. Dans plusieurs de ses écrits, il a reproduit les mêmes tours de langage, les mêmes métaphores et hyperboles, les mêmes expressions tirées du Coran, les mêmes historiettes, bien que ces fleurs de rhetorique et ces ornements soient parfois des emprunts.'[23] In Ṣafadī's list, many titles differ only slightly from those of others, and even allowing for the fact that the rhyming and often meaningless titles of some of the works effectively conceal the real nature of their contents, we can discern that many of the compositions deal with the same subject. It is very likely that some titles are the names of chapters or sections of larger books rather than titles of independent works. Thus Ṣafadī's *Mā jarā bain al-Mutanabbī wa Saif ad-Daula* 'Al-Mutanabbī's relations with Saif ad-Daula' is obviously identical with the long section on the great poet in the fifth *bāb* of the first *qism* of the *Yatīmat ad-dahr*. In GAL, I, 337-40, Suppl. I, 499-502, Brockelmann lists as extant fifty-four of Tha'ālibī's works, and this is still a considerable total. The extensiveness of his output makes the almost complete silence of later authorities on the details of his life and career all the less explicable.

The titles of Tha'ālibī's compositions show that his interests covered a fairly well-defined sector of Islamic learning. He was not primarily a theologian, traditionist, jurist or philosopher, although he was far from being ignorant of these sciences. It was not for nothing that he had been a disciple of the great grammarian and authority on Sibawaih's *Kitāb*, Ibn Fāris (d. 390/1000 or 395/1004-5). In his own career, Tha'ālibī was concerned above all with those branches of traditional Arabic lore which dealt with the handling of words in the widest possible sense. Prominent amongst his works are those dealing with the Arabic language in all its rich and manifold aspects. He wrote copiously on grammar and philology, on *balāgha* or rhetoric and composed what we would call 'classified vocabularies' of certain expressions or categories of words. His *Thimār al-qulūb fi'l-muḍāf wa'l-mansūb*,

[22] Introd. to their text of the *Laṭā'if*, 14-20.

[23] *Ghurar as-siyar*, tr., Preface, xii ff.

roughly translatable as 'The fruits of the hearts concerning words used coupled together and attributively', lists and explains commonly used or proverbial phrases and names which consist of one word and a second dependent on it, and deals similarly with the relative adjectival forms frequently and proverbially used, e.g. *'Azīz Miṣr* 'the Mighty One of Egypt' (sc. in the Qur'ānic story of Joseph), *afā'ī Sijistān* 'the vipers of Sīstān' and *kaid an-nisā'* 'women's wiles'. Another extensive work, *at-Tamthīl wa'l-muḥāḍarāt* 'The use of proverbial sayings and elegant conversation', is a collection of aphorisms, often-cited lines of verse, etc., classified under subject matter for easy use. Zakī Mubārak calls the whole work, 'sans réserves, un chef d'œuvre rare dans notre littérature'. Similarly, his *Fiqh al-lugha* 'Systematic principles of language' deals with such groups of words as synonyms; words which are nearly synonymous but which exhibit fine shades of meaning; Arabic words which were in Tha'ālibī's time used in place of their Persian equivalents; Persian words used where no native Arabic words existed; and words used in Arabic which were considered to be of Greek origin. This work was extremely popular; in the 8th/14th century it was put into verse as the *Naẓm fiqh al-lugha,* and various modern printed editions have appeared in the East.[24]

The Arabic science of rhetoric, drawing to some extent on Greek models, came to give inordinate importance to the figurative and allusive use of words and to their use alliteratively or assonantally. Tha'ālibī's works in this field do not rival the great compositions of such literary theorists of the previous two or three generations as Ibn al-Mu'tazz and Qudāma b. Ja'far, but they do include a *Kitāb at-tajnīs* 'Book on paronomasia'; a *Kitāb siḥr al-bayān* 'Book on the charm of eloquent expression'; a *Miftāḥ al-faṣāḥa* 'Key to correct usage'; a *Kitāb al-kināya wa't-ta'rīḍ* 'Book of hinting and allusion', i.e. the conveyance of meaning through metaphor; and a *Kitāb al-iqtibās* 'Book concerning the use in literary style of Qur'ānic quotations'. As well as this more theoretical and analytical side of linguistic science, Tha'ālibī was interested also in creative literary composition. In the *Laṭā'if,* as in many others of his works, he several times quotes his own verses, and examples of his poetry appear also in 'Utbī's *Yamīnī.* Bākharzī mentions that a volume (*mujallada*) of Tha'ālibī's poetry found its way into his hands after the author's death, and in his biography of his master and guardian he quotes several examples of this verse. Ṣafadī mentions too a *dīwān* or collection of

[24] On the *Fiqh al-lugha,* see J. A. Haywood, *Arabic lexicography* (Leiden 1960), 113. It is likely that Tha'ālibī's choice of title here was influenced by that of one of his teacher Ibn Fāris's works, the *Kitāb aṣ-Ṣāḥibī fī fiqh al-lugha al-'arabiyya*; cf. H. Loucel, 'L'origine du langage d'après les grammariens arabes, II', *Arabica,* x (1963), 253 ff.

Tha'ālibī's poetry; this has not apparently survived.[25] One of Tha'ālibī's friends and contemporaries was Abū'l-Fatḥ Bustī, a secretary and official in Ghaznavid service and universally famed in the eastern Islamic literary and administrative world for his dazzling epistolary style. Tha'ālibī thrice quotes him in the *Laṭā'if* (tr. below, pp. 135, 136, 144), and he also made a collection of the outstanding parts of his poetry, the *Kitāb aẓ-ẓarf* (? *aṭ-ṭuraf*) *min shi'r al-Bustī* 'Book of the elegancies in al-Bustī's verse'.

But the most ambitious of Tha'ālibī's works in the field of pure literature, comparable only with the *Ghurar as-siyar* in its extensiveness, was his *Yatīmat ad-dahr fī maḥāsin ahl al-'aṣr* 'The unique pearl concerning the elegant achievements of contemporary people'. This is a vast anthology of the leading poets of his time, with copious quotations from their verses linked by passages of biographical information or literary criticism relevant to the poetry cited. Tha'ālibī often revised or added to his compositions in later years, and it is difficult to construct a chronology of his work; but the first version of the *Yatīma* was produced, according to the author himself, in 384/994, and it was probably put in its final form some time between 402/1011-12 and 407/1016-17 (see above, pp. 4-5).[26] It is arranged geographically and deals successively in its four sections with the poets of Syria and al-Jazīra, of Iraq, of western Persia and of Khurāsān and Transoxania (Egypt and the Islamic lands further west are not treated). Many of the poets mentioned are now unknown or little-known apart from Tha'ālibī's quotations, and the whole work is supremely valuable as a panorama of literary activity in the central and eastern lands of Islam during the second half of the 4th/10th century and the early decades of the ensuing one, the age which the Swiss orientalist Adam Mez called the 'Renaissance of Islam'. The popularity of the *Yatīma* and its usefulness to contemporaries ensured firstly that it would be widely copied (Brockelmann enumerates seventeen extant manuscripts) and secondly that continuations of it would be undertaken. Tha'ālibī himself led the way with his own *Tatimmat al-yatīma* 'Completion of the *Yatīma*', written in the last years of his life between 424/1033 and his death five years later. Continuing in it the geographical arrangement of the parent work, he was now able to include many of the scholars and literary men who had risen to fame under Ghaznavid patronage in the twenty years or so since the *Yatīma* had been completed. Following on Tha'ālibī, Abū'l-Ḥasan 'Alī al-Bākharzī (d. 467/

[25] Bākharzī, *Dumyat al-qasr*, 183; Safadī, cited by Abyārī and Ṣairafī in Introd. to their text of the *Laṭā'if*, 16.

[26] On the date of the composition of the *Yatīma*, see Zotenberg, *Ghurar as-siyar*, tr., Preface, xvii, n. 2.

1075) composed his *Dumyat al-qaṣr wa 'uṣrat ahl al-'aṣr* 'Statue of the palace and refuge of the people of the present age', and a century later 'Imād ad-Dīn al-Kātib al-Iṣfahānī (d. 597/1201) wrote his *Kharīdat al-qaṣr wa jarīdat ahl al-'aṣr* 'Virgin pearl of the palace and register of the people of the present age'.

It is convenient at this point to consider Tha'ālibī's position as a native Persian and to consider his attitude, so far as it is discernible, towards the use of Persian language and culture. The fact that he was born and bred in eastern Persia, at a time when the Persian national consciousness was beginning once more to express itself after three centuries' submergence under the at first predominantly Arab religion and culture of Islam, did not necessarily dispose him to express himself at the scholarly level in his native tongue, and for centuries to come Arabic remained the language for much of the scholarship produced in Persia. It is, moreover, true that by the beginning of the 5th/11th century the heritage of non-Islamic Persian culture had been largely incorporated into Arabo-Islamic administrative practices, social habits and literary subject-matter. The central and eastern lands of the Caliphate were now dominated by an Arabo-Persian, and not a purely Arab culture, so that participation in the renaissance of New Persian language and literature did not involve a break with the mainstream of Islamic religion and culture; indeed, the ethos of this renaissance remained overwhelmingly Islamic.

In his scholarly attitudes, Tha'ālibī shows himself as an Arab traditionalist; his primary concern was, as we have seen, with the older Islamic sciences and especially with those revolving round the Arabic language. He was doubtless proud of the glories of the ancient kings of Persia, and their history, mythical and real, takes up a very large part of the *Ghurar as-siyar*. In his investigation of the sources of the *Ghurar as-siyar*, Zotenberg concluded that Tha'ālibī must have drawn indirectly on Ibn al-Muqaffa''s Arabic translation of the Middle Persian national epic, the *Khudāy-nāma* or 'Book of Kings'. Furthermore, in two places in the part of the text edited by Zotenberg, Tha'ālibī mentions 'the author of the book of the *Shāh-nāma*', although this was probably not Firdausī's masterpiece but one of the several works of this name known in Persia during the 4th/10th century.[27] Yet on the whole, Tha'ālibī kept to the well-trodden Arabo-Islamic ways. The *Laṭā'if al-ma'ārif*, for instance, contains nothing, beyond one or two references to the pre-Islamic Sāsānid emperors and an undue concentration on Persia in the geographical section, that

[27] *Ibid.*, xxiii ff.

would specifically suggest to the reader that its author was a Persian. In displaying such an attitude, Tha'ālibī was only following the example of earlier scholars of purely Persian descent, such as the philologist and literary critic Ibn Qutaiba (d. 276/889); although his father came from Merv in Khurāsān, Ibn Qutaiba's works include an opuscule called the *Faḍl al-'Arab 'alā 'l-'Ajam* 'Superiority of the Arabs over the non-Arabs (sc. the Persians)'.[28] Many other Persian scholars devoted themselves wholly to the Arab sciences, and in the disputes of the Shu'ūbiyya, the literary and cultural conflicts between the partisans of Arab culture and those of non-Arab and especially Persian culture, they often aligned themselves decisively with the former.

In Ṣafadī's list of Tha'ālibī's compositions occurs the title *al-Fuṣūl al-fārisiyya* 'Chapters in Persian' or perhaps 'Chapters on Persian subjects', but this would appear to be the only work, apart from the first part of the *Ghurar as-siyar*, which dealt specifically with Persian topics. However, 'Abbās Iqbāl has pointed out that the information in the third and fourth sections of the *Yatīmat ad-dahr* is of the highest value for the literary and cultural history of Persia during Tha'ālibī's time. He adds that Tha'ālibī usually notes which poets were *Dhū'l-lisānain* 'Two-tongued', i.e. equally proficient writers in both Arabic and Persian, sometimes giving Arabic translations of their Persian poetry and occasionally even giving actual examples of Persian verses.[29]

Despite his special interest in linguistic and literary topics, Tha'ālibī did not by any means neglect the other branches of traditional Arabic knowledge. His work *al-Jawāhir al-ḥisān fī tafsīr al-Qur'ān* 'The beautiful gems concerning the interpretation of the Qur'ān' represents an incursion into the field of exegesis, and this commentary was highly praised by Ḥājjī Khalīfa, who thought himself fortunate personally to possess the first half of it[30]; and his *Makārim al-akhlāq* represents one into the field of ethics. The *Ta'rīkh ghurar as-siyar* (see above, pp. 3, 6) was an isolated foray into the sphere of universal and Islamic history, but it was conceived on a grand scale. By the early 5th/11th century, Muslim historiography was no longer so dominantly didactic and theocentric as it had been in the first centuries of Islam. At the beginning of the 4th/10th century, the historian, traditionist and exegete Abū Ja'far aṭ-Ṭabarī had still felt constrained to call his monumental historical work the *Ta'rīkh ar-rusul wa'l-mulūk* 'History of apostles and rulers'; but, as the century progressed, a new form of historical writing appeared, less concerned with the

[28] Printed by M. Kurd 'Alī in his *Rasā'il al-bulaghā'*⁴ (Cairo 1374/1954), 344-81 under the alternative titles of *Kitāb al-'Arab* 'Book of the Arabs' or *ar-Radd 'alā 'sh-Shu'ūbiyya* 'Refutation of the Shu'ūbiyya'.

[29] *Tatimmat al-yatīma*, Introd., I, 4.

[30] *Kashf aẓ-ẓunūn*, ed. Flügel (Leipzig 1835-58), No. 4279, II, 642-3.

unfolding of God's plan on the general stage of history and more interested in human actions and the temporal causation of events. This new attitude is exemplified in the Būyid historians Thābit b. Sinān, Hilāl b. al-Muḥassin aṣ-Ṣābi' and Miskawaih, and the Ghaznavid one Abū'l-Faḍl Baihaqī, all of whom were officials and administrators by profession and no longer primarily theologians, traditionists or jurists.[31] Tha'ālibī's scholarly attitudes and training made him fit better into the older pattern of historian, but what is still preserved of the *Ghurar as-siyar* (the first two of its four books, carrying the narrative up to the end of the Caliphate of al-Manṣūr in 158/775; cf. G. Gabrieli in RCAL, Ser. 5, Vol. XXV [1917], 1138-43) shows it as a splendidly constructed work, and the information which the lost second half no doubt gave on the eastern Islamic world during the two centuries before the author's own time would be most valuable to us today.[32]

In addition to being a pure scholar, Tha'ālibī was a teacher. One late source, the *'Uyūn at-tawārīkh* of Ibn Shākir al-Kutubī (d. 764/1363), says that in his early days, Tha'ālibī was compelled to earn his living by teaching children, and it is unlikely that a figure of his eminence would in his maturer years fail to collect around him an eager band of students. As a native of Nīshāpūr, he was born into one of the most intellectually vital cities of eastern Islam. The whole province of Khurāsān, before the 4th/10th century rather backward materially and culturally in comparison with western Persia,[33] became under the Sāmānids not only the centre of a renaissance of New Persian language and literature (a movement which did not, as we have just seen, significantly affect Tha'ālibī), but also a centre for the traditional Arabic literary, legal and theological sciences. Perhaps because the frontier with Central Asian and Indian paganism was never very far away, Khurāsān was a centre of Sunnī orthodoxy, producing in the 5th/11th century such outstanding figures as the Ash'arī scholars Abū Muḥammad 'Abdallāh al-Juwainī and his son the Imām al-Ḥaramain Abū'l-Ma'ālī 'Abd al-Malik, the Ṣūfī publicist al-Qushairī and the great Seljuq Vizier Niẓām al-Mulk. In the last decades of Tha'ālibī's life, Nīshāpūr was in a particular ferment caused by an intense struggle for power in the city between the orthodox Sunnī ulema and the conservative literalist sect of the Karāmiyya. Khurāsān further became at this time the starting-point for Sunnī orthodoxy's counter-offensive against Shī'ism, which under dynasties like the Būyids, Ḥamdānids and Fāṭimids had during the second half of the 4th/10th century

[31] Cf. D. S. Margoliouth, *Lectures on Arabic historians* (Calcutta 1930), 128ff.

[32] On Tha'ālibī's historical technique in this work, see Rosenthal, *A history of Muslim historiography* (Leiden 1954), 81-2, 123-4; he places him below Miskawaih in historical insight and feeling, but states that the *Ghurar* is preserved in too fragmentary a state to allow a definitive judgement on Tha'ālibī as a historian.

[33] See on this backwardness, E. Herzfeld, 'Khorasan: Denkmalsgeographische Studien zur Kulturgeschichte des Islam in Iran', *Der Islam*, XI (1921), 107-74. However, M. Sprengling has truly noted ('From Persian to Arabic', AJSL, LVI [1939], 326) that the poetry quoted in the *Yatīmat ad-dahr*, IV, 64, on the superiority of the culture of Iraq over that of Sāmānid Transoxania, should not be taken at its face value, as does Browne in *Lit. Hist. of Persia*, I, 465-6; Tha'ālibī goes on to point out that the poet in question was a disappointed and therefore embittered office-seeker in Bukhārā.

secured almost unbroken political power over that part of the Middle East running from central Persia to Egypt. After the middle of the 5th/11th century, the attack on the intellectual plane was given material impetus through the formation in Persia and Iraq of the Great Seljuq empire. An important aspect of this Sunnī reaction was the spread of madrasas, colleges of instruction which had arisen from (and were as yet hardly disassociated from) the teaching aspect of the mosque. Niẓām al-Mulk's name has been especially linked with this movement, and the sources make prominent mention of the nine Niẓāmiyyas which he founded in Iraq and Persia during the reign of Sultan Malik Shāh (465-85/1073-92); but it is clear that the madrasa-building movement had begun long before his Vizierate. In the opening years of the century, a madrasa was built in Nīshāpūr for the scholar Ibn Fūrak al-Iṣfahānī when he was invited to teach in the city.[34] The stimulus to the growth of madrasas must have arisen towards the end of the 4th/10th century, probably in response to the challenge of the Fāṭimid educational institutions and training centres for their *dā'īs* or propagandists, prominent amongst which was al-Azhar in Cairo, nucleus of the later university there.

[34] Ibn Khallikān, tr. II, 673-4, cf. Bosworth, 'The rise of the Karāmiyyah in Khurasan', *Muslim World*, L (1960), 8.

It is not our concern here to follow the course of this Sunnī reaction, but it is relevant to note that Tha'ālibī in his mature years must inevitably have been caught up in an atmosphere of intellectual endeavour and even, within the limits prescribed by Islamic views on the nature of knowledge, of adventure. So far as we know, he did not act as a theological disputant with Shī'a or Karāmiyya or Ismā'īlīs, but he cannot have failed to be influenced by the intellectual currents of the time, with their stress on the inculcation of orthodoxy and the traditional Arabic sciences. The linguistic sciences were Tha'ālibī's own special province, and many of his works on Arabic grammar, vocabulary, rhetoric, etc. are clearly meant as reference works or as teaching manuals, texts upon which a teacher could lecture to his circle of pupils. The stress on madrasa building shows how important was the educational aspect of the Sunnī reaction, and a scholar-statesman like Niẓām al-Mulk aimed at building up and training a corps of officials and secretaries who would administer the Seljuq empire on orthodox lines and thus counteract the pernicious influence of Shī'ī-tinged bureaucracies in western Persia and Iraq.

Hence we pass to the other chief group of Tha'ālibī's compositions, a group which includes the *Laṭā'if al-ma'ārif*: works which were written, often on a modest scale, with the needs in mind of students, secretaries, officials, etc. A desideratum for the Muslim seeking either a general education or else specific training for such professions as those of secretary or official, was a knowledge of *adab*, the body of learning necessary to give social or professional polish; there are a large number of works by Muslim authors on the *adab* required by such groups as rulers, viziers, soldiers, mystics and contemplatives, and even court jesters and raconteurs. The scope of *adab* was very wide: it embraced all the traditional Islamic linguistic, religious and legal sciences, together with the whole stage of human history as it was known to the Muslims, beginning with the Creation and ranging over such non-Islamic cultures as those of ancient Greece and Persia. This wideness in part explains why a work like the *Laṭā'if* appears rather a rag-bag of unrelated snippets of information.[35]

Before turning to a specific consideration of the *Laṭā'if*, we may note the titles of some others of Tha'ālibī's works in the above field. The fact that they were written with a broadly didactic aim did not imply a ponderous approach on Tha'ālibī's part; many of them are short and concise and contain a good deal of light and entertaining matter. There were dull pedants amongst Muslim scholars as amongst those of every culture. But the ideal of most writers who wrote in fields outside the heavier theological or legal or philosophical ones was to keep their readers' interest. This they achieved by such devices as introducing amusing anecdotes into their subject-matter, setting strange and titillating items of information before their readers, and abruptly leaving a topic if they felt that boredom might result from an undue dwelling upon it. Indeed, the student of Islamic literature is not infrequently on the track of important or intriguing information in some work, only to find the author breaking off and turning to a new subject for fear he become too prolix and lose his readers' sympathy.

For the special use of officials, Tha'ālibī composed his *Kanz al-kuttāb* 'Treasure house for secretaries' containing 2,500 passages from 250 different poets; and in his *Khāṣṣ al-khāṣṣ* 'Outstanding extracts from outstanding authors' he gave characteristic excerpts from the works of great stylists. In both these compositions, he aimed to provide secretaries in the chanceries of Muslim rulers with a ready-to-hand compendium of useful quotations and stylistic models, for much of these secretaries' work involved inditing correspondence in a highly artificial rhymed prose, replete with quotations from and allusions to earlier authors. His works on

[35] For general discussions on *adab*, see G. E. von Grunebaum, *Mediaeval Islam* (Chicago 1946), 250-7, and F. Gabrieli in EI² s.v.

rhetoric and stylistics (see above, pp. 8-9) were no doubt intended as similar handbooks. For specific classes of statesmen like rulers and viziers he composed his *Sirāj al-mulūk* (see above, p. 5), his *Kitāb as-siyāsa* 'Book on political conduct' and his *Sirr al-wizāra* 'Secret of the vizier's office'. A large subdivision of these *adab* works comprises, however, collections of anecdotes, facetiae, curious occurrences and odd or striking pieces of information; the well-educated man was expected to have a good stock of these with which to season his style or speech. Included in this category are the *Ghurar al-maḍāḥik* 'Best funny stories'; *aẓ-Ẓarāʾif wa'l-laṭāʾif* 'Amusing and curious stories' (not identical with the *Laṭāʾif al-maʿārif*, despite a similarity in title); the *Ḥilyat al-muḥāḍara wa-ʿunwān al-mudhākara wa-maidān al-musāmara* 'Ornament of conviviality and foremost part of conversation and field of story-telling'; and the *Aḥāsin kalim an-nabī wa'ṣ-ṣaḥāba wa't-tābiʿīn wa-mulūk al-Jāhiliyya wa-mulūk al-Islām wa'l-wuzarāʾ wa'l-kuttāb wa'l-bulaghāʾ wa'l-ḥukamāʾ wa'l-ʿulamāʾ* 'Finest examples of the sayings of the Prophet, the Companions, the Successors, the pre-Islamic rulers, the Islamic rulers, the Viziers, the secretaries, the eloquent ones, the philosophers and the scholars'.

3. *The* Laṭāʾif al-maʿārif *and its contents.*

We have seen that Thaʿālibī was an indefatigable compiler of works which would be useful for various classes and professions, ranging from those people concerned with such highly-technical subjects as Arabic grammar to those simply wishing to add a veneer of *adab* to their education. In the century and a half before his time, several works had appeared which were compendia of useful information. The Baghdad scholar Muḥammad b. Ḥabīb (d. 245/859-60) wrote his *Kitāb al-muḥabbar* 'The ornamented book' and included in it much material later inserted in the *Laṭāʾif*. He was particularly concerned to give lists of groups of the pre-Islamic and early Islamic Arabs who were characterised by some striking attribute or activity; accordingly, the *Muḥabbar* is a mine of genealogical information, much of it not found in other sources. Thaʿālibī included in the fifth, sixth, eighth and ninth chapters of the *Laṭāʾif* many such lists. In his eighth chapter, the lists of rulers and prominent persons who had physical defects follows Muḥammad b. Ḥabīb very closely, often verbatim; his list of the members of Quraish famous for their shrewdness (*ad-*

duhāt) is identical with that of the *Muḥabbar*, and his list of those notorious for their lack of judgement (*al-ḥamqā*) is an abridgement.[36]

Tha'ālibī seems to have taken material equally freely from Ibn Qutaiba's *Kitāb al-ma'ārif* 'Book of items of knowledge'. This is a compendium of historical information from the Creation onwards, intended as a concise reference work for secretaries and officials, and containing little material not found in the more extensive historical works; G. Lecomte has justly spoken of 'sa sécheresse et son caractère de *muḫtaṣar* pedagogique'.[37] A Persian author of a generation or so later, Abū 'Alī Aḥmad b. 'Umar, known as Ibn Rusta, wrote an encyclopaedia, the *Kitāb al-a'lāq an-nafīsa* 'Book of the rich and costly robes', in Iṣfahān some time after 290/903. Its seventh section is a geographical one, but the purely geographical part of this section is finished off by several lists of people outstanding for some aspect of lineage, for some action or for some physical defect, etc.; the whole section was extensively drawn upon by Tha'ālibī, both for his own geographical chapter and for the lists of people and snippets of curious information which abound in the *Laṭā'if*.

It is not until the middle years of the 4th/10th century, towards Tha'ālibī's own lifetime, that we get systematic attempts to define and classify the various branches of knowledge and to give lists and interpretations of the technical terms of the sciences. These attempts are represented by al-Fārābī's *Iḥṣā' al-'ulūm* 'Enumeration of the sciences' (widely known in mediaeval Europe in Latin translations as the *De scientiis* or *Compendium omnium scientarum*); the enigmatic Sha'yā or Isaiah b. Farīghūn's *Jawāmi' al-'ulūm* 'Connections of the sciences'; and Abū 'Abdallāh Muḥammad al-Khwārazmi's *Mafātīḥ al-'ulūm* 'Keys of the sciences', which was written shortly after 367/977-8.[38] The latter two works were both written in the north-eastern corner of the Iranian world, in the first case, for the Muḥtājid Amīr of Chaghāniyān on the upper Oxus, in the second one, for a Vizier of the Sāmānids of Bukhārā. Tha'ālibī could conceivably have known the authors of both works personally, but there is no sign of their influence in the *Laṭā'if*. The disciplined approach of Ibn Farīghūn and al-Khwārazmī is poles apart from the mélange of curious information purveyed in the *Laṭā'if*, a book which has little inner coherence but is simply a collection of chapters on disparate topics.

De Jong, who edited the text of the *Laṭā'if* in the 19th century, Zotenberg, who edited part of the *Ghurar as-siyar*, and now

[36] Cf. I. Lichtenstädter, 'Muḥammad Ibn Ḥabîb and his Kitâb al-Muḥabbar', JRAS (1939), 1-27.

[37] 'L'Ifrîqiya et l'Occident dans le Kitâb al-Ma'ârif d'Ibn Qutayba', *Les Cahiers de Tunisie*, Nos. 19-20 (1957), 253.

[38] On these works, see Bosworth, 'A pioneer encyclopedia of the sciences: al-Khwārizmī's Keys of the Sciences', *Isis*, LIV/1 (1963), 100-1.

Abyārī and Ṣairafī, who have recently edited the text of the *Laṭā'if*, have all put forward as the dedicatee of the *Laṭā'if* the famous Ṣāḥib Ismā'īl b. 'Abbād, Vizier to the Būyid Amīr Fakhr ad-Daula of Ray and Jibāl and a famed Arabic stylist, being known as the *Kāfī al-Kufāt* 'Supremely-capable one'. Tha'ālibī's dedication simply says that his book is 'honoured by the exalted name of the Ṣāḥib Abū'l-Qāsim'. It is unlikely that this person could be the Ṣāḥib Ismā'īl b. 'Abbād, even though the latter did, it is true, have the very common patronymic Abū'l-Qāsim (a much-favoured *kunya* because it had been the Prophet Muḥammad's one). So far as we know, Tha'ālibī passed his life in the north-eastern part of the Iranian world, and had no particular connections with the Būyids and their lands in central and western Persia. Moreover, the great Būyid Vizier died in 385/995, and there are various references in the text of the *Laṭā'if* to events and people at dates later than this (e.g. tr. below, pp. 114–15, 143), not all of which can have been later additions or insertions. The true dedicatee can in fact be incontestably identified as the celebrated Ghaznavid Vizier Abū'l-Qāsim Aḥmad b. Ḥasan Maimandī, known as *Shams al-Kufāt* 'Sun of the capable ones' (see above, p. 6). Maimand was a small place in the province of Zamīndāwar in south-east Afghanistan, lying between Bust and Qandahār, and Maimandī's father had been *'āmil* or tax-collector of Bust under Sebüktigin.[39] In the tenth, geographical chapter of the *Laṭā'if*, Tha'ālibī deals with Bust and praises it as the region which has given birth to 'the unique figure of the age, the crown of the epoch, the outstanding figure of both this inferior world and the superior one, the Ṣāḥib Shams al-Kufāt' (tr. below, p. 136). The *Laṭā'if* must therefore come from the latter period of Tha'ālibī's life when he had been drawn into the orbit of the Ghaznavids, but it must have been written before Maimandī's death in 424/1032.

[39] See Bosworth, *The Ghaznavids*, 73.

The ten chapters of the *Laṭā'if* fall roughly into three groups:

(1) The biggest group comprises chapters one, four, five, six, eight and nine, which give information about the originators of certain practices and about outstanding exponents of certain professions, give lists of people with some common quality or link of relationship, describe strange coincidences and set down anecdotes containing unusual or striking items of information.

(2) Chapters two, three and seven deal with personal names; the explanation of curious nicknames given to poets and other

well-known figures, and a consideration of remarkable coincidences and patterns in the giving of names.

(3) Chapter ten is an extended geographical section, treating of the regions and cities of the central and eastern lands of Islam, with particular emphasis on their characteristic products and specialities.

The first chapter deals with the *awā'il*, the first occurrences of certain things or phenomena and the first persons to perform certain acts, both in the pre-Islamic period – many of these *awā'il* are placed in the age of the Old Testament Prophets – and in the time of Muḥammad and his successors the Caliphs. Muslim interest in the first occurrence of things seems to have had three bases: a natural curiosity about origins; a general feeling that the ancients were the repositories of much wisdom which it was the duty of later generations to recover; and a legal and historical necessity, viz. the need to justify practices and to ground them on such sound authorities as the Patriarchs and Prophets, Muḥammad and his Companions, and the early Caliphs.

Studies on the *awā'il* crystallised into a minor branch of Islamic literature, at first merely as sections of larger works (as here in the *Laṭā'if*) and then as independent works, beginning with the *Kitāb al-awā'il* of Abū Hilāl al-Ḥasan al-'Askarī (written in 395/1005). 'Askarī was also the author of a famous treatise for secretaries, the *Kitāb aṣ-ṣinā'atain al-kitāba wa'sh-shi'r* 'Book of the two arts, secretaryship and poetry', and knowledge of the *awā'il* was accounted part of a secretary's general education. Hence the 9th/15th century Mameluke author al-Qalqashandī in his monumental guide to the secretary's art, the *Ṣubḥ al-a'shā fī ṣinā'at al-inshā'* 'Dawn of the night-blind one concerning the art of inditing correspondence', devotes a section to it, noting with approval the pioneer efforts of Tha'ālibī in the *Laṭā'if* and of 'Askarī.[40] Much of Tha'ālibī's material in this first chapter accords with that in Ibn Qutaiba's *Ma'ārif* and in Ibn Rusta's *al-A'lāq an-nafīsa*, both of which have a special chapter on the *awā'il*. There are also many parallels with lists in Muḥammad b. Ḥabīb's *Muḥabbar*, e.g. the list of those prophets born clean and circumcised; and that part of Tha'ālibī's chapter dealing with the prophets before Muḥammad overlaps the literature of the *Qiṣaṣ al-anbiyā'* 'Tales of the prophets' of such authors as Abū Isḥāq Aḥmad b. Muḥammad ath-Tha'labī (d. 427/1035) and Muḥammad b. 'Abdallāh al-Kisā'ī (lived in the 5th/11th century).[41]

The second chapter deals with the nicknames (*alqāb*) of Arab

[40] *Ṣubḥ al-a'shā* (Cairo 1331-40/1913-22), I, 412-36.

[41] The only monograph on the *awā'il* literature is the very outdated and inaccessible one of R. Gosche, 'Die Kitâb al-awâil, eine litterar-historische Studie', in *Festgabe zur XXV. Versammlung deutscher Philologen, Orientalisten und Schulmänner zu Halle* (Halle 1867), which deals mainly with the works of Ibn Qutaiba, 'Askarī and Suyūṭī (who abridged 'Askarī); see now Rosenthal, in EI² s.v.

poets which were taken from their own poetry, and the third one with the nicknames given in Islamic times to great leaders and prominent men. The Arab system of nomenclature was for a person to have a name proper (*ism 'alam*) e.g. 'Alī, Zainab, plus a patronymic (*kunya*) e.g. Abū Aḥmad, Umm Ḥabīb, and finally a by-name showing origin or relationship (*nisba*) or nickname (*laqab, nabaz*). The *nisba* might be a plain statement of trade or profession, e.g. *al-Qalānisī* 'the hat-maker', or it might show personal or family origin, e.g. *al-Ḥalabī* 'the man from Aleppo'. The *laqab* might be an honorific, the use of which was becoming widespread in eastern Islam during Tha'ālibī's day, e.g. *Zain al-Milla* 'Ornament of the religious community', or it might be satirical or derisory, e.g. *al-Farazdaq* 'the man with the pasty complexion' (the term *nabaz* is only used for nicknames with a clearly derogatory meaning).[41a]

[41a] The composition of the Arabic name is discussed in great detail and with a wealth of examples, by L. Caetani and G. Gabrieli in their *Onomasticon arabicum*. I *Fonti – Introduzioni* (Rome 1915), 73ff.; the *laqab* is dealt with on pp. 144–222.

The *alqāb* of poets dealt with by Tha'ālibī in his second chapter are mainly neutral in tenor, being derived from striking phrases or rare words in their poems which later became attached to their author; a well-known one of this type is that of the pre-Islamic warrior-poet Thābit b. Jābir al-Fahmī, known as *Ta'abbaṭa Sharran* 'He carried an evil under his arm', for which various explanations are given (see below, p. 53). The *alqāb* explained in the third chapter are, however, mainly uncomplimentary or mocking, for, as Tha'ālibī notes at the beginning of the chapter, the men of Mecca had the practice of giving offensive nicknames, and this became general, despite a Qur'ānic prohibition (Sūra xlix, 11).

In fact, the Arabs seem to have given each other epithets and nicknames from the earliest times, sometimes to highlight praiseworthy qualities, sometimes with a satirical intent. Not infrequently, these appellations were *nomina boni augurii*, aimed at attracting a favourable omen and at avoiding the evil eye.[42] In this connection, the words of Ibn Duraid in his *Kitāb al-ishtiqāq* 'Book of the derivation of names' are noteworthy: 'Abū Ḥātim Sahl b. Muḥammad as-Sijistānī related to us that someone once said to al-'Utbī "How is it that the Arabs give their sons names which are considered unpleasant (*mustashna'a*) yet give their slaves pleasant (*mustaḥsana*) ones?" He was told that they give their sons names with their enemies in mind, whereas they give their slaves the names they want (sc. without any ulterior motive in mind).' Ibn Duraid then goes on to give examples of names given to sons which would augur well against enemies (*tafā'ul*^{an}

[42] Names of this type are examined from a general point of view by Sir James Frazer in *The golden bough*, Pt. II 'Taboo and the perils of the soul', Ch. 6 'Tabooed words'; in the Islamic context, see the comments of Caetani and Gabrieli in their *Onomasticon arabicum*, I, 64–5.

'alā a'dā'ihim), i.e. names expressing toughness, bellicosity, etc.[43]

In Islamic times it came to be believed that a man's nickname gave a good indication of his nature. Tha'ālibī twice quotes in this third chapter of the *Laṭā'if* a line of poetry which must have become a popular saying: 'It is rare that your eyes light upon a man whose character is not revealed, if you consider the matter, in his nickname' (tr. below, pp. 62-3). A fair-sized literature grew up on the explanation and formation of both patronymics and nicknames; amongst this literature, for instance, is a work by the great Ḥanbalī scholar Abū'l-Faraj Ibn al-Jauzī (d. 597/1200), the *Kashf an-niqāb 'an al-asmā' wa'l-alqāb* 'Removing of the veil from names and nicknames'.[44] At the end of this third chapter, Tha'ālibī makes the curious observation that the people of Baghdad and Nīshāpūr were celebrated for the inventiveness and freedom with which they bestowed nicknames, and he gives several examples, all of them bizarre and one or two of them very gross; since he does not explain them, the stories behind the names must remain forever unknown.

The short fourth chapter is concerned with the class of secretaries (*kuttāb*) through the ages, and it traces the development of the profession from the time of Idrīs, the first man to use the pen, and of Joseph, secretary to the Mighty One in Egypt, down to the secretaries of the Umayyad period. Here is a clear instance of a practical motive for delvings into the *awā'il*, the first persons in this case to act as secretaries: the class of secretaries, numerous and influential in the *dīwāns* or government departments of the Abbasid Caliphate, was concerned with the prestige of its calling and wished to demonstrate its long pedigree.[45] Much of the technical knowledge and expertise of the Islamic secretaries in fact went back to the secretaries of Sāsānid Persia, the *dibhērān*, for there were few purely Arab foundations here to build upon. However, Tha'ālibī in this chapter ignores entirely the Persian heritage, and jumps from the secretaries of Old Testament times to the Arabs of the Prophet's time, without reference to any intervening cultures. In addition to upholding the prestige of the class of secretaries, there was a historical reason for the study of past adepts of the craft: the amanuenses of the Prophet had been entrusted with the recording of the successive revelations making up the Qur'ān, and the secretary Zaid b. Thābit played the leading part in collecting together and collating the various extant versions of the divine revelation, producing under the Caliph 'Uthmān the recension of the text which became standard.[46]

[43] Ed. Wüstenfeld (Göttingen 1850), 4-5; see also Jāḥiẓ, *Kitāb al-ḥayawān* (Cairo 1356-64/1938-45), I, 324-7.

[44] Barbier de Meynard examines this literature on nicknames at the beginning of his monograph 'Surnoms et sobriquets dans la littérature arabe', JA, Ser. 10, Vol. IX (1907), 173-244, 365-428, Vol. X (1907), 55-118, 193-273; he includes in his alphabetical list of names many of those given by Tha'ālibī in the second and third chapters of the *Laṭā'if*. To the sources used by Barbier de Meynard, there should be added the short section on *alqāb ba'ḍ ash-shu'arā'* in Jāḥiẓ, *al-Bayān wa't-tabyīn* (Cairo 1366/1947), I, 351-3, and the *Kitāb al-mukāthara 'ind al-mudhākara* 'Book of profuse speech in literary discussions' of Ja'far b. Muḥammad aṭ-Ṭayālisī (d. 282/895), first edited by R. Geyer in SBWAW, CCIII (1927), No. 4, and now by M. T. aṭ-Ṭanjī in Supplement to *Sarkiyat Mecmuasī*, I (Istanbul 1956). The Islamic literature on *kunyas* is also extensive; see the bibliographical note in Caetani and Gabrieli, *op. cit.*, I, 132-3.

[45] Sourdel has observed that the class of secretaries, very much in the background during the Umayyad period, pushed itself into prominence during the early Abbasid period, a process criticised by the contemporary writer Ibn al-Muqaffa' (*Le vizirat 'Abbāside*, I, 60-1).

[46] Cf. Nöldeke-Schwally, *Geschichte des Qorans* (Leipzig 1909-19), II, 11ff.; R. Bell, *Introduction to the Qur'ān* (Edinburgh 1953), 38-43.

With regard to sources, it is clear from correspondences in the texts that Tha'ālibī drew on the *Kitāb al-wuzarā' wa'l-kuttāb* 'Book of viziers and secretaries' of Abū 'Abdallāh Muḥammad b. 'Abdūs al-Jahshiyārī (d. 331/942-3). Jahshiyārī also begins his book with Idrīs, as being the first to write with the pen (Adam, he says, scratched on clay tablets), and likewise passes on to the amanuenses of the Prophet and the officials and secretaries of later times up to the time of the Abbasids; but unlike Tha'ālibī, Jahshiyārī does notice *en passant* the rôle of the Persian secretaries of the Sāsānid emperors. At the end of his chapter, Tha'ālibī mentions those authors who have written about the secretaries of recent times (his own brief account has terminated with a mention of the secretaries of the Umayyad governor al-Ḥajjāj b. Yūsuf, d. 95/714): he names Jahshiyārī, the *Kitāb al-wuzarā'* 'Book of Viziers' of Abū Bakr Muḥammad b. Yaḥyā aṣ-Ṣūlī (d. 335/946-7 or 336/947-8) and his own *Yatīmat ad-dahr*.[47]

[47] Unfortunately, the second part of Jahshiyārī's book, beginning with the reign of al-Ma'mūn, is lost, but several citations in later authors are known; these have been collected by M. 'Awwād in RAAD, XVIII (1943), 318-32, 435-42, and by Sourdel in *Mélanges Louis Massignon* (Damascus 1956-7), III, 271-99. Ṣūlī's work is wholly lost, but fragments of it from later works have been gathered together by Sourdel in *Bulletin d'Études Orientales*, XV (Damascus 1956-7), 99-108.

The fifth chapter bears the Arabic title *Fī'l-a'raqīn min kull ṭabaqa wa'l-mutanāsiqīn fī aḥwāl mukhtalifa*, which can only be translated into English in a ponderous fashion as something like 'Concerning those with the longest family traditions of possessing certain qualities or of exercising certain functions, and concerning those who could trace back the longest unbroken lines of descent in regard to various functions or qualities'. The Arabs always took a pride in their ancestry, and the ability to trace back unbroken lines of non-servile ancestors was much prized. This pride is clearly seen in one example adduced by Tha'ālibī, that of the Umayyad Caliph Yazīd III (reigned 126/744). Because of his paternal descent from several Caliphs and their marriage connections with princesses from non-Arab dynasties, he was able to boast:

> I am the descendant of the Persian emperor, my forefather was Marwān [b. al-Ḥakam], and both the Emperor of Byzantium and the Khāqān of the Turks were my ancestors. (tr. below, p. 73)

In the early Caliphate, the skill of the *nassāba* or genealogist (the first Caliph, Abū Bakr, is said to have been very knowledgeable here) was no mere academic attainment. The payment of stipends to the Arab warriors from the central treasury, the Dīwān system instituted by the Caliph 'Umar, took into account, for purposes of computing the stipends, closeness of relationship to the Prophet. Moreover, since the money was handed out in a lump sum to the tribal chiefs, who then distributed it to the rank-and-file, it was necessary for everyone to enrol in one or other of the Arab tribes.[48] All this was a great stimulus to genealogical research. Genealogical lists figure prominently in Muḥammad b. Ḥabīb's *Muḥabbar,* from which Tha'ālibī derived material for this chapter, and the desire to connect oneself as closely as possible with the Prophet and his entourage is seen in Tha'ālibī's section on the man with the longest chain of forefathers, all of whom could claim to have been Companions of Muḥammad (tr. below, p. 73).

48 Cf. Cl. Cahen, EI² Art. ''Aṭā'', and A. S. Tritton, 'Notes on the Muslim system of pensions', BSOAS, XVI (1954), 170-2.

But there was yet a further motive in the search for long lines of predecessors in some special activity or office. There was a strong feeling in the Islamic world that the arcana of many offices and professions were best preserved within certain families. Rulers often chose their ministers from families in which traditions of official service were deep-rooted; thus the Abbasids took several of their Viziers from the Barmakīs, the Wahbīs, the Khāqānīs, the Furātīs and the Jarrāḥīs, and the Sāmānids had their Jaihānīs, Bal'amīs and 'Utbīs. That rulers should recruit their Viziers, Mustaufīs, Ḥājibs, Qāḍīs, etc. from families who retained their skills hereditarily is a frequent recommendation of the 'Mirrors for Princes'.[49]

49 E.g. in Niẓām al-Mulk's *Siyāsat-nāma*, ch. xli, tr. H. Darke, *The book of government or rules for kings* (London 1960), 178-9.

The greater part of this chapter of the *Laṭā'if* is devoted to men with unbroken pedigrees in some activity or office. For the ruler with the longest pedigree, Tha'ālibī had to go to the Sāsānid emperors. The early Arabs had no feeling for primogeniture, indeed, they positively disliked it; direct succession from father to eldest son was found, but equally often, power passed to uncles or brothers or younger sons. In this chapter, some of Tha'ālibī's chains of people are linked only by some curious or rather inconsequential feature, e.g. the man with the longest chain of ancestors who died violent deaths, but others are based on family traditions in certain offices such as those of Vizier or Qāḍī. Finally, he devotes a fair amount of space to the family with the longest poetic pedigree, that of Abū Ḥafṣa, who from the time of the Caliph 'Uthmān to the end of the 3rd/9th century counted ten generations of poets, all of whom were favoured and patronised by the Caliphs.

The sixth chapter, *Fī'l-ghāyāt min ṭabaqāt an-nās* 'Concerning outstanding levels of achievement or character reached by various classes of people', also deals with 'records': records in regard to nobility of lineage, exaltedness of marriages, giving birth to many sons who subsequently became Caliphs, etc. Just before the end of the chapter there is an interesting and detailed description of the unparalleled pomp and lavishness with which the Ḥamdānid princess Jamīla bint Nāṣir ad-Daula performed the Pilgrimage to Mecca in 366/976-7, and then Tha'ālibī gives the story of her later unhappy fate at the hands of the Būyid 'Aḍud ad-Daula, vanquisher of Jamīla's brother Abū Taghlib. Tha'ālibī's narrative here was explicitly quoted by the later historian adh-Dhahabī (d. 748/1347-8), but the authenticity of the tale has been doubted by modern orientalists (see below, p. 83, n. 19). Finally, on the authority of Abū Manṣūr al-Barīdī, Tha'ālibī quotes 'Aḍud ad-Daula – certainly the most powerful ruler of eastern Islam in the early part of Tha'ālibī's lifetime – as an example of a monarch acquiring by conquest or inheritance an unrivalled number of territories.

The short seventh chapter, *Fī ẓarā'if al-ittifāqāt fi'l-asmā' wa'l-kunā* 'Concerning curious coincidences and patterns in names and patronymics', reverts to the topic of unusual aspects of nomenclature. Much of the information conveyed here again seems inconsequential, if not downright futile, but a knowledge of such items of information as these was clearly considered an integral part of an *adīb*'s education. The sections where Tha'ālibī treats of men who were involved in certain actions and whose names all began with a certain letter of the alphabet, show a connection with Muslim speculations on the mystical and prophetic values of letters and numbers. His examples relate to the change of régime in 132/750 when the Abbasids overthrew the Umayyad dynasty; at this time, there was circulating in the Islamic world a considerable popular literature of predictions (*malāḥim*) in which the protagonists of the coming struggle were denoted by initials in this mysterious manner (see below, pp. 86-7). A section just before the end of the chapter is about prominent men who had two or three patronymics instead of the usual single one, and is based on the section with the same title in Ibn Qutaiba's *Ma'ārif*.

The eighth chapter is quite a long one and contains various items of striking and curious information about the Prophet, his fellow-tribesmen of Quraish and the rulers of the Arabs. It includes many lists of those men of Quraish who were involved in the events of Muḥammad's prophetic career and in his subsequent victory over those who had mocked at and rejected him. The elaborate story of the five members of Quraish who derided Muḥammad and his preaching and who all mysteriously died on the same day, seems to be an attempt to explain Qur'ān, xv, 95, 'Indeed, We have relieved you of the mockers', and perhaps also to emphasise the early Islamic disapproval of frivolity and scoffing (*hazl, mujūn*).[50] It also injects a miraculous element into Muḥammad's life story, a process which, so scholars like Tor Andrae and R. A. Nicholson have claimed, began soon after the Prophet's death, and which sprang from a natural human feeling that Muḥammad could not have been exactly like other mortals.[51] The list of these five scoffers, and many other lists in this chapter, appears in Muḥammad b. Ḥabīb's *Muḥabbar*, but the explanatory stories detailing how the five scoffers met their fates appear not in the *Muḥabbar* but in the same author's *Kitāb al-munammaq* 'The embellished book'. The lists of persons with physical defects given here by Tha'ālibī are also found in Ibn Qutaiba's *Ma'ārif* and in Ibn Rusta, as well as in the *Muḥabbar*, and, indeed, Islamic literature contains special books devoted to this class of people (see below, pp. 93, n. 26; 94, n. 29).

A dwelling on physical defects and on disreputable traits of character (cf. Tha'ālibī's lists here of the notorious liars, fornicators and heretics of Quraish) was a tactic of the anti-Arab party in their literary battles with the pro-Arabs, the controversies of the Shu'ūbiyya, which were at their height in the 3rd/9th century. From seeking *taswiya*, equality, with the Arabs, the Shu'ūbīs passed to *tafḍīl*, the vaunting of their own particular nation, Persian, Nabataean, Greek, etc. over that of the Arabs. We have noted how much importance the Arabs attached to purity of lineage. The Persian *mawālī* or clients took up the study of genealogies enthusiastically, and the Shu'ūbīs then carried the war directly into the enemy's camp and attacked many of the Arab genealogies as spurious, as being linked by invalid marriages or as being tainted by slave blood.[52] Tha'ālibī quotes as his source for his section on the notorious sodomites and pathics of Quraish a work on the *mathālib* or disreputable characteristics of the Arabs by the polemicist and philologist Abū 'Ubaida Ma'mar b. al-Muthannā (110-209/728 to 824-5), himself a *maulā* of Mesopotamian, presumably Nabataean, origin. The exact rôle played by Abū 'Ubaida in the Shu'ūbiyya controversies is still a matter for dispute (see below, p. 91, n. 16), but his name is widely linked with the *mathālib* literature, and it is clearly from material of this type that Muḥammad b. Ḥabīb and later Tha'ālibī drew the subject-matter of their lists.

In the latter part of the chapter, Tha'ālibī goes on to consider

[50] On this attitude, see Pellat, 'Seriousness and humour in early Islam', *Islamic Studies*, II/3 (Karachi 1963), 353-6 (=an enlargement of his EI² article 'al-Djidd wa'l-hazl').

[51] Cf. Andrae, *Die Person Muhammads in Lehre und Glauben seiner Gemeinde* (Stockholm 1918), 290ff., and Nicholson, 'The Perfect Man', in *Studies in Islamic mysticism* (Cambridge 1921), 77-142.

[52] Cf. Goldziher's masterly chapter in *Muhammedanische Studien* (Halle 1888-90), I, 101ff., still the best starting-point for a consideration of the Shu'ūbiyya movement.

certain other topics The dominant traits and interests of the Umayyad Caliphs and the treasure hoards amassed by the Abbasids (one of his sources here was aṣ-Ṣūlī's *Kitāb al-aurāq* 'Book of the written sheets') are discussed. Then comes a detailed description of two of the most dazzling celebrations ever given in Islam, whose splendour became proverbial: that given by al-Ma'mūn's minister al-Ḥasan b. Sahl on the occasion of the Caliph's consummation of his marriage to al-Ḥasan's daughter Būrān, and that given by al-Mutawakkil at the circumcision of his son al-Mu'tazz. The description of the festivities organised at Fam aṣ-Ṣilḥ by al-Ḥasan follows closely that given by the Egyptian author Abū'l-Ḥasan 'Alī b. Muḥammad ash-Shābushtī (d. 390/1000) in his work on the Christian monasteries of the Near East and especially of Iraq, the *Kitāb ad-diyārāt*. Finally, there is a brief reversion to the lists of the earlier part of the chapter, with sections on the sons born of slave mothers (after the time of al-Amīn, it became the norm that the Abbasid Caliphs were born of slave mothers, usually non-Arab women) and on the trades and crafts of prominent early Muslim leaders and scholars.

The ninth chapter is also long and is devoted to interesting and entertaining pieces of information about unusual happenings and remarkable coincidences. Much of this material is presented in the form of historical anecdotes, in which the Caliphs loom large; the intricacies of relationship and succession, the turns of fortune brought about by depositions and restorations, form the staple of these stories. Striking facts about ages, lengths of tenure of power in certain offices, and a series of moral tales about the deaths of prominent rulers and military leaders, then follow. The chapter ends with several verses by Tha'ālibī himself on the great mortality amongst Muslim rulers and commanders in the two years 387/997 and 388/998, again pointing a suitable moral about the transience of human power.

The tenth and last chapter is the longest of the book and is a geographical one. It is a highly selective survey, with almost exclusive emphasis on the beauties and imperfections (*maḥāsin wa masāwī*) of the places dealt with, and on their characteristic products and specialities (*khaṣā'iṣ*). The area covered is only a limited part of the Islamic world, and the coverage obviously reflects Tha'ālibī's own sphere of interest and knowledge. It was a convention observed by many earlier geographers (e.g. the early 4th/10th century ones Qudāma b. Ja'far, Ibn Rusta and Ibn al-Faqīh) to begin with the cradles of Islam, the two Holy Cities or Ḥaramain of Mecca and Medina; Thaʻālibī follows this, but apart from a few lines on the products of the Yemen, he has no further interest in the Arabian peninsula. Egypt and Syria are accorded sections, but the whole of the Maghrib and Africa is otherwise ignored; nor are the Fāṭimid Caliphs of Cairo, whose political and cultural influence was dominant in the western Islamic world and in much of the region of Syria and Palestine during Thaʻālibī's time, ever mentioned here.

Only when he moves eastwards to Iraq does Thaʻālibī become more detailed, usually dealing with specific towns rather than with whole countries or provinces. He was not of course a professional geographer and so was unaffected by the great strides made in Islamic geographical techniques during the course of the 4th/10th century. He adopts neither of the two main approaches of the classical Islamic geographers, the first one based on the Greek system of zones or climes (Arabic *iqlīm* pl. *aqālīm*), and the second one based on the Persian division of the earth into seven concentric circles (*haft kishvar*) centred on Iraq, where had lain the capital of the Sāsānid empire.[53] Instead, Thaʻālibī's survey is purely territorial, moving from west to east and becoming increasingly detailed the nearer he approaches to Khurāsān and the eastern Iranian lands, those with which he had personal acquaintance. However, Baghdad, the seat of the Abbasid Caliphate and the cultural centre of the non-Fāṭimid Islamic world, could not be dismissed summarily. Geographers like Yaʻqūbī and Masʻūdī considered Baghdad and Iraq as 'the navel of the earth' (*surrat al-arḍ*), placed in the central and most equable clime of the world, and Thaʻālibī is equally enthusiastic about it as the focal point of skill and knowledge in the Islamic world. He cites the famous Būyid Vizier and literary stylist Abū'l-Faḍl Muḥammad, known as Ibn al-ʻAmīd, who accounted approval of Baghdad and its rôle as the home of the arts and sciences of mankind as one of the two indispensable criteria for scholarship (the other being approval of Jāḥiẓ and his writings).[54] From Iraq, Thaʻālibī passes into Persia proper and becomes fuller in his treatment of its towns, ranging as far east as Ghazna and Bust in eastern Afghanistan and as far north as Samarqand, Bukhārā and Khwārazm. Short sections on the specialities of India, China and the Turkish lands conclude the geographical survey.

The earlier 'road-book' type of geography had concentrated on the routes linking towns and provinces and on administrative boundaries, as the favoured name for several geographies of this

[53] Cf. S. Maqbul Ahmad, EI[2] Art. 'Djughrāfiyā'.

[54] According to Thaʻālibī, *Yatīmat ad-dahr*, III, 158, Ibn al-ʻAmīd was himself known as the Jāḥiẓ of his age (*al-Jāḥiẓ al-akhīr*).

type, *Kitāb al-masālik wa'l-mamālik* 'Book of roads and provinces' shows (cf. the works of Ibn Khurradādhbih, Jaihānī and Iṣṭakhrī); these works had often in fact been practical handbooks for travellers, administrators and agents of the *Barīd* or state postal and intelligence service. Tha'ālibī was not concerned with topography and communications or with fixing the exact geographical location of places; his aim was merely to give the modicum of geographical information required by a student of *adab*. The nearest he gets to an interest in physical geography is in his comments on the fertility and pleasantness or otherwise of places, and on weather and climate, whenever these presented special points of interest (e.g. the excessive cold of Khwārazm, in regard to which he quotes some of his own poetry, tr. below, p. 143).

As the appearance of the word *khaṣā'iṣ* in the chapter heading would lead one to expect, the bulk of Tha'ālibī's material is on the crops, products and manufactures for which each town or region was famed; it thus forms in some degree an economic geography. Amongst these specialities, foodstuffs (fruits, vegetables, herbs, etc.), luxury articles (perfumes, jewels, furs, etc.) and textiles (cloths, carpets, etc.) figure most prominently. Many of the towns of Persia were considerable centres of industrial activity on the part of small craftsmen, artisans and shopkeepers, and there were few places which did not produce textiles of some sort: rugs and carpets in north-western Persia, Armenia and Kurdistan, cotton and woollen cloths almost everywhere. Textiles played a great part in the lives of mediaeval Muslims, for the accumulation of a store of rich carpets or garments was one way of keeping wealth in a fairly liquid form. Some of the cloths produced in Persia achieved fame all over the Islamic world, e.g. the gold-threaded *mulḥam* cloth of Merv, the *munayyar* silken cloth of Ray and the fine *ḥafī* and *sāburī* cloths of Nīshāpūr (see below, tr. p. 133); in his *Bard al-akbād* Tha'ālibī links *mulḥam* and *ḥafī* cloths with *Wadhārī* ones from Samarqand and *'attābi* ones from Fārs as the only four materials fit for rulers and nobles to wear.[55]

[66] *Khams rasā'il*, 129, tr. Rescher, *Orientalistische Miszellen*, 11, 77.

Tha'ālibī frequently repeated himself in his many works, utilising items of information taken from one composition in another. Thus quite a lot of the material in this chapter of the *Laṭā'if* also appears, more or less verbatim, in his philological work the *Thimār al-qulūb* (see above, pp. 8-9). In the forty-fourth chapter of this work, 'Concerning dwellings, buildings and places', Tha'ālibī deals *inter alia* with the lighthouse of Alexandria, the great church of Edessa, the Umayyad mosque at Damascus and the Wādī'l-Qaṣr at Basra. In the forty-fifth chapter, 'Concerning various items and products connected with particular lands and places', he treats of the taxative capacity of Egypt, its cotton, asses and papyrus; the apples, glassware and olive oil of Syria; the aloes wood and swords of India; the sapphires of Ceylon; the cloaks and swords of the Yemen; the garments of Rūm; the ambergris of ash-Shiḥr (on the coast of the Ḥaḍramaut); the sugar-cane of Ahwāz; the roses of Jūr; the honey of Iṣfahān; the carpets of Armenia; the cloaks of Ray; the edible earth of Nīshāpūr; the jet of Ṭūs; the *qishmish* currants of Herat; the garments of Merv; the fine paper of Samarqand; the curious contrivances and *objets d'art* made in China; and the musk of Tibet. Finally, in the forty-sixth chapter, 'Concerning various states and conditions connected with different regions', he mentions the submissiveness of the people of Syria, the ease of life at Medina, the fevers of Ahwāz and the climate of Gurgān.[56]

[56] *Thimār al-qulūb* (Cairo 1326/1908), 409-41.

Despite the unsystematic and selective nature of Tha'ālibī's approach in this tenth chapter of the *Laṭā'if*, many of his snippets of information can be combined with other material from contemporary geographers and historians to give a picture of the vitality of eastern Islam's economy at this time. Distances were great and communications hazardous, but the pacification of the Persian countryside, achieved in some measure by forceful dynasties like the Sāmānids, the early Būyids and the Ghaznavids, tempted merchants to invest money in operations beyond their own home towns and thus allowed a long-distance trade to develop. The rise of Baghdad as the supreme centre of production and consumption favoured the growth of this traffic. Tha'ālibī records that the superlative *bāranj* melons of Khwārazm were exported to Iraq, a distance of 1,600 miles, as early as the Caliphates of al-Ma'mūn and al-Wāthiq (i.e. the first half of the 3rd/9th century); these melons were packed around with snow inside leaden containers (tr. below, p. 142). Likewise, he speaks of the famous edible earth of Zauzan in the Nīshāpūr district, presumably a diatomaceous or similar light clay, and says that it is exported as far as Egypt and the Maghrib, where a *riṭl* of it fetches as much as a dinar (tr. below, pp. 131-2).

The pagan lands beyond the eastern borders of Islam were chiefly known to the Muslims, at least before the Ghaznavid campaigns into India, through trade connections, and Tha'ālibī's sections on India, China and the Turkish lands are devoted exclusively to a consideration of their products. The Siberian steppes and the Central Asian and Tibetan mountain massifs were chiefly known as sources for Turkish slaves, furs, hides and precious stones and metals; Tha'ālibī details these articles, with particular emphasis on the various fur-producing animals whose pelts found their way into the Islamic world as luxury articles. India supplied the Muslims with many wonderful things, such as jewels, hardwoods, aromatics and other products of its tropical fauna and flora. The Chinese had a reputation as skilful and ingenious artisans; according to Tha'ālibī, 'The Arabs used to call every delicately or curiously-made vessel and such like, whatever its real origin, "Chinese", because finely-made things are a speciality of China.' He mentions the fine, translucent pottery made in China under the T'ang (and at a later period, under the K'i-tan or Liao and Sung) which, as the excavations of Sarre and Herzfeld revealed, was used in the palaces of the Abbasids at Sāmarrā in Iraq; and in his section on Samarqand he records how the manufacture of fine paper was introduced into that city by Chinese artisans captured in the Arab-Chinese warfare of the 2nd/8th century (see below, tr. p. 140).

Although Tha'ālibī mentions various informants who gave him items of information on the different towns and their products, or who recited to him verses about them (the chapter is liberally sprinkled with poetry), he mentions none of the great geographers of the 4th/10th century specifically by name. His nearest approach to this is a mention of 'the author of the Book of provinces and roads', *ṣāḥib Kitāb al-mamālik wa'l-masālik* (tr. below, p. 140), and since the passage here quoted does not appear in the extant geographies bearing this name or a similar one, the work in question is most likely the lost *Kitāb al-masālik wa'l-mamālik* of the Sāmānid Vizier Abū 'Abdallāh Aḥmad b. Muḥammad al-Jaihānī.

Nevertheless, Tha'ālibī does cite frequently in this chapter, as elsewhere in the *Laṭā'if*, the great littérateur of the previous century, Abū 'Uthmān 'Amr b. Baḥr al-Jāḥiẓ (d. 255/868). Jāḥiẓ was the author of a *Kitāb al-amṣār wa 'ajā'ib al-buldān* 'Book on the great cities and wonders of the lands' in which he discussed the characteristics and relative advantages and defects of the regions of Islam; it is probably this work which Maqdisī had in mind when he cited Jāḥiẓ on the characteristics of each of the *amṣār* (*Aḥsan at-taqāsīm*, 33, cf. 241), and it is quoted explicitly by Mas'ūdī (*Murūj adh-dhahab*, I, 206-7, and *Kitāb at-tanbīh*, 55, tr. Carra de Vaux, 82).[57] The only work by Jāḥiẓ which Tha'ālibī specifically names is the *Kitāb at-tabaṣṣur bi't-tijāra* 'An enquiry

[57] A *Kitāb al-buldān* by Jāḥiẓ is partially extant in a British Museum ms., and it is possible that this is identical with the *Kitāb al-amṣār wa 'ajā'ib al-buldān*; cf. Pellat, 'Ǧāḥiẓiana III. Essai d'inventaire de l'œuvre ǧāḥiẓienne', *Arabica*, III (1956), 154, No. 35.

into commercial practice', quoting from it that the best felts come from China, the Maghrib and Ṭālaqān in that order (tr. below, p. 142). The *Kitāb at-tabaṣṣur* is a brief work which deals with certain products, items of commerce and manufactures according to groups: precious metals, jewels, perfumes, textiles, falcons, etc., and Tha'ālibī's citation does indeed appear in its text. But the foremost authority of our time on Jāḥiẓ and his work, Professor Ch. Pellat, has on stylistic grounds doubted its attribution to Jāḥiẓ; at best, he thinks, Jāḥiẓ might have been commissioned to write an opuscule on articles of commerce and then have entrusted its composition to a third party.[58] Whatever the truth may be, the evidence from Tha'ālibī is that the *Kitāb at-tabaṣṣur* was commonly attributed to Jāḥiẓ within 150 years of his death.

Tha'ālibī's tenth chapter moves to its close with a short selection of anecdotes about various places and the peculiar phenomena recorded there. He winds up with an account of a disputation at the court of 'Aḍud ad-Daula in Shīrāz between one Abū 'Alī al-Hā'im and the well-known traveller and raconteur Abū Dulaf Mis'ar b. Muhalhil al-Khazrajī, who overwhelms his opponent with an orational *tour de force* in which he inserts a great number of the special products of the various regions of the Islamic world.

[58] Cf. *idem*, 'Ǧāḥiẓiana I. Le *Kitāb al-tabaṣṣur bi-l-tiǧāra* attribué à Ǧāḥiẓ', *Arabica*, I (1954), 153-65, giving a translation of the work.

The *Laṭāʾif al-maʿārif*

Exordium.

In the name of God, the Merciful, the Compassionate
Our trust is in the Lord of Mankind, the Beneficent One

Beginning with praise to God and the invocation of His assistance, and with salutations on the Prophet, the Chosen One, at the opening of the day and at its end.

This is a book about entertaining and subtle aspects of the various branches of knowledge, their striking features and their strange ones, their amusing sides and their wondrous ones. The material for this book has been taken from works dealing with historical accounts and traditions which go back a long way in time, and the book is now at this moment honoured by the exalted name of the Ṣāḥib Abū'l-Qāsim ⌜Aḥmad b. Ḥasan al-Maimandī⌝.[1] With it I pay homage to his elevated presence, a presence which is too lofty for any book to be laid before it except for works which even kings would be proud to accept and which both a free man and a slave would be emboldened to put forward.

Nevertheless, all the choicest fruits of literature and the elegancies of polite learning which are gathered before his presence are just like a pitcher of brackish water brought to the foaming waters of the wide Euphrates. Despite this fact, the book may perhaps be offered to the master of the age, the unique one amongst mankind, the one who encompasses within himself all the rare beauties of the world, the one who unites harmoniously within himself all the disparate elements which go to make up nobility of character, the one who is superior to the noble souls and men of power of past ages and present times[2] as much as the sun is superior to the full moon and the ocean to a rain drop! Mere words and phrases are inadequate to describe all his qualities, and his unparalleled merits cannot be brought under the

[1] The pious wish 'May God have mercy on him!' of J must be, as noted in AS, a later copyist's addition, for Maimandī was clearly alive when Tha'ālibī wrote this dedication.

[2] Reading with J *al-bāqīn* for the *al-'āfīn* of AS.

heading of the normal or the commonplace; but everyone gives a present according to his merit, and seeks the favour of the benevolent patron with the utmost of his determination.

May God, His name is magnified, be pleased to lengthen his days, [so that he may remain] secure in his power and serenity, his authority firmly-established and his tranquillity assured, his mind fixed on lofty things and his hand kept supreme, and with his cup of happiness filled both now and for ever! [4

This book is divided into ten chapters. God alone is the One who guides us to a right conclusion of affairs!

Chapter One concerning the first occurrences of various things and the first persons to do various things (*al-awā'il*)

Chapter Two, concerning the nicknames (*alqāb*) given to poets which were taken from their own poetry

Chapter Three, concerning the nicknames further given in Islamic times to great leaders and prominent figures

Chapter Four, concerning the secretaries of former ages

Chapter Five, concerning those with the longest family traditions of possessing certain qualities or of exercising certain functions, and concerning those who could trace back the longest unbroken lines of descent in regard to various functions or qualities

Chapter Six, concerning outstanding levels of achievement or character reached by various classes of people

Chapter Seven, concerning curious coincidences and patterns in names and patronymics

Chapter Eight, concerning diverse items of curious and striking information about the Prophet, Quraish and the rulers of the Arabs

Chapter Nine, concerning interesting and entertaining pieces of information about various unusual happenings and strange coincidences

Chapter Ten, concerning some examples of the specialities of the different lands, together with something about the excellences and imperfections of these places.

With this, the book closes.

In a short while, there will doubtless follow books which will be superior to this one in excellence and which will remedy[3] its defects. The humble slave awaits the command of the exalted one (may God Most High increase him in power and influence) to produce a [further] book by the composition of which he may render service [to the exalted one], and in the composition of which nothing will possibly be kept back to embellish and polish

[3] Reading with AS, *yajburu*.

it – all this through God's granting ability and through His will, and through our master's power (may God prolong his days), and through the felicity of attachment to his service.

Chapter One.

Concerning the first occurrences of various things and the first persons to do various things.

The first sin committed in heaven and earth against God. A certain man of former times has said, Beware of envy, for it was the first sin committed in heaven and earth against God. In regard to heaven, there was Iblīs's envy of Adam, which led Adam to become puffed up and cease bowing down to God. In regard to earth, there was Cain's envy of his brother Abel, because Abel's sacrifice was accepted and his was not, which eventually led to Cain's killing his brother, a deed for which he afterwards, however, became full of remorse.[1]

The first person to use inferential reasoning. Sufyān b. [6
'Uyaina[2] has said, and other people relate likewise, Beware of inferential reasoning (*qiyās*), for the first person who employed it was Iblīs when he said, 'I am superior to him (sc. to Adam), for You have created me from fire, but him from clay.'[3]

The first person who planted date palms and raised cotton was Anūs b. Shīth b. Ādam (sc. Enos). It is also related that he was the first to put a door on the Ka'ba and to speak words of divine wisdom.[4]

The first person who expounded the science of the stars,

[1] Allusion to Qur'ān v, 34/31. On the story of Iblīs and Adam as conceived in Muslim lore, see Tha'labī, *'Arā'is al-majālis fī qiṣaṣ al-anbiyā'* (Cairo 1347/1928), 21-30, and on that of Cain and Abel, *ibid.*, 30-3.

Abū Muḥammad Sufyān b. 'Uyaina al-Hilālī, allegedly a *maulā* in origin and a famous traditionist of Kufa; d. at Mecca in 198/814 (cf. Ibn Khallikān, tr. I, 578-80).

[3] Allusion to Qur'ān, vii, 11/12. The position of *qiyās* as one of the sources of Islamic law was the subject of much acrimonious dispute amongst early legal scholars.

[4] An alternative tradition to this one on Enos and the door of the Ka'ba is one in which the Tubba' king of Yemen, As'ad Abū Karib, is said to have come to Mecca and provided the Ka'ba with a veil, a door and a lock (see below, tr. p. 42). The Ka'ba itself is said either to have existed archetypally in Paradise before the descent of Adam to earth, or else to have been first raised by Abraham and Ishmael in the spot indicated by God (cf. Tha'labī, *op. cit.*, 60, and A. J. Wensinck, EI[1] Art. 'Ka'ba').

pointed out the patterns of the heavenly spheres, plotted the paths of the stars, revealed their various influences on human affairs and brought forward information on the wonders of their construction, was Idrīs (? Enoch), peace be upon him. He was also the first to use writing and to sew garments, whereas previously people had only worn skins and hides; and he was the first to make use of weapons, make war and capture people as slaves.[5]

The first person who clipped his moustaches, parted his hair, rinsed out his mouth, cleaned his teeth with a *miswāk*, trimmed his nails and washed himself after performing natural functions, things which later became considered as established practice (*sunna*), was Ibrāhīm (sc. Abraham), peace be upon him.[6] He was also the first to be circumcised, and it is related that he circumcised himself at al-Qaddūm (al-Qaddūm is a place, one of the villages of Canaan, and not, as some people hold, the [7 tool which is used like an axe) (sc. an adze, *qadūm*).[7] One of the popular tales says that a man once circumcised his son, and the latter cried out, 'You have killed me, O father!' The father replied, 'I haven't killed you, it is Abraham, the Friend of God, who has killed you!' Abraham is said to have been the first to give hospitality to guests, so that he acquired the patronymic Abū'ḍ-Ḍaifān ('Father of Guests'); the example which he set is followed at Jerusalem to this day.[8] He was the first person to become white-haired. In this connection, it is said that his son Isḥāq (sc. Isaac) was exactly like him in appearance, so that only someone who considered him at great length or who peered at him with deep penetration, could tell them apart; hence God marked him out with a hoary head, making this a feature by which the two of them could be distinguished. It is related that Abraham was startled when he saw his white hair, and exclaimed, 'O Lord, what is this?' God Most High sent down the message to him, 'This is [a sign of] venerableness', so Abraham replied, 'Increase me in venerableness, O Lord!' Some witty and eloquent person has said, 'Praise be to God who has made pitch[-black hair]

[5] See Tha'labī, *op. cit.*, 34-5, on Idrīs's scientific and cosmological lore. Post-Qur'ānic Muslim authors unanimously identified Idrīs with the Biblical Enoch, and because the consonants of the name 'Enoch' suggest a meaning of 'the initiated', they made him the originator of various sciences and crafts; Nöldeke, however, pointed out that the name 'Enoch' probably conceals that of 'Andreas'. Cf. Wensinck, EI[1] Art. 'Idris'. [*see also* Addenda and Corrigenda, below, p. 147]

[6] On these Abrahamic 'firsts' of personal hygiene, see Tha'labī, *op. cit.*, 70. The use of a *miswāk* or piece of wood to clean the teeth, though not obligatory in Islamic law, was highly commended and was considered to be one of the prescriptions of the 'natural religion' or *fiṭra*; see Wensinck, EI[1] s.v.

[7] According to Muslim tradition, several of the prophets, culminating in Muḥammad himself, were born circumcised; see the lists in Muḥammad b. Ḥabīb, *Kitāb al-muḥabbar* (Hyderabad 1361/1942), 131-2. According to Tha'labī, *op. cit.*, 69, Abraham circumcised himself at a hundred years old, with an adze at al-Qaddūm (thus satisfying both explanations!), after a battle with the Amalekites, so that in future, all the people of the natural religion of Islam would be identifiable as such if slain on the battlefield.

[8] Cf. Tha'ālibī, *Thimār al-qulūb*, 196, s.v. 'Abū'ḍ-Ḍaifān', and Tha'labī, *'Arā'is al-majālis*, 69: 'It is said in the Tradition that someone once addressed the Prophet as "O Lord of Mankind", but the Prophet corrected him, saying, "That title belongs to Abraham, Abū'ḍ-Ḍaifān; he would never eat his morning or evening meal unless he could find a guest to eat with him, and often he would walk two miles or more until he found a guest to invite. His example of hospitality will last until the day of resurrection; it is the 'blessed tree' of which God Most High says, 'It is lit from a blessed tree . . . etc.' (Qur'ān, xxiv, 35)." '

(*qār*) white and called it venerableness (*waqār*)!'[9] Finally, it is related that Abraham was the first person to cast stones [at Satan[10]], and the first to levy taxation; but other people say that, in regard to the last point, it was Mūsā (sc. Moses), peace be upon him.

The first person to speak in Arabic was Ismā'īl (sc. Ishmael), peace be upon him; all the Arabs came subsequently from his progeny, except for three tribes, those of al-Auzā', Ḥaḍramaut and Thaqīf.[11] He was the first to ride horses, these mounts being originally wild horses which had never been ridden before. [8

The first free-born person to be sold as a slave and reduced to servitude was Yūsuf (sc. Joseph), peace be upon him; a poet of our own time has said in allusion to this (metre *Ṭawīl*): *I say, when my spirit is overwhelmed with sorrow, 'O my Lord, if You were to sell my friendship for a song, / One of the prophets, may the blessing of the God of mankind rest upon him, was sold for a vile price too.'*

Joseph was the first person to bring into use papyrus (*al-qarāṭīs*) and employ it for writing; he acted as a scribe for the Mighty One of Egypt, the man who had the dream.[12]

The first person who fashioned a mailed coat and wore it was Dā'ūd (sc. David), peace be upon him; previously in battle, they had worn only cuirasses made of iron plates. He was also the first to use the introductory phrase *Ammā ba'd . . .* ('As follows . . .') in his discourses; this is reputedly the 'trenchant speech' (*faṣl al-khiṭāb*) which God Most High mentions.[13]

The first person to use millstones and set up baths was Sulaimān b. Dā'ūd (sc. Solomon son of David), peace be upon him. He also introduced the use of depilatories. Bilqīs (sc. the Queen of Sheba) had a thick growth of hair on her legs, which was considered ugly and unsightly; so because of this, he ordered the use of depilatories. This is referred to by a certain poet who was satirising a tribe (metre *Basīṭ*): *On the day when the corn is being trampled out, bread is more precious amongst them than depilatories in the time of Bilqīs.*[14]

Solomon, peace be upon him, was also the first person to use soap. [9

The first person after David, peace be upon him, who delivered orations and homilies and spoke eloquently and concisely, was Luqmān the Wise, whose outstanding wisdom and homilectic powers have become proverbial. It is said that neither he nor anyone else ever uttered anything more eloquent and concise than

[9] Cf. *Thimār al-qulūb*, 556, s.v. 'Waqār ash-shaiba'.

[10] See below, tr., p. 117.

[11] The genealogists regard Ismā'īl as the progenitor of the North Arabs of 'Adnān, *al-'Arab al-musta'riba*, 'arabised', whereas Qaḥṭān's descendants of the South Arabs are designated as 'true Arabs', *al-'Arab al-'āriba*. Auzā' are usually accounted a South Arabian tribe, but Thaqīf were in early Islamic times attributed to the North Arabian groups of either Iyād or Hawāzin; satirists and enemies of Thaqīf, and especially of the Umayyad governor al-Ḥajjāj b. Yūsuf, said that they were the remnants of Thamūd, the people destroyed in the Qur'ān for their impiety, and this tale may have been in Tha'ālibī's mind here (cf. H. Lammens, *La cité arabe de Ṭāif à la veille de l'Hégire* [Beirut 1922], 57-68).

[12] On Joseph in Muslim lore, see Tha'labī, *'Arā'is al-majālis*, 75-99.

[13] In *ibid.*, 194, it is said that God gave David the faculty of using iron so that it became 'just like wax or dough or dampened clay, completely malleable in his hands to whatever form he wished without the need of fire or hammering'; and in *ibid.*, 193, Tha'labī gives several theories on the meaning of *faṣl al-khiṭāb* (=Qur'ān, xxxviii, 19/20).

[14] See on this anecdote about Bilqīs, Tha'labī, *op. cit.*, 216-18, and E. Ullendorff, 'The Queen of Sheba', *Bulletin of the John Rylands Library*, XLV/2 (1963), 493-4, 496.

his words, 'O man! Night and day are both at work upon you (i.e. the ravages of time are devouring you), so strive within them!'[15]

The first person who spoke about predestination (*qadar*) was the prophet 'Uzair (sc. Ezra), peace be upon him; but when he kept on talking about it with great insistence and with polemical arguments, his name was removed from the roll of the prophets, so that he is no longer listed as being one of them, although he does in fact belong there.[16] Ibn ar-Rūmī once satirised someone and compared him to 'Uzair in these words (metre *Mutaqārib*): *Ibn 'Ammār has in him a trait of 'Uzair; he uses it to dispute with God about predestination.*[17]

The first person who wore his robes long and trailed them along the floor was Qārūn (sc. Korah). He was also the first to take up the study of alchemy, and he alludes to it when he says in the Word of God, His name is magnified, 'I have been given it because of knowledge which I have.' He was also the first to wear scarlet-coloured robes: 'So he went forth to his people in all his finery.'[18]

The first person who laid down that the central place in a social gathering should be given to a guest was Bahrām Gūr; he called such a guest the *mihmān*, i.e. 'lord of the house'.[19] A poet has said concerning this (metre *Basīṭ*): *The Persians only called the guest of honour* mihmān *out of respect for that guest, whoever he might be; | The element* mih *means 'greatest one' and* mān *means 'dwelling'* [10 *and a guest is accounted their lord whilst ever he remains in their house.*

The first person who consumed *sawīq* was al-Iskandar (sc. Alexander the Great).[20] He was also the first to make use of gelded horses for ambushes, to plant spies in the armies of his foes and to order his commanders not to pursue fugitives.

The first Arab ruler to sit on a throne was Jadhīma al-Abrash. He was also the first person to set up mangonels as siege-engines, and he originated the use of wax candles for lighting. He grew too proud to associate with human beings, and so took as his boon companions the Farqadān (sc. the two stars β and γ near the pole of the Little Bear); he used to drink one cup, then pour out two

15 On Luqmān, see Tha'labī, *op. cit.*, 243-6, and B. Heller, EI[1] s.v., noting this mysterious figure's various rôles as a sage, as Vizier to King David, as a writer of Aesop-like fables, etc.

16 On 'Uzair, see Heller in EI[1] s.v.; he is unanimously identified by the Muslim commentators with Ezra, although Casanova plausibly suggested that 'Uzair is really Uzail-Azael-Azazel, one of the fallen angels.

17 Aḥmad b. 'Ubaidallāh b. Muḥammad, called Ibn 'Ammār, was an author and also filled minor offices under the patronage of the Banū Wahb in al-Mu'taḍid's reign, dying in 314/926 (R. Guest, *Life and works of Ibn er Rûmî* [London 1944], 28, 94). The occasion of Ibn ar-Rūmī's saying this line is given in Yāqūt, *Irshād al-arīb*, ed. Margoliouth (London 1907-31), I, 223-8.

18 Qur'ān, xxviii, 79. In this *sūra*, Qārūn is the Biblical Korah (Num. xvi) and behaves arrogantly towards the people of Moses because of his great wealth; in two other Qur'ānic passages he is Pharaoh's minister and oppresses the Israelites. Cf. D. B. Macdonald in EI[1] s.v.

19 The hospitality of Bahrām Gūr, and the festivities which he organised, were renowned; cf. Tha'ālibī, *Ta'rīkh ghurar as-siyar*, ed. and tr. H. Zotenberg, *Histoire des rois des Perses* (Paris 1900), 564ff.

20 According to J. Ruska, EI[1] s.v., *sawīq* was 'in the first place barley flour, then wheat flour, then a soup made with flour and water, with honey, oil or pomegranate syrup added'; from Ṭabarī, *Ta'rīkh ar-rusul wa'l-mulūk*, ed. de Goeje, etc. (Leiden 1879-1901), III, 1199, tr. E. Marin, *The reign of al-Mu'taṣim (833-42)* (New Haven, Conn. 1951), 31-2, 40, it appears that *sawīq* was often issued to troops on campaign as a sort of iron ration. In *Ghurar as-siyar*, 444-5, on the authority of Ibn Khurradādhbih, Alexander is said to have have been the first to have had it prepared from wheat, barley and almonds.

for them, until at last he came across Mālik and 'Uqail and took them as his drinking companions.[21]

The first person who had made for himself iron spear-points was Dhū Yazan al-Ḥimyarī, after whom Yazanī lances are named. Previously, the Arabs used the horns of oxen as spear-points.

The first person who ground up and mixed (*hashama*) *tharīd* was 'Amr b. 'Abd Manāf, and he therefore became called Hāshim (literally, 'He who crushes up'); it has been said of him (metre *Kāmil*): *'Amr, the noble one, made up* tharīd *for his people, at a time when the inhabitants of Mecca were starving and emaciated.*[22] [11
It has been further said of him,

There is certainly no-one like Hāshim, however he may crush up tharīd (hasham), *just as there is certainly no-one like Ḥātim, however much he may try to be magnanimous like him* (ḥatam).[23]

He was also the first to introduce the system of two annual trading caravans, one in winter and the other in summer, and the first member of Quraish to go forth to Syria, visit princes, travel far from home, pass through hostile tribes and negotiate with those princes the treaties of peaceful relations (*al-īlāf*), as mentioned by God Most High.[24]

The first person who covered over the Ka'ba with leather strips and fabric pieces was Abū Karib As'ad al-Ḥimyarī; he was a faithful believer in the Prophet, God's prayers and peace be upon him, a long while before the latter was actually sent. He lived for more than 300 years, and it was he who said (metre *Mutaqārib*): *I bear witness that Aḥmad is a messenger from God, the Creator of all mankind; / If only my allotted span could reach up to his lifetime, I would act as his helper and cousin.*[25]

The first person who put a cover of silk and brocade over the Ka'ba was Nutaila bint Janāb b. Kulaib, the mother of al-'Abbās b. 'Abd al-Muṭṭalib. Once when al-'Abbās was small, he had got lost, and she had vowed that if she found him again, she would cover the Holy House with silk and brocade. She did in fact find him, and accordingly fulfilled her vow.

[21] Cf. Tha'ālibī, *Thimār al-qulūb*, 143-4, s.v. 'Nadīmā Jadhīma', and on the man himself, an Arab ruler in Iraq who probably flourished in the 3rd century A.D., see I. Kawar, EI[2] Art. 'Djadhīma al-Abrash'.

[22] The line is attributed in Ṭabarī, I, 1088, to 'Abdallāh b. az-Zabar'ī b. Qais as-Sahmī. On *tharīd*, a dish of meat minced up with bread, grain or dates and one of the favourite dishes of Quraish at Mecca, see Jāḥiẓ, *Kitāb al-bukhalā'*, ed. Ṭ. Ḥājirī (Cairo 1958), 57, 230-2 and *passim*; Jāḥiẓ describes it as the food *par excellence* of the old, young and toothless, and there is a tradition of the Prophet in Bukhārī, *Kitāb al-aṭ'ima*, that 'the superiority of 'Ā'isha over other women is like the superiority of *tharīd* over all other food'.

[23] There is a possible parallelism of the first hemistich with the second in that *wa-in ḥatam* may mean 'however much he may have food left over from his table (sc. as a sign of his great hospitality)'; *taḥattama* = 'eat crumbs left on the table, crumble food' (Lane, s.v.).

[24] Allusion to Qur'ān, cvi, 1-2; cf. M. Hamidullah, '*Al-Īlāf*, ou les rapports économico-diplomatiques de la Mecque pré-islamique', in *Mélanges Massignon* (Damascus 1956-7), II, 293-311.

[25] This paragraph appears substantially in Mas'ūdī, *Murūj adh-dhahab*, ed. and tr. Barbier de Meynard and Pavet de Courteille (Paris 1861-77), I, 133. It was an ancient Semitic usage to cover idols and their shrines with garments or cloths, and this must in fact have been the origin of the covering of the Ka'ba; cf. Wellhausen, *Reste arabischen Heidentums*[2] (Berlin 1897), 78. But early Islamic tradition had to seek the beginnings of the practice in the gifts of the Tubba' kings, who whilst living in the pre-Islamic period, could be cherished for their royal lineage and patronage of the shrine and for having, as Tha'ālibī here maintains, *animae naturaliter muslimae*. The first coverings certainly seem to have been of tanned leather and Yemenī cloth, attesting to the early trade connections of Mecca and the Yemen. Cf. M. Gaudefroy-Demombynes, 'Le voile de la Ka'ba', SI, II (1954), 6-8.

The first person in the Jāhiliyya who took off his sandals before entering the Ka'ba was al-Walīd b. al-Mughīra. People followed his example, and under Islam, they all took off their sandals. Especially noteworthy in this respect was Abū Muslim, the organiser of the [Abbasid] revolution, who took them off, [12
saying, 'This spot is holier than Ṭuwā, where God Most High ordered Moses to take off his sandals.'[26] Al-Walīd was also the first to mutilate thieves as a punishment; then the revelation came down under Islam, 'As for thieves, of whichever sex, cut off their hands.'[27]

The first person in Mecca to use black dye-stuffs on his person was 'Abd al-Muṭṭalib b. Hāshim. A man of Ḥimyar applied it to him when he was in the Yemen, and when he used it at Mecca, the people imitated him; previously, they had dyed themselves with red.

The first adult person who believed in the Messenger of God, God's prayers and peace be upon him, was Abū Bakr the Veracious[28]; the first youth, Zaid b. Ḥāritha; the first child, 'Alī b. Abī Ṭālib, who was nine years old at the time; and the first woman, Khadīja bint Khuwailid. The precedence of these four cannot be controverted in any way.[29]

The first child born under Islam after the Hijra was 'Abdallāh b. az-Zubair, his mother being Asmā' bint Abī Bakr.[30] People had been wont to say that the Jews had cast a spell over the Muhājirūn, so that no children had been born amongst them, but when 'Abdallāh was born, this sort of talk was stopped, and joy was unbounded.

The first person who shed blood fighting in the way of God was Sa'd b. Abī Waqqāṣ. He was the first to whom the Messenger of God, God's prayers and peace be upon him, spoke and linked both his own father and mother together in his exhortation, 'Let fly, may my father and mother be your ransom!' [13

The first person called after the Prophet's own name, Muḥammad, God's prayers and peace be upon him, was Muḥammad b. Ḥāṭib, who was born in Abyssinia.[31] The one who named the child was reproached for doing this, but he replied that he had

[26] Allusion to Qur'ān, xx, 12; the Ṭuwā referred to is perhaps meant for Syriac Ṭūrā 'Mount [Sinai]'.

[27] Qur'ān, v, 42/38.

[28] I have followed here, as elsewhere, the conventional translation of *aṣ-Ṣiddīq* by 'the Veracious'; but according to Ibn Isḥāq (tr. A. Guillaume, *The life of Muhammad* [Oxford 1955], 182-3), it really means 'the one testifying to Muḥammad's prophethood and his truthfulness', sc. when many other Muslims were dubious about accepting Muḥammad's story of the night journey (*isrā'*) with Gabriel.

[29] Contrary to Tha'ālibī's glib statement here, the question of the first converts to Islam was hotly debated; cf. W. Montgomery Watt, *Muhammad at Mecca* (Oxford 1953), 86-8.

[30] This accords with what is said in Muḥammad b. Ḥabīb's *Muḥabbar*, 275-6.

[31] In his list of the sons of the Muhājirūn who were first given the name 'Muḥammad', Muḥammad b. Ḥabīb places first the son of 'Alī's brother Ja'far b. Abī Ṭālib (*Muḥabbar*, 274-5).

heard the Messenger of God, God's prayers and peace be upon him, say, 'Use my name, and use my patronymic, but don't use both of them together.'[32]

The first time that the Messenger of God, God's prayers and peace be upon him, got ready a battle standard for an expedition was when he gave one to Ḥamza b. 'Abd al-Muṭṭalib, and said, 'Take it, O Lion of God!'

The first martyr amongst the Muslim community was 'Umair b. al-Ḥubāb[33] al-Anṣārī, killed at Badr. The occasion of his martyrdom was when on that day the Prophet, God's prayers and peace be upon him, made a speech and then went on to say, 'God, His name is magnified, has stipulated paradise as the reward of the one who dies fighting, calmly and determinedly, pressing forward and not retreating.' 'Umair was eating a handful of dates at that moment, and he sprang up and exclaimed, 'Bravo! Only the munching of these few dates separates me from entering paradise!' Then he began to stuff them in his mouth, hurled the stones away, seized his sword and fought furiously till he was killed.

The first woman martyr was Sumayya Umm 'Ammār. She proclaimed openly at Mecca her Muslim faith, and was persecuted by Quraish. She refused to recant; Abū Jahl speared her in the upper part of her breast and she died.

The first person who was called *Amīr al-Mu'minīn* ('Commander of the Faithful') was 'Umar b. al-Khaṭṭāb, may God be pleased with him. Abū Bakr, may God be pleased with him, used to be called *Khalīfat Rasūl Allāh* ('Successor of the Messenger of God'). After his death, 'Umar was nominated ruler over the community, but he exclaimed, 'How can I be called "Successor of the Successor of the Messenger of God" – it's far too lengthy!' Al-Mughīra b. Shu'ba said to him, 'You are our commander, and we are the faithful believers, so you are the commander of the faithful.' 'Umar thereupon agreed to this title.[34] 'Umar [14 was also the first to compute dates from the Hijra, to seal documents with clay, to levy the land-tax and to arrange the People of the Poll-Tax (*Ahl al-Jizya*) in [taxable] categories, from which, however, he excluded children, women, the aged and infirm, and the destitute.

The first person to be hailed by the title *Amīr* was al-Mughīra b. Shu'ba. Before this time, they simply greeted governors by their patronymics, but al-Mughīra laid down, 'It is fitting that there should be a gulf fixed between the governor and the subjects.' So he compelled the people under his jurisdiction to address

[32] The various forms of this tradition are discussed in detail by A. Fischer, 'Vergöttlichung und Tabuisierung der Namen Muḥammad's bei den Muslimen', *Beiträge zur Arabistik, Semitistik und Islamwissenschaft*, ed. R. Hartmann and H. Scheel (Leipzig 1944), 314ff.; cf. also Goldziher, 'Gesetzliche Bestimmungen über Kunja-Namen im Islam', ZDMG, LI (1897), 260-3, and on the use together of 'Abū'l-Qāsim' and 'Muḥammad' or 'Aḥmad', A. Mez, *Abulḳâsim, ein bagdâder Sittenbild* (Heidelberg 1902), xxv-xxvi, noting that this *kunya* became especially used in revolutionary Shī'ī circles.

[33] Corrected by AS, in the light of Ṭabarī and Ibn Hishām, from the 'al-Ḥumām' of J.

[34] These questions of titulature are discussed by Ibn Khaldūn, amongst many others, in his *Muqaddima*, tr. F. Rosenthal (New York 1958), I, 388-9, 465-6; see also M. van Berchem, 'Titres califiens d'Occident', JA, Ser. 10, Vol. IX (1907), 258ff., and Sir Thomas Arnold, *The Caliphate* (Oxford 1924), 31ff. A widespread tradition makes the Companion 'Abdallāh b. Jaḥsh, victor of the clash at Nakhla in 2/624, the first recipient of the title *Amīr al-Mu'minīn*, but it seems only to have become a Caliphal title with 'Umar.

him as *Amīr*. Then the rest of the Muslims adopted the practice when addressing their respective governors. He was also the first in Islam to give bribes, for he would say, 'Often the coin sweats in my palm for me to give it to Yarfā, 'Umar's doorkeeper.'

The first occasion when an act of oppression was perpetrated in the community of Muḥammad, God's prayers and peace be upon him, was when they shouted, 'Get out of the road!' This is supposed to have occurred in the time of 'Uthmān, may God be pleased with him.

The first person to appropriate money for himself from the public treasury of the Muslims was Abū Huraira 'Abdallāh b. 'Amr ad-Dausī. 'Umar, may God be pleased with him, had appointed him governor of Baḥrain, but whilst there, he took money from the public treasury. So 'Umar dismissed him, had his accounts thoroughly investigated and compelled him to disgorge the sum totted up against him. He beat Abū Huraira until he had got 1,500 dinars from him. Abū Huraira protested, 'I'll [15
never fill any public office for you again!' 'Umar retorted, 'A better person than you once acted as a public official (meaning Joseph) for a worse person than me (meaning the Mighty One of Egypt).'

The first of the Arabs to cross the river of Balkh was Sa'īd b. 'Uthmān b. 'Affān when Mu'āwiya appointed him governor of Khurāsān.[35]

The first of the Arabs to wear dark-coloured silken robes was 'Abdallāh b. 'Āmir b. Kuraiz. He was governor of Basra under 'Uthmān, may God be pleased with him, and when he addressed the people of Basra from the pulpit wearing a robe of this material, people said that the Amīr had put on the skin of a bear.

The first person to change one of the decisions of the Messenger of God, God's prayers and peace be upon him, was Mu'āwiya when he adopted [as his own half-brother] Ziyād b. 'Ubaid ath-Thaqafī, proclaiming Abū Sufyān as his putative father. By doing this, he altered the Messenger of God's decision of 'The child to the bed, and stoning for the adulterer and fornicator.' Mu'āwiya was also the first to partition off a section in the mosque (*maqṣūra*) for his own personal use, because he saw one day a dog climbing up into his own pulpit; and he was the first to proclaim the [16
name of his successor (*walī al-'ahd*), even though he was still hale and hearty at the time, and the first to appoint in this way his own son.[36]

Mu'āwiya also originated the Dīwān of the Seal. The reason

[35] Sa'īd's expedition across the Oxus took place in 56/676, when the Soghdians were defeated and their city (? Kish, Samarqand) captured; but Abū 'Ubaida, in Balādhurī, mentions a raid on Māymurgh in Soghdia as early as 33/654. Cf. H. A. R. Gibb, *The Arab conquests in Central Asia* (London 1923), 15ff.

[36] All these are accusations frequently hurled at the Umayyads by later, hostile writers, e.g. by Mas'ūdī in *Murūj*, v, 20-7, 69-73. An alternative reason for Mu'āwiya's partitioning off a *maqṣūra* is often said in the sources to be as a protective measure after an assassination attempt by one of the Khawārij; cf. Ibn Khaldūn, *op. cit.*, tr. II, 69-70, and Lammens, *Études sur le règne du Calife Omaiyade Mo'âwia Ier* (Paris 1908), 203-8.

for this was that 'Amr b. az-Zubair b. al-'Awwām came to him, and Mu'āwiya placed the sum of 100,000 dirhams to his credit, writing at the same time to Ziyād in Iraq to arrange for its payment [from the revenues there]. Now 'Amr took the letter and broke it open, and changed the '100,000' to '200,000'. When Ziyād came and presented his accounts to Mu'āwiya for inspection, these included a payment of 200,000 dirhams to 'Amr. Mu'āwiya expostulated that he had only ordered Ziyād to pay out 100,000 dirhams, until the latter showed him his own letter. So Mu'āwiya wrote to the governor of Medina, Marwān b. al-Ḥakam, requiring him to get the extra 100,000 dirhams back from 'Amr, and this was done. Mu'āwiya then ordered the Dīwān of the Seal to be set up.[37]

Furthermore, Mu'āwiya was the first person to have *maḍīra* prepared (literally, 'thickened') for him. Abū Huraira, may God be pleased with him, used to be avidly fond of it, and at the time of the Battle of Ṣiffīn, would go over to Mu'āwiya's side to eat it, and over to the side of 'Alī b. Abī Ṭālib, may God be pleased with him, to perform the prayers under 'Alī's direction. People remonstrated with him about this, but Abū Huraira replied that Mu'āwiya's *maḍīra* was the finest, whereas it was more meritorious to perform the prayers under 'Alī. Hence he became called, 'Shaikh of the *Maḍīra*'.[38]

The first person who took vengeance on someone under his protection for another person under his protection, and took vengeance on an innocent man, for an evil-doer was Ziyād [b. Abīhi]. He used to say, 'Many a rightful due has been extracted from the loins of some unlawful act.' He was also the first [17 to have people walking before him with staffs, the first to wear robes made of *Dabīqī* cloth and the first to erect at Basra buildings of fired brick and stucco.[39]

The first person who had men walking before him whilst he himself was mounted, was al-Ash'ath b. Qais, chief of the people of the Yemen. He was once captured in battle and ransomed for 3,000 she-camels, thus becoming the first man to ransom himself with such a sum. He was moreover the first person to be interred within his own house and not borne away to the burial-ground. The reason for this was that when he died at Medina, the great press of people prevented his corpse from being brought out and buried. Al-Ḥasan b. 'Alī was unable to get through to him, until he got in through some neighbour's house. Al-Ḥasan saw a man dismount and then slay his horse, and another lead in his camel

[37] This story is given in many of the historical sources, e.g. Ṭabarī, II, 206, and Jahshiyārī, *Kitāb al-wuzarā' wa'l-kuttāb* (Baghdad 1357/1938), 15; see the discussion on the use of the ruler's seal in Ibn Khaldūn, *op. cit.*, tr. II, 60-5.

[38] On *maḍīra*, a dish of meat cooked with sour milk or yoghourt, and Abū Huraira's weakness for it, see Mas'ūdī, *Murūj*, VIII, 403-4, giving verses in praise of it; Tha'ālibī, *Thimār al-qulūb*, 86-7, s.v. 'Shaikh al-Maḍīra'; and Badī' az-Zamān al-Hamadhānī's *Maqāma al-Maḍīriyya*, where it is said that *maḍīra* 'bears witness to Mu'āwiya's being truly an Imām' (ed. Muḥ.'Abduh [Beirut 1924], 109, tr. F. Gabrieli, 'La «Maqāma maḍīriyya» di al-Hamadhānī', RCAL, Ser. 8, Vol. IV [1949], 511).

[39] The perfect security reigning in Basra during Ziyād's governorship is stressed even in the anti-Umayyad sources; cf. Lammens, 'Ziād ibn Abīhi, Vice-roi de l'Iraq, lieutenant de Mo'āwia I', in *Études sur le siècle des Omayyades* (Beirut 1930), 72-5. On *Dabīqī* linens from the Nile delta, see Mez, *The renaissance of Islam*, Eng. tr. (Patna 1937), 459-61, and on Ziyād's building operations at Basra, Lammens, *op. cit.*, 119-24, and Pellat, *Le milieu basrien et la formation de Ǧāḥiẓ* (Paris 1953), 8-11.

and then kill it; he feared lest people start sacrificing beasts wholesale at al-Ash'ath's graveside, so he ordered that he should be buried in his own house.[40]

The first person in the Islamic period who relinquished half his possessions was 'Ubaidallāh b. al-'Abbās b. 'Abd al-Muṭṭalib. Mu'āwiya once cut off the allowance paid to al-Ḥasan b. 'Alī b. Abī Ṭālib, may God be pleased with him, and in that year, al-Ḥasan's circumstances became very straitened. So he wrote to 'Ubaidallāh about it; the latter wept and exclaimed, 'Shame on you, Mu'āwiya! You are living in luxury and opulence, whilst al-Ḥasan is lamenting his miserable condition and his inability to support his numerous family!' Then he told the intendant of his finances, 'Convey half of my possessions to al-Ḥasan, and that should solve all his worries; but if it doesn't, then make over [18 the other half to him.' When the gift reached al-Ḥasan, he exclaimed, 'Indeed we belong to God! I have made myself a burden upon my own cousin! Would that I had never written to him about my affairs!' He accepted the half-share which 'Ubaidallāh had offered him of his wealth.[41] 'Ubaidallāh was also the first to provide food for his neighbours on the morning after the end of the Ramaḍān fast (sc. the *'Īd al-Fiṭr*); and he was the first person in the Islamic period to set up tables in public thoroughfares and summon people to come up and eat, the first to make the food free so that it could be carried away, and the first to employ men to bear it away because of its profuseness.

The first person to have the legends on dirhams and dinars stamped in Arabic was 'Abd al-Malik b. Marwān; he devoted his personal attention to this question and wrote to al-Ḥajjāj ordering him to see that the new practice was henceforth observed.[42] He was also the first person in Islam to bear the name ''Abd al-Malik' and the first Caliph to have the honorific *al-Muwaffaq bi'llāh* ('He who is helped by God to success').[43]

[40] According to H. Reckendorff, EI² s.v., al-Ash'ath died at Kufa during al-Ḥasan's brief period of power there in 40/661. The fears expressed here by al-Ḥasan are clearly of a recrudescence of pagan Arabian funeral practices in which beasts were slaughtered or tethered and left to die at the graves of great men; cf. Maḥmūd Shukrī al-Alūsī, *Bulūgh al-arab fī ma'rifat aḥwāl al-'Arab*³ (Cairo n.d.), II, 309-11, and EI² Art. 'Baliyya' (J. Hell-Ch. Pellat).

[41] 'Ubaidallāh's attachment to the Alid family is stressed here, and this confirms the conclusion of Wellhausen, *The Arab kingdom and its fall*, Eng. tr. (Calcutta 1927), 106, 109-10, that 'Ubaidallāh's name was substituted in later historical accounts for that of his brother 'Abdallāh b. al-'Abbās when the latter deserted al-Ḥasan for Mu'āwiya in 40/661. On 'Ubaidallāh's renowned generosity, see the anecdotes in Mas'ūdī, *Murūj*, v, 371-3.

[42] Cf. Wellhausen, *op. cit.*, 217-18, and J. Walker, *A catalogue of the Muhammadan coins in the British Museum. II Arab-Byzantine and post-reform Umaiyad coins* (London 1956), lii ff., who concludes from the historical sources and an examination of coins that the earliest gold reform coinage dates from 77/696-7 and the earliest silver from 79/698-9.

[43] The use of honorific titles (*alqāb*) by the Caliphs only became the rule with the Abbasids, who wished to emphasise the theological justification for their power. There is thus no evidence to support Tha'ālibī's assertion here that 'Abd al-Malik had a title. Hilāl aṣ-Ṣābi', whose knowledge of official practice and protocol was outstanding in his day, says bluntly, 'None of the Umayyads ever used honorifics', *lam yatalaqqab aḥad min Banī Umayya* (*Rusūm dār al-khilāfa*, ed. M. 'Awwād [Baghdad 1384/1964], 129). The information in Mas'ūdī's *Kitāb at-tanbīh wa'l-ishrāf*, ed. de Goeje (Leiden 1894), 335-6, tr. Carra de Vaux (Paris 1897), 431-2, that the Umayyads had honorifics exactly as the Abbasids had (according to this, 'Abd al-Malik's *laqab* was *al-Mu'thir li-amri'llāh*), is clearly an invention of 'Uthmāniyya elements concerned to assert the legitimacy of the Umayyads' power; cf. Caetani and Gabrieli, *Onomasticon arabicum*, I, 184-6, and A. Abel, 'Le Khalife, présence sacrée', SI, VII (1957), 33ff.

The first person to mint base dirhams was 'Ubaidallāh b. Ziyād,
at the time when he fled from Basra. Encamping by a well, he was
afraid of being attacked by the Bedouins, so he shared out these
coins amongst them.[44]

The first person to found an infirmary for the sick was al-Walīd
b. 'Abd al-Malik. He further inaugurated the giving of pensions
to the Qur'ān readers and custodians of mosques, and he similarly
granted allowances to the blind and crippled, providing each of
them with a personal attendant. He was the first Caliph to [19
act autocratically, and strutted forth amongst the people in a
haughty and tyrannical manner. This was the reverse of previous
rulers' conduct, and marked a contrast with how people used
formerly to speak to Mu'āwiya, Yazīd and 'Abd al-Malik, addressing
them by their personal names and conversing with them on
equal terms. In connection with this, al-Walīd went up into the
pulpit and spoke to the populace in these terms: 'You used to
address the Caliphs before me as your equals, saying "O Mu'āwiya",
"O Yazīd" or "O 'Abd al-Malik"! But now I call God
to witness and to hold me to my vow, let no-one talk to me in
this fashion, or I will have him put to death; for by my life, if the
people behave familiarly with their rulers in this fashion, they will
go further, relax their obedience and venture on acts of rebellion!'
Some time afterwards, a man from the Banū Murra exhorted him,
'Fear God, O Walīd, for pride is an attribute of God alone!' Al-Walīd
had him trampled to death, and the people took warning
and regarded him with fear.[45]

The first Caliph to establish a system of ranks at court was
al-Manṣūr. The Umayyads had residences with no barriers or
special procedure of seeking permission to enter; people used
merely to wait at their doors until they were either summoned
inside or turned away. But when the Abbasids came to power and
al-Manṣūr built Baghdad, he built specific waiting-rooms in his
palace, and this has become the practice down to the present day.[46]
It was also for al-Manṣūr that the use of canvas sheets (*khaish*)
was introduced. The Persian emperors used to have the roof of
a summer-house plastered over with clay each day during the hot
summer, and used to take their siestas within. They used to have
willow laths placed upright round the walls of the buildings, and
then large lumps of snow would be placed in the interstices. [20
The Umayyads followed a similar practice. When al-Manṣūr first
became Caliph, a summer-house was prepared for his siestas by
being plastered over in the traditional way, but then Abū Ayyūb

[44] The tradition that 'Ubaidallāh was the first to strike dirhams of base alloy (*zuyūf*) is referred to by Sauvaire, these coins being minted when 'Ubaidallāh fled to Syria after the Zubairid *putsch* in Basra in 64/686 and lodged amongst the Bedouin. But Walker says that there is no trace of this base coinage amongst the surviving dirhams of this governor (*A catalogue of the Muhammadan coins in the British Museum*. I *A catalogue of the Arab-Sassanian coins* [London 1941], xlviii-xlix).

[45] Al-Wāqidī, in Ṭabarī, II, 1178, reports the harsh, minatory tone of al-Walīd's oration to the people at the burial of his father and the ceremony of allegiance to himself; but in II, 1271, Ṭabarī mentions the social measures described here by Tha'ālibī and states that the Syrians considered al-Walīd as the best of their Caliphs.

[46] On al-Manṣūr's withdrawal from the public gaze, see Pseudo-Jāḥiẓ, *Kitāb at-tāj*, tr. Pellat, *Le livre de la couronne* (Paris 1954), 61-2.

al-Mūryānī[47] took some thick fabric material which had been wetted and then draped over the contrivance which is called in Persian *sipāya* ('tripod, trivet'). Al-Manṣūr felt the coolness from it and found it very pleasant. Then he commented, 'It seems to me that if sheets of heavier material than this were used, they would hold more water and give off more coolness.' So they got some thick canvas for him and stretched it over a dome-shaped frame. Then after that, the practice arose of using a suspended matting of woven reeds, and the use of this became general.[48]

The first person to combine the duties of military governor and civil collector of taxes was Khālid b. Barmak when al-Manṣūr appointed him governor of Fārs with responsibility both for its defence and for the collection of its revenues. Furthermore, the registers in government offices were previously made up of rolls of sheets fastened together; Khālid made the innovation of having the registers composed of parchment and papyrus sheets bound together into codices or books.[49]

The first Caliph to take Turkish slaves into his service was al-Manṣūr, who had Khumār[50]; al-Mahdī had Mubārak; and then subsequent Caliphs and people in general imitated them.[51]

The first Caliph's daughter who was taken from one place to another when given to her husband, was al-'Abbāsa, al-Mahdī's daughter. When he gave her in marriage to Muḥammad b. Sulaimān b. 'Alī,[52] he brought her to her husband at Basra.

The first person to make use of swift camels (*jammāzāt*) was Umm Ja'far Zubaida. She ordered the camel drivers to urge [21 on faster the Bactrian camels which were transporting her, as she feared lest ar-Rashīd might be dead. When the beasts were urged on, they went along with a mixture of walking and trotting, interspersed with periods of galloping (*fa-jamazat*). This happened to please her, since she was a woman of discrimination and wide knowledge of affairs, and she found that galloping was quite comfortable, and even enjoyable. So she ordered the camel drivers to urge the beasts along in this way. Hence they kept on trying to get them to gallop, at times managing to do it properly, at times unable to manage it. Meanwhile, she was giving the drivers directions as best she could, pointing out when they were handling the beasts faultily and then putting them right, until they had

[47] Abū Ayyūb Sulaimān b. Makhlad al-Mūryānī, a Persian from Khūzistān, was Vizier to al-Manṣūr 138-53/755-70; cf. Ibn Khallikān, tr. I, 595-6, and Sourdel, *Le vizirat 'Abbāside*, I, 78-87.

[48] This anecdote appears in Ṭabarī, III, 418; cf. also, Mez, *The renaissance of Islam*, 380-1, and Pellat's long note on *khaisha* in the glossary to his translation of Jāḥiẓ's *Bukhalā'*, *Le livre des avares* (Paris 1951), 316-17.

[49] Khālid was apparently appointed to Fārs early in al-Manṣūr's reign after he had been dismissed from the headship of the Dīwān in favour of his enemy Abū Ayyūb al-Mūryānī, and spent two years there (Jahshiyārī, *al-Wuzarā' wa'l-kuttāb*, 67; Ibn al-Abbār, *I'tāb al-kuttāb* [Damascus 1380/1961], 67). Again according to Jahshiyārī, *op. cit.*, 59, Khālid had made his innovation in the keeping of the registers during the preceding reign of as-Saffāḥ (cf. also, B. Lewis, EI² Art. 'Daftar').

[50] Following J; AS has 'Ḥimār'.

[51] The trickle of Turkish slaves (*ghilmān, mamālīk*) employed by the first Abbasids were essentially domestic slaves, but the flood of Turks introduced into the Caliphate by al-Mu'taṣim (218-27/833-42) were used as military guards; according to Maqrīzī, al-Mu'taṣim ordered the names of the Arab warriors or *muqātila* to be struck off the pay-rolls in Egypt, and used the money saved to buy Turkish mercenary troops (R. Levy, *The social structure of Islam* [Cambridge 1957], 417).

[52] The texts have the name in incorrect order as 'Muḥammad b. 'Alī b. Sulaimān'. Muḥammad was himself a member of the Abbasid family and cousin of Ibrāhīm b. Ṣāliḥ b. 'Alī (see below, tr. p. 50); he filled various provincial governorships in Iraq, Arabia and Persia, and was the first husband of al-'Abbāsa, dying in 173/789-90.

more or less got the right idea about driving the beasts in this way Then she left them alone to complete the journey, until all went smoothly and the journey was over.[53]

The first person to sit directly on the under-carpet (*bisāṭ*),[54] without any sur-carpet or mattress (*namaṭ*), in times of mourning and calamity, was ar-Rashīd when he heard the news of Ibrāhīm b. Ṣāliḥ b. 'Alī's death.[55] He went along to Ibrāhīm's house, and refused to sit down on any of the mattresses or cushions which were arranged on the under-carpet, but would only support himself by leaning on his sword. Then he ordered the mattresses and cushions to be taken away, and he sat down directly on the under-carpet. He commented that it was not seemly that anyone should sit down on mattresses and cushions in the house of a dear friend and relative on such a day of misfortune; one should not sit down on anything but the under-carpet. The Abbasids therefore established this as a regular practice in times of calamity.

The first person in the time of the Abbasids to become the grandfather of a grandfather was Mu'ādh b. Muslim, and then al-Faḍl b. ar-Rabī', despite his being perceptibly younger than Mu'ādh. After this, Zainab bint Sulaimān b. 'Alī became the grandmother of a grandmother, and finally 'Alī b. 'Īsā b. Māhān became the grandfather of a grandmother.

The first person to bestow a million dirhams or more was Mu'āwiya, and after him, Yazīd. The occasion for this was that Mu'āwiya used to make an allowance of one million dirhams [22 per annum to al-Ḥasan, al-Ḥusain, 'Abdallāh b. 'Abbās and 'Abdallāh b. Ja'far b. Abī Ṭālib. When he died and Yazīd became Caliph, 'Abdallāh b. Ja'far came to him and said, 'O commander of the Faithful, Mu'āwiya used to recognise the claims of my lineage by allotting me a million dirhams each year.' Yazīd replied, 'You shall have that million and a further two millions.' 'Abdallāh exclaimed, 'You are dearer to me, O Commander of the Faithful, than my own father and mother! By God, I have never spoken this oath to any human being before this occasion.' Yazīd said, 'Take another million', so 'Abdallāh received a total of four millions.

The next person after Mu'āwiya and Yazīd to give a million dirhams or more was Abū Ja'far al-Manṣūr, despite the fact that he was notorious for his avarice and was nicknamed by the people Abū'd-Dawānīq ('Father of Farthings').[56] Muḥammad b. Sallām[57] has mentioned that no Caliph before al-Manṣūr had ever bestowed ten million dirhams. Financial drafts were issued for this sum, and

[53] This paragraph is based on Jāḥiẓ, *Kitāb al-ḥayawān* (Cairo 1356-64/1938-45), I, 83-4. On the use of *jammāzāt*, see Mez, *The renaissance of Islam*, 502. A few years after Zubaida's time, in the reign of al-Mu'taṣim, Muḥammad b. 'Abd al-Malik az-Zayyāt is mentioned as being in charge of the manufacture of equipment for these animals (*ālat al-jammāzāt*); as his father had been under al-Ma'mūn (Ṭabarī, III, 1183, tr. Marin, *The reign of al-Mu'taṣim*, 19; cf. Sourdel, *Le vizirat 'Abbāside*, I, 255-6).

[54] On the terminology of the various kinds of carpet, see R. Ettinghausen, EI[1] Suppl. Art. 'Ḳālī'; it is possible that, in this context, *bisāṭ* simply means 'floor'.

[55] Ibrāhīm b. Ṣāliḥ b. 'Alī al-Hāshimī acted as governor of Egypt for al-Mahdī and of Syria for ar-Rashīd, and was the second husband of al-'Abbāsa bint al-Mahdī (Ibn Qutaiba, *Kitāb al-ma'ārif* [Cairo 1960], 380).

[56] The unknown author of the *Kitāb at-tāj* is at pains to correct the impression given by a book on royal misers, which he cites, that al-Manṣūr was in fact niggardly, and he gives details of his immense gifts to his family (*Le livre de la couronne*, tr. Pellat, 160-2).

[57] Abū 'Abdallāh Muḥammad b. Sallām al-Jumaḥī al-Baṣrī (d. 231/845-6 or 232/846-7), well-known author of the *Ṭabaqāt ash-shu'arā'*; cf. Yāqūt, *Irshād*, VII, 13-14, and Brockelmann, GAL, Suppl., I, 43, 165.

these were registered in the Dīwāns. Al-Manṣūr also in one single day gave each of his paternal uncles ten million dirhams each, and then gave ʿĪsā b. Mūsā[58] one million and ordered that he should be accounted one of his uncles. Later, the Barmakīs gave away millions, as did al-Ma'mūn and al-Ḥasan b. Sahl; but gifts on this scale then ceased.

The first person to go back on his promises and disappoint prominent men over the granting of governorships and tax-collecting rights, and generally to evade fulfilling his promises, was Ismāʿīl b. Ṣubaiḥ, ar-Rashīd's secretary.[59] Before this, great men had never been confronted with broken promises.

The first person to increase the secretaries' salaries was al-Faḍl b. Sahl Dhū'r-Riyāsatain. In the time of al-Manṣūr, their allowances were fixed at 300 [dirhams] each, which had been the figure prevailing at the time of the Umayyads. They re- [23
mained at this level till al-Ma'mūn's time, when al-Faḍl raised them.[60]

The first qāḍī executed in Islam was the Qāḍī Abū'l-Muthannā. He had done homage to Ibn al-Muʿtazz, and when the latter fell from power,[61] [the restored Caliph] al-Muqtadir ordered Abū'l-Muthannā to be brought in with his hands pinioned behind him and killed. No-one in the time of the Umayyads or Abbasids had ever suffered such a fate as this.

[58] ʿĪsā b. Mūsā, son of the brother of as-Saffāḥ and al-Manṣūr, and *walī al-ʿahd* during the reigns of al-Manṣūr and al-Mahdī; d. 167/783-4.

[59] Ismāʿīl b. Ṣubaiḥ al-Ḥarrānī had an influence with ar-Rashīd comparable with that of al-Faḍl b. ar-Rabīʿ, being in charge of the chancery, finance and crown lands and acting as the Caliph's confidential secretary; he later, however, fell into obscurity under al-Amīn. Cf. Ibn al-Abbār, *Iʿtāb al-kuttāb*, 102-4, and Sourdel, *Le vizirat ʿAbbāside*, I, 185, 190-3.

[60] Cf. A. A. Dūrī, EI[2] Art. 'Dīwān. i. The Caliphate' On al-Faḍl b. Sahl, see Sourdel, *op. cit.*, I, 196-213. The *laqab* of *Dhū'r-Riyasātain* was solemnly conferred on him, together with a grant of all the eastern territories, by al-Ma'mūn in 196/812 (Ṭabarī, III, 841, who explains that the two *riyāsas* are over the conduct of war, *ḥarb*, and over state affairs and administration, *tadbīr*).

[61] See for these events, below, p. 107.

Chapter Two.

Concerning the nicknames given to poets which were taken from their own poetry.[1]

Al-Muraqqish. His name was ʻAuf b. Saʻd b. Mālik. He was given this nickname because of his line (metre *Sarīʻ*) : *The encampment lies bare and deserted, and its traces are just as if a pen had traced patterns* (raqqasha) *on the surface of a skin.*[2]

Al-Mumazziq. He was Sha's b. Nahār al-ʻAbdī. He was given
this nickname because of his line (metre *Ṭawīl*) : *If I am to* [25
to be eaten, then be the best of those who devour [*my flesh*]; *but if not, then hurry and save me before I am torn to pieces* (wa-lammā umazzaq).[3]

Al-Mukharriq. His name was ʻAbbād. He was given this nickname because of his line (metre *Basīṭ*) : *I am the one who rips away* (al-mukharriq) *the honour of the ignoble ones, just as my father was the one who used to tear away their honour.*[4]

Al-Mutalammis. He was Jarīr b. ʻAbd al-Masīḥ aḍ-Ḍubaʻī. He was given this nickname because of his line (metre *Ṭawīl*) : *This is the time of our encamping at al-ʻIrḍ, when it was alive with flies and wasps and with bluebottles, avidly seeking out* (al-mutalammis)
their food.[5] [26

An-Nābigha. He was Ziyād b. Muʻāwiya adh-Dhubyānī. He was given this nickname because of his line (metre *Ṭawīl*) : *She alighted amongst the Banū Ḳain b. Jasr, at a time when they had brought upon us* (qad nabaghat *'there had arisen'*) *many serious difficulties.*[6]

Ufnūn. He was Ṣuraim b. Maʻshar at-Taghlibī. He was given this nickname because of his line (metre *Basīṭ*) : *O Madnūn, you have bestowed on us your love grudgingly; in our time, youths wore their hair long and flowing* (ufnūnā).[7]

[1] This chapter has been annotated by Abyārī and Ṣairafī in great detail, with profuse parallel citations of the lines of poetry and their variants; see also Caetani and Gabrieli, *Onomasticon arabicum*, I, 159-62, who note that the *Fihrist* of Ibn an-Nadīm mentions a book by the historian al-Madā'inī which was specifically devoted to the poets whose nicknames were derived from their own poetry, the *Kitāb man qāla shiʻran fa-summiya bihi.*

[2] Cf. Barbier de Meynard, 'Surnoms et sobriquets dans la littérature arabe', JA, Ser. 10, Vol. X (July-Dec. 1907), 214-15.

[3] Cf. *ibid.*, 232-3.

[4] Cf. *ibid.*, 209-10.

[5] Cf. *ibid.*, 201.

[6] Cf. *ibid.*, 238-40.

[7] Cf. *ibid.*, Vol. IX (Jan.-June 1907), 216.

Ta'abbaṭa Sharran. He was Thābit b. Jābir. He was given this nickname because of his line (metre *Ṭawīl*): *He tucked something evil under his arm* (ta'abbaṭa sharr^{an}), *then he returned home in the evening or next morning.*[8]

A'ṣur. He was Munabbih b. Sa'd. He was given this nickname because of his lines (metre *Kāmil*): *Umaima said, 'What is the matter with your head, now that hoary old age has come swiftly on, and has brought such a regrettable change of colour?' / O Umaima, indeed the passing of the nights and the constantly-changing revolutions of time* (ikhtilāf al-a'ṣur) *have altered your father's colour.*[9] [27

Al-Mustaughir. He was 'Umar b. Rabī'a b. Ka'b. He was given this nickname because of his line (metre *Wāfir*): *The sweat steams on its stout haunches, just as a heated stone steams in milk heated up by placing hot stones in it* (al-laban al-waghīr).[10]

Al-A'sar. He was Marthad b. Abī Ḥumrān al-Ju'fī. He was given this nickname because of his line (metre *Ṭawīl*): *Do not number me, O my tribe, amongst the descendants of Sa'd b. Mālik, lest I incite* (u'sir) *and kindle war amongst them.*[11]

Ṭarafa. He was 'Umar b. 'Abd. He was given this nickname because of his line (metre *Basīṭ*): *Do not [O my two friends] hasten now to raise the tears of one who has recently departed* (muṭṭaraf), *nor the tears of your two chiefs when they halt at the encampment.*[12] [28

Al-Musayyab. He was Zuhair b. 'Alas. He was given this nickname because of his line (metre *Ṭawīl*): *If you desire that a she-camel should not return in the evening with empty udders, then send off your camel and let it pasture freely* (al-musayyab *'camel which is allowed to pasture freely'*).[13]

'Uwaif al-Qawāfī. He was 'Uwaif b. Mu'āwiya b. 'Uqba. He was given this nickname because of his line (metre *Ṭawīl*): *I shall brand as mendacious the accusation of those who allege that when I say poetry, I do not get the rhymes* (al-qawāfī) *correct.*[14]

Al-Muzarrid. He was Yazīd b. Ḍarīr, the brother of ash-Shammākh. He was given this nickname because of his line (metre *Ṭawīl*): *I said, 'O Ḍirār, gulp down* (tazarrad) *[this creamy milk,* zubda*], for I am the one who provides this nourishment for the aged and toothless* (muzarrid) *clients of the tribe in years of dearth.'*[15] [29

Al-Ba'īth. He was Khidāsh b. Bashīr. He was given this nickname because of his line (metre *Ṭawīl*): *It [sc. poetry] has flowed out* (taba''atha) *from me after my physical powers have declined, though my resolution is still firm.*[16]

[8] Cf. *ibid.*, 233-4.

[9] Cf. *ibid.*, 213-14.

[10] Cf. *ibid.*, Vol. x, 217-18.

[11] Cf. *ibid.*, Vol. IX, 209.

[12] Cf. *ibid.*, Vol. x, 72.

[13] Cf. *ibid.*, 220.

[14] Cf. *ibid.*, 91.

[15] Cf. *ibid.*, 215-16. I follow J in reading the poet's name as 'Yazīd b. Ḍirār' and not '. . . b. Ṣirār' as in AS.

[16] Cf. *ibid.*, Vol. IX, 228.

Dhū'r-Rumma. He was Ghailān b. 'Uqba. He was given this nickname because of his line (metre *Rajaz*): . . . *a split and splintered* [*tent-peg*], *with the remnants of a rope* (rumma) *still attached round it like a necklace.*[17] [30

Jirān al-'Aud. He was al-Mustaurid al-'Uqailī. He was given this nickname because he once said to his two wives (metre *Ṭawīl*): *Beware, O my two wives, for I see that the lash* (jirān al-'aud, literally, '[*a whip made from*] *the hair of the neck of an aged camel'*) *is almost got ready for you.*[18]

Al-Quṭāmī. He was 'Umair b. Shuyaim. He was given this nickname because of his line (metre *Rajaz*): *He drives them down at one side, and then at the other, just as the falcon* (al-quṭāmī) *attacks the partridges when they come down to their watering-places.*[19] [31.

Mūsā Shahawāt. He was a client of Quraish. He was given this nickname because he once said to Yazīd b. Mu'āwiya (metre *Khafīf*): *You are not one of us, nor is your maternal uncle one of us, O you who neglect the prayers for your pleasures* (shahawāt).[20]

Al-'Ajjāj. He was 'Abdallāh b. Ru'ba. He was given this nickname of his line (metre *Rajaz*): . . . *so that those who cry repeatedly for help* ('aj'aja) *shout desperately in their distress* (ya'ajja).[21]

Ar-Ruqayyāt. He was 'Abdallāh b. Qais. He had this nickname attributed to him because he was associated with three women of Quraish, each called Ruqayya. However, others say that he got it because of his line (metre *Wāfir*): *This Ruqayya, not that Ruqayya, nor that Ruqayya, O man!*[22] [32

Al-Akhḍar. He was al-Faḍl b. al-'Abbās b. 'Utba b. Abī Lahab. He was given this nickname because of his line (metre *Madīd*): *I am the dusky one* (al-akhḍar), *as is well known, a dark-skinned one* (akhḍar al-jilda), *born of the nobility of the Arabs.*[23]

'Ā'id al-Kalb. He was Muṣ'ab b. 'Abdallāh az-Zubairī. He was given this nickname because of his line (metre *Kāmil*): *How is it that I was ill, but none of you came to visit me* (fa-lam ya'udnī 'ā'id), *yet if your dog* (kalb) *were to be sick, I would visit it.*[24]

[17] Cf. *ibid.*, 396-7.

[18] Cf. *ibid.*, 239.

[19] I follow AS and many parallel citations in reading 'Shuayim' instead of the 'Shatīm' of J.

[20] Cf. *ibid.*, Vol. x, 237-8. Yazīd is accused of impiety, debauchery and other crimes in all the anti-Umayyad sources, and the poet here, who according to Ibn Qutaiba, *Kitāb ash-shi'r wa'sh-shu'arā'*, ed. de Goeje (Leiden 1904), 366-7, was a *maulā* from Azerbaijan, represents the attitude of the 'pious opposition' and Zubairid partisans in the Medina where he lived. The reference to Yazīd's maternal uncle is to Mālik b. Baḥdal b. Unaif, brother of the Caliph's mother Maisūn and leader of the Kalbī or Yemenī party during the reigns of Mu'āwiya and Yazīd; and the poet alludes indirectly to the Christian origins of the family of Ibn Baḥdal; cf. Lammens, *Études sur le règne du Calife Omaiyade Mo'âwia Ier*, 286ff.

[21] Cf. Barbier de Meynard, *op. cit.*, Vol. x, 82-3.

[22] Cf. *ibid.*, Vol. IX, 413-14.

[23] Cf. *ibid.*, 204-5. Some sources state that al-Faḍl did in fact have a dark-skinned Ḥabashī forebear, but the point here seems to be that the poet is boasting of noble Arab ancestry; to be dark and swarthy (*akhḍar*) was considered a sign of pure Arab blood, whereas a ruddy-faced, light colouring (*ḥumra*) was considered an attribute of non-Arab peoples like the Persians and Greeks. Cf. Goldziher's excursus, 'Schwarze und Weisse', in *Muhammedanische Studien*, I, 268-9, K. Vollers, 'Über Rassenfarben in der arabischen Literatur'; in *Centenario della nascità di Michele Amari* (Palermo 1910), I 85-8; and A. Morabia, 'Recherches sur quelques noms de couleurs en arabe classique', SI, XXI (1964), 79, who describes *akhḍar* as 'l'un des [adjectifs les] plus riches de sens de langue arabe'. Also, Jāḥiẓ in his *Kitāb fakhr as-sūdān 'alā 'l-bīḍān* 'Book of the vaunting of the blacks over the whites', in *Tria opuscula*, ed. Van Vloten (Leiden 1903), 74ff., tr. Rescher, *Orientalistische Miszellen*, II (Istanbul 1926), 168ff., discusses the question of the exact meaning of *akhḍar*.

[24] Cf. Barbier de Meynard, *op. cit.*, Vol. x, 80.

Ṣarī‘ al-Ghawānī. He was Muslim b. al-Walīd b. al-Anṣārī. Ar-Rashīd gave him this nickname because of his line (metre *Ṭawīl*): *Is life anything more than being swept along by* [33
passion, or being prostrated (ṣarī‘) *by the wine-cup and by wide-eyed beauties?*
A man once asked him, 'Why are you called Ṣarī‘ al-Ghawānī?' So he began reciting to him (metre *Khafīf*): *The rosy flush of the cheeks, the wide, alluring eyes, and the teeth gleaming like the flower of the camomile, / The jet black of the ringlets falling over the temples on the white cheek, the breasts gently-rounded like pomegranates, / [All these beautiful features] have left me prostrated in the presence of these maidens* (ladā 'l-ghawānī ṣarī‘an), *and because of this, I am called 'He who is left prostrated by the maidens'.*[25]

Ghubār al-‘Askar. He was Marwān al-Aṣghar Abū's-Simṭ. He was given this nickname because of his line (metre *Kāmil*): *When someone asks me about my white hair, I reply that it is dust left there from the dust raised by armies* (ghubār al-‘askar).[26] [34

Muqabbil ar-Rīḥ. I cannot recall his name. He was given this nickname because of his lines (metre *Basīṭ*): *O Hind, what do you command*[27] *in the case of a man of whose heart sadness has taken its fill? / The north wind blew, and people said, 'In whichever land you may be, may it be blessed!' / Then out of the depth of his emotion, he kissed the wind* (qabbala 'r-rīḥa), *whereas no-one before him had ever kissed the wind.*

[25] Cf. *ibid.*, 64-5.

[26] Cf. *ibid.*, 92-3.

[27] Following the emendation here of AS. In company with Abyārī and Ṣairafī, I have been unable to trace the proper name of this poet.

Chapter Three.

Concerning the nicknames further given in Islamic times to great leaders and prominent figures.

Although God, He is exalted and magnified, had prohibited the practice, the men of Quraish used to give each other derisory nicknames (*tatanābazu bi'l-alqāb*).[1]

[An-Na'thal 'the long-bearded one'.] 'Uthmān b. 'Affān, may God be pleased with him, was very hirsute, i.e. he had a lot of hair on his body and a flowing beard; hence they gave him the nickname of 'the long-bearded one', and sometimes he was called 'the long-bearded one of Quraish'.[2]

[Abū Turāb 'father of dust, dusty one'.] The members of the Umayyad clan used to call 'Alī b. Abī Ṭālib, may God be pleased with him, by this name. It arose because one day, the Prophet, God's prayers and peace be upon him, while in the course of one of his journeys, saw 'Alī asleep in the dust and covered over with it. So he said to him in a bantering way, 'Arise, O dusty one!'[3]

Khaiṭ Bāṭil 'incorporeal threads which seem to shimmer in the air during the heat of the day'. Marwān b. al-Ḥakam was inordinately tall and thin, so he was given this nickname. A [36
poet once said concerning him (metre *Ṭawīl*): *May God curse a people who have appointed as their ruler a* khaiṭ bāṭil, *giving him unfettered power to bestow or to withhold!*[4]

Abū'dh-Dhibbān 'father of flies'. 'Abd al-Malik b. Marwān was notorious for his foul breath, and was given this nickname. He was also notorious for his avarice, and was known as *Rashḥ*

[1] Cf. Qur'ān, xlix, 11, 'Do not scoff at each other or revile each other with derisory nicknames (*lā tanābazū bi'l-alqāb*)', and also Caetani and Gabrieli, *Onomasticon arabicum*, I, 144-5, 150-1, on the satirical origins of the *laqab* and *nabaz*.

[2] Cf. Barbier de Meynard, 'Surnoms et sobriquets dans la littérature arabe', JA, Ser. 10, Vol. X, 244-5, and Goldziher, 'Spottnamen der ersten Chalifen bei den Schî'iten', WZKM, XV (1901), 327.

[3] Cf. *ibid.*, Vol. IX, 190-1, and Nöldeke, 'Zur tendenziösen Gestaltung der Urgeschichte des Islām's', ZDMG, LII (1898), 29-30. Nöldeke takes 'Abū Turāb' as originally an insulting designation, connected with such expressions as *taribat yadāhu* 'May his hands be earthy!' = 'May he be felled to the ground!' In Bukhārī and in Ṭabarī, I, 1272, it is said that the name was given to 'Alī by his enemies, but that very soon explanations such as the one given here by Tha'ālibī grew up, thus turning the original insult into a term of honour.

[4] Cf. Barbier de Meynard, *op. cit.*, Vol. IX, 377. In Mas'ūdī, *Murūj*, V, 200, this line of verse is attributed to Marwān's own brother, 'Abd ar-Raḥmān b. al-Ḥakam.

al-Ḥajar ('sweat from a stone'). He got the name 'Father of flies' because flies used to buzz past his mouth and drop down dead because of the concentrated foulness of his breath. It is related that he once took a bite out of an apple, and then passed it over to one of his wives. She called for a knife to be brought, so he asked her what she intended to do. She retorted that she was going to cut out the bad bit; upon which he immediately divorced her. Another of his wives asked him, 'O Commander of the Faithful, why don't you brush your teeth clean?' He replied, 'I'll brush them with you (i.e. kiss you).' 'Abd al-Malik was called 'Sweat from a [37
stone' because, of course, stones do not sweat, or if they do, this is very exceptional. One uses the sobriquet 'Sweat from a stone' just as one says 'Dog's wool', 'Ant's marrow' or 'Bird's milk' for something difficult or impossible to find.[5]

Laṭīm ash-Shaiṭān 'touched by a blow from Satan'. According to al-Jāḥiẓ, when one wants to insult someone who has a twisted mouth or inverted eyelids, one says, 'O wretch, marked by Satan'. 'Amr b. Sa'īd b. al-'Āṣ al-Ashdaq used to be called by this nickname. When 'Abdallāh b. az-Zubair heard the news that 'Abd al-Malik b. Marwān had procured 'Amr b. Sa'īd's murder,[6] he exclaimed in the course of the Friday sermon which he was making, 'We have just heard that the Father of Flies has killed the One marked by Satan – "In this way we place some of the evildoers in the power of others, as a penalty for what they have gained for themselves." '[7]

'Ajūz al-Yaman 'the old woman of Yemen'. Wahb b. Munabbih relates[8]: "Abdallāh b. az-Zubair appointed as governor over us one of our own chiefs. This man was extremely ugly and had been given the nickname "Old woman of Yemen". I came to Ibn az-Zubair as a member of a delegation from Yemen, and found [38
'Abdallāh b. Khālid b. Usaid[9] with him. This latter person greeted me, "O Abū 'Abdallāh, how is the old woman of Yemen?" I disdained to reply, but he repeated the question several times, insistently, so in the end I quoted, "I have submitted myself, with Solomon, to God, the Lord of the Worlds".[10] and then added, "And how is the old woman of Quraish?" He asked whom it was that I meant by this, and I told him, "Umm Jamīl (sc. the wife of Muḥammad's enemy in Mecca, Abū Lahab), 'the one who carries

[5] Cf. Barbier de Meynard, *op. cit.*, Vol. IX, 193-4; Tha'ālibī, *Thimār al-qulūb*, 197, s.v. 'Abū'dh-Dhibbān', and 443, s.v. 'Rashḥ al-Ḥajar'. According to Jāḥiẓ, *Ḥayawān*, III, 381-2, the former *laqab* became proverbial for any foul-breathed person.

[6] *Ashdaq* = opening the sides of the mouth widely in order to articulate clearly and deliberately (Lane). This paragraph is based on Jāḥiẓ, *al-Bayān wa't-tabyīn* (Cairo 1366/1947), I, 303-4, on 'Amr b. Sa'īd and his *tashāduq fī'l-kalām*, and *Ḥayawān*, VI, 178; cf. also Barbier de Meynard, *op. cit.*, Vol. X, 194-5. 'Amr was a member of the Umayyad family and especially hated by 'Abdallāh b. az-Zubair because he had led Umayyad armies against him and his brother Muṣ'ab b. az-Zubair. According to Mas'ūdī, *Murūj*, v, 198-9, 'Amr had supported Marwān b. al-Ḥakam's succession to the Caliphate on condition that Marwān made him the *walī al-'ahd* after Khālid b. Yazīd b. Mu'āwiya; 'Abd al-Malik therefore feared 'Amr's pretensions and had him executed in 70/689-90 (cf. K. Zetterstéen, EI^{2} s.v.).

[7] Qur'ān, vi, 129.

[8] Wahb b. Munabbih (d. 110/729-30 or 114/732), was a *qāṣṣ* or popular story-teller of Yemenī origin and at one stage of his life qāḍī of Ṣan'ā'; he was a great authority on the scriptures and lore of the Jews and Christians (J. Horovitz, EI^{1} s.v.).

[9] 'Abdallāh b. Khālid b. Usaid b. Abī'l-'Aiṣ b. Umayya had been temporarily governor of Kufa on Ziyād b. Abīhi's death in 53/673 until the latter's son 'Ubaidallāh took over, but later went over to the Zubairids; cf. Balādhurī, *Ansāb al-ashrāf*, I, ed. M. Ḥamīdallāh (Cairo 1959), 496.

[10] Qur'ān, xxvii, 45/44.

firewood, with a rope of palm-fibre round her neck'."[11] Ibn az-Zubair burst out laughing, and he turned to Ibn Khālid, saying, "You asked a silly question, but he gave a good answer!" '[12]

Al-Qubā' 'the huge one'. When al-Ḥārith b. 'Abdallāh b. Abī Rabī'a became governor of Basra,[13] he peered one day at one of the measures in use there for grain and commented, 'This measure of yours is certainly *qubā'*', i.e. very wide. From this, he was given the nickname of al-Qubā', and it became so well-known that it replaced his proper name. It was said of him (metre *Wāfir*): *O Commander of the Faithful, may you be recompensed with good, deliver us from the huge one* (qubā') *of the Banū 'l-Mughīra.*[14]

Babba. When civil strife broke out at Basra between the partisans of the Marwānids and the Zubairids, the people there eventually came together and agreed to give allegiance to 'Abdallāh b. al-Ḥārith b. Naufal b. al-Ḥārith b. 'Abd al-Muṭṭalib as their Amīr, until the question of the Caliphate was finally settled.[15] This man's nickname was Babba, given to him because his mother Hind bint Abī Sufyān b. Ḥarb used to dandle him as a baby on her knees and say to him (metre *Rajaz*): *I'll marry off my* [39 *baby* (babba) *to a beautiful maiden, who will deprive the Muslims* (literally, *'People of the Ka'ba'*) *of their living allowances.*

I.e. she will be so beautiful that when men see her, they will hate their own wives, divorce them and have to give them back their dowries; in this way, she will despoil them, i.e. cause them to expend their living allowances.

Other people say that he was called Babba simply because he used, as an infant, to repeat this word; his mother used to address him by it, and it became attached to him. Al-Farazdaq refers to him when he says (metre *Ṭawīl*):

In the past, I have given my allegiance to many people and served them faithfully; now I have given allegiance to Babba and will not betray him.

We have given ourselves to him for our temporal preservation and for our eternal salvation, and what better protector could we have against sudden dangers and catastrophes?

He is the noble one who bears the burdens of his people, the chosen one of Quraish, descended from the families of both Ḥarb and Ḥārith.[16]

When Muṣ'ab b. az-Zubair made himself ruler of Iraq and entered Basra,[17] he was afraid lest the people there might give him some opprobrious nickname, as they had given to al- [40 Qubā' and Babba. So one day, in the course of the Friday sermon, he threatened them with these words, 'You have acquired the

[11] *Ibid.*, cxi, 4-5.

[12] Cf. Barbier de Meynard, *op. cit.*, Vol. x, 83-4; this story appears also in *Thimār al-qulūb*, 241, s.v. ''Ajūz al-Yaman'.

[13] Sc. in 44/664-5 during Mu'āwiya's reign; cf. Pellat, *Le milieu basrien et la formation de Ǧāḥiẓ*, 278.

[14] Cf. on this nickname, Barbier de Meynard, *op. cit.*, Vol. x, 102. The reference to the Banū'l-Mughīra in the line of verse is to al-Ḥārith's relative and fellow-member of the clan of Makhzūm of Quraish, al-Mughīra; al-Mughīra was a prominent opponent of the Prophet in his early years at Mecca and father of the scoffer al-Walīd, on whom see below, tr., p. 89 (Ibn Duraid, *Kitāb al-ishtiqāq*, ed. Wüstenfeld, 60-1).

[15] This was in 65/684-5, cf. Pellat, *loc. cit.* Babba later joined the rebellion of Ibn al-Ash'ath (see below, p. 59), and, after the latter's defeat, fled before al-Ḥajjāj to 'Umān (Ibn Qutaiba, *Ma'ārif*, 127).

[16] Cf. Barbier de Meynard, *op. cit.*, Vol. IX, 223-5. Farazdaq refers in his last line to Babba's descent from the two noble clans in Mecca of Umayya or 'Abd Shams or Ḥarb on one side, and of al-Ḥārith or al-Muṭṭalib on the other. The ultimate common parentage of the two clans from 'Abd Manāf is not infrequently stressed in early literature; in *Murūj*, VI, a descendant of the Umayyads recites verse to ar-Rashīd and stresses the fact that 'Abd Shams was the paternal uncle of 'Abd al-Muṭṭalib.

[17] Sc. in 67/686-7 when Muṣ'ab became governor of Basra for his brother 'Abdallāh and just before his suppression of al-Mukhtār's rising in Kufa.

habit of giving your governors nicknames, so you may as well call me here and now "The Butcher" (*al-Jazzār*), for by God, if I hear that any of you has given me any other nickname, I will have him executed just as a camel meant for slaughter (*jazūr*) is disposed of.' They accordingly refrained from nicknaming him.

Ẓill ash-Shaiṭān 'Satan's shadow'. Muḥammad b. Sa'd b. Abī Waqqāṣ had this name because of his height, his swarthiness and his stout build.[18] He joined the rebellion of Ibn al-Ash'ath,[19] and used to act as his muezzin and as his prayer-leader. When Muḥammad was captured, he was brought before al-Ḥajjāj, who reproached him with the words, 'O vile one, O shadow of Satan! You used to be the proudest of men, yet you have agreed to act as muezzin for a weaver, himself the son of a weaver!' (Al-Ḥajjāj meant 'Abd ar-Raḥmān b. Muḥammad b. al-Ash'ath, because he was a Yemenī, and the people of Yemen are all contemptuously called 'weavers'.)[20]

[Al-Faqīr 'the destitute one'. This was] 'Abdallāh al-Faqīr, who was 'Abdallāh b. Muslim, the brother of Qutaiba b. Muslim. He got the name because whenever his brother Qutaiba was sharing out the booty in Khurāsān amongst his retainers and troops, 'Abdallāh would say, 'O Amīr, give me an extra share, for I'm a poor man (*faqīr*).' So they called him that. Now Qutaiba appointed him governor of Samarqand, and he remarked to his companions, 'Do you think that this nickname will no longer be given to my brother, now that he has been raised to the governorship of Samarqand?' They replied decisively, however, 'Indeed no, O Amīr, not even if he became governor of all Khurāsān; this nickname will stick to him more tenaciously than debts or the quartan fever stick to a man, and more inescapably than hair grows again on the upper part of the chest [after it has been cut off].'[21] [41

Latīm al-Ḥimār 'marked by a blow from a wild ass'. This was 'Umar b. 'Abd al-'Azīz b. Marwān, whose mother was Umm 'Āṣim bint 'Āṣim b. 'Umar b. al-Khaṭṭāb.[22] It is related that 'Umar [b. al-Khaṭṭāb], may God be pleased with him, used to say, 'One of my descendants will have the same name and patronymic as myself, will have a blemish on his face, and will fill the earth with justice where previously it was filled with tyranny.' When 'Umar [b. 'Abd al-'Azīz] was still a child, he was wounded on the face by a wild ass and was left with scarring on his forehead. His brother Aṣbagh said, 'God is most great! You must be the "scar-faced one of the Umayyad dynasty".' 'Umar's detractors

[18] Cf. Barbier de Meynard, *op. cit.*, Vol. x, 77-8. According to Jāḥiẓ, *Ḥayawān*, vi, 178-9, *Ẓill ash-Shaiṭān* was used for inordinately proud and massively-built people, and *Ẓill an-Na'āma* 'Ostrich's shadow' for excessively tall ones.

[19] Ibn al-Ash'ath was in revolt during the years 80-2/699-701, having turned the so-called 'Peacock Army' in Sīstān against al-Ḥajjāj and raised the Arabs of Iraq against the Umayyads; cf. Sir William Muir, *The Caliphate, its rise, decline and fall*[4] (Edinburgh 1915), 336-8, and Wellhausen, *The Arab kingdom*, 232-49.

[20] The trade of weaver was traditionally regarded with contempt in Islam; see R. Brunschvig, 'Métiers vils en Islam', SI, XVI (1962), 50-5, cf. C. Bouyahia in *Arabica*, x (1963), 209-10.

[21] Cf. Barbier de Meynard, *op. cit.*, Vol. x, 98-9. According to Ya'qūbī, *Ta'rīkh*, ed. M. T. Houtsma (Leiden 1883), II, 344, it was 'Abd ar-Raḥmān b. Muslim whom Qutaiba appointed governor of Samarqand (cf. Gibb, *The Arab conquests in Central Asia* [London 1923], 35, 38, 46). Balādhurī, *Futūḥ al-buldān* (Cairo 1959), 410, says that 'Ubaidallāh b. Muslim was appointed by Qutaiba governor of Khwārazm after the conquest of 93/712, but in his enumeration of the thirteen sons of Muslim, Ibn Qutaiba, *Ma'ārif*, 406-8, mentions only an 'Abdallāh and not an 'Ubaidallāh.

[22] Cf. Tha'ālibī, *Thimār al-qulūb*, 88, s.v. 'Ashajj Banī Umayya'.

therefore called him 'the one one marked by the wild ass'. 'Umar once spoke about Yazīd b. al-Muhallab and remarked, 'Is there any 'Irāqī who doesn't have some element of perfidiousness in his character?' This eventually reached Yazīd and he became enraged, saying, 'Who will be my helper[23] against the one marked by the wild ass?'

[Jarāda 'locust'.] This was Maslama b. 'Abd al-Malik, so-called on account of his pallid, yellowish complexion.[24]

['Āshiq Banī Marwān 'the impassioned lover of the Marwānids'.] This was Yazīd b. 'Abd al-Malik, so-called because of his enduring devotion to his two slave girls, Sallāma and Ḥabāba.[25] [42

[Khalī' Banī Marwān 'the outcast, the debauchee of the Marwānids'.] Al-Walīd b. Yazīd was thus called.[26]

[Yazīd an-Nāqiṣ 'Yazīd the reducer'.] Yazīd b. al-Walīd was thus called because he reduced the stipends of the Arab warriors.[27]

Khudhaina 'the lady'. This was Sa'īd b. 'Abd al-'Azīz b. al-Ḥārith b. al-Ḥakam b. Abī'l-'Āṣī b. Umayya. Maslama b. 'Abd al-Malik appointed him governor of Khurāsān, so he crossed the Oxus [to take up his post]. Since he was bisexual and effeminate by nature, and led a debauched, sybaritic life, the people of Samarqand nicknamed him *Khudhaina*.[28] In the parlance of the people of Samarqand, *khudhain* is used for a noble, free-born lady, just as the Turks use the term *khātūn*; the *tā' marbūṭa* is added to it either for feminisation or to show intensiveness, giving *khudhaina*.[29]

Az-Zāgh 'the jackdaw'. Asad b. 'Abdallāh al-Qasrī was appointed governor of Khurāsān by his brother Khālid b. 'Abdallāh, viceroy of Iraq.[30] Asad was very dark and swarthy, and he used to wear a red silk turban, the ends of which he wrapped over the lower part of his face as a veil. When they first saw him, certain Khurāsānīs exclaimed, 'Our Amīr is just like a jackdaw', and this nickname for him became generally current. Hence one day, Asad threatened in the course of the Friday sermon, 'I shall certainly bring trouble (*la-uzayyighanna*) for anyone who calls me *az-Zāgh*.' Notwithstanding, they paid no attention to him[31] and continued applying the nickname to him. [43

Muqawwim an-Nāqa 'he who fixes the she-camel's value'. A

23 Reading, with AS, *'adhīrī* for the *ghadīrī* of J.

24 Cf. Barbier de Meynard, *op. cit.*, Vol. IX, 237-8, and below, p. 62.

25 Cf. *ibid.*, Vol. X, 79-80.

26 Cf. *ibid.*, Vol. IX, 375-6.

27 Cf. *ibid.*, Vol. X, 240-1. According to M. Sprengling, 'From Persian to Arabic', AJSL, LVI (1939), 218-20, Tha'ālibī's explanation here of *nāqiṣ* is not the correct one, but the nickname refers to the fact that Yazīd's reign marked the end (*naqṣ* 'fall, ruin') of the Umayyad dynasty.

28 Cf. Barbier de Meynard, *op. cit.*, Vol. IX, 371. Sa'īd was appointed governor in 102/720-1, cf. Gibb, *The Arab conquests in Central Asia*, 61-2, and Barthold, *Turkestan*, 188-9. According to Balādhurī, *Futūḥ*, 417, he was given his nickname by one of the dihqāns of Transoxania who came into Sa'īd's presence and found him with his face made up with yellow dye and his hair combed into curls. Sa'īd was Maslama's son-in-law, and according to Ṭabarī, II, 1417-18, this was the only reason why he got the governorship.

29 In Soghdian, 'queen, lady' was *γwt'ynh*, pronounced *khwatēn*, the final *h* being, according to Henning, an unpronounced determinative of feminine words. This would be rendered in Arabic script as *khudain* and the final *a* presumably added as a kind of hypercorrection by Arabising scholars. (I am indebted to Sir Gerard Clauson for this note.)

30 In 105/723-4, according to Balādhurī, *Futūḥ*, *loc. cit.*, and Ṭabarī, II, 1480. Cf. on this nickname, Barbier de Meynard, *op. cit.*, Vol. IX, 416-17.

31 Following here the emendation of AS, *fa-lam yaktarithū bihi*.

man from the tribe of Kalb, whose name is not known to me, was governor of Yamāma.[32] He once delivered the Friday sermon to his people, and in the course of it said, 'O my people! Beware of growing insolent and disobeying God Most High, for God destroyed a whole people because of a she-camel worth a mere 300 dirhams.'[33] Because of this, he acquired the nickname 'He who fixes the she-camel's value'.

Marwān al-Ḥimār 'Marwan the wild ass', also called *al-Ja'dī*. He was Marwān b. Muḥammad b. Marwān, last of the Umayyad Caliphs.[34] Two explanations are given of how he got the name *al-Ḥimār*.

The first is that the Arabs used to call the culmination of each period of a hundred years *ḥimār*, and when the Umayyad dynasty's period of power approached the hundred year mark during Marwān's reign, they nicknamed him after that. People interpreted God Most High's words in the story of 'Uzair as a reference to the beginning of the Abbasids' period of power: 'Look at your ass (*ḥimār*) – in order that We may make you a miraculous sign to the people . . .', i.e. you have remained dead for a hundred years, but then you have been raised to life, just as He has previously said in the same verse, 'So God caused him to die for a hundred years, and then raised him to life again.'[35]

The other explanation is that Marwān was continually involved (literally, 'never allowed his saddle felt to get dry') in combatting the Khawārij and Musawwida[36] (sc. the supporters of the Abbasids, 'those who wear black'). He was always out making forays, riding furiously and experiencing the rigours of warfare, so that he acquired the nickname of 'the wild ass', an animal proverbially famous for its endurance; one says 'more hardy than the wild ass'.

As for his other nickname, *al-Ja'dī*, this was after al-Ja'd b. Dirham, one of the Marwānids' clients, notorious as a [44 heretic; he is said to have taught Marwān his heretical doctrines, so that Marwān became known as one of his adherents.[37]

Abū'd-Dawānīq 'father of farthings'. Abū Ja'far al-Manṣūr had this nickname because of his carefulness over the smallest sums of money (*tadnīq*) and his practice of demanding detailed accounts,

[32] Cf. Barbier de Meynard, *op. cit.*, Vol. x, 228-9. In Balādhurī, *Ansāb al-ashrāf*, v, ed. S. D. F. Goitein (Jerusalem 1936), 155, 189, 355, Muqawwim an-Nāqa is identified as 'Abdallāh b. 'Ubaidallāh b. Abī Thaur, described as a *ḥalīf* of the Banū 'Abd Manāf, and appointed governor by the anti-Caliph 'Abdallāh b. az-Zubair.

[33] Alluding to the hamstringing of the divinely-sent she-camel by the people of Thamūd when they rejected the prophet Ṣāliḥ; cf. Qur'ān, vii, 75/77, xi, 67-8/64-5, xxvi, 155-7, xci, 13-15.

[34] Cf. Barbier de Meynard, *op. cit.*, Vol. IX, 239-40, 367-8, and H. von Mžik, 'Einiges über Marwâns II. Beinamen: al-Ḥimâr und al-Ǧa'dî', WZKM, XX (1906), 310-13.

[35] Qur'ān, ii, 261/259.

[36] Both J and AS have the meaningless *Musawwira* for *Musawwida*. On the Abbasid adoption of black, see G. van Vloten, *Recherches sur la domination arabe, le chiitisme et les croyances messianiques sous le Califat des Omeyyades* (Amsterdam 1894), 63-5; a popular explanation of it came to be that it was a sign of mourning for the martyrs of Karbalā', al-Ḥusain b. 'Alī and his children.

[37] Al-Ja'd was accused of heretical beliefs and at the instigation of the Caliph Hishām was in 125/743 executed by Khālid b. 'Abdallāh al-Qasrī; he seems to have held that the Qur'ān was created and that knowledge of a thing is in itself an act without an agent ('Abd al-Qāhir b. Ṭāhir al-Baghdādī, *al-Farq bain al-firaq* [Cairo 1328/1910], 262, tr. A. Halkin [Tel-Aviv 1935], 101-2; Ibn an-Nadīm, *Fihrist* [Cairo 1348/1929-30], 472-3; A. S. Tritton, *Muslim theology* [London 1947], 54-5, 59).

down to the last farthings (*dawānīq*) and grains, from his provincial governors as well as from his personal agents and stewards. Yet on the other hand he was, as we have noted, capable of bestowing as a gift millions of dirhams.[38]

Mūsā Aṭbiq 'Mūsā, shut your mouth!'. This was Mūsā al-Hādī, son of al-Mahdī, son of al-Manṣūr. His upper lip was contracted and puckered, so that he could only close his mouth by making a special effort. Hence al-Mahdī attached to him a servant, who had to stay with him night and day, and who told him at regular intervals, 'Mūsā, shut your mouth!' As this went on for a long time, the phrase became applied to him as a nickname, and even stuck to him after he became Caliph and ruler of the world.

Utrujja 'citron', Shaḥm al-Ḥazīn 'fat of the sorrowing man' and Ka'b al-Baqar 'ox's knuckle-bone'. Dā'ūd b. 'Īsā b. Mūsā was called 'Citron' because of his yellowish complexion and pleasant personal odour. 'Abd as-Samī' b. Muḥammad b. Manṣūr was called 'Fat of the sorrowing man', and Muḥammad b. Aḥmad b. 'Īsā was called 'Ox's knuckle-bone'. All three were supporters of al-Musta'īn, but went over to al-Mu'tazz,[39] who thereupon recited (metre *Mutaqārib*): *Utrujja, Shaḥm al-Ḥazīn and* [45 *Ka'b al-Baqar have come to me seeking safe conduct; / So welcome to all who rally to us, and may those who fail to come be in hellfire!*[40]

Karb ad-Dawā' 'the unpleasantness of medicine'.[41] [The Caliph] al-Muktafī had a passion for giving people nicknames, and prided himself on being able to devise appropriate ones. He used to say, 'The person who said that nicknames come down from heaven was perfectly right.' He was thus expressing in prose what a poet has said (metre *Basīṭ*): *It is rare that your eyes light upon a man whose character is not revealed, if you consider the matter, in his nickname.*

So al-Muktafī called his Vizier al-'Abbās b. al-Ḥasan[42] 'the Unpleasantness of medicine', his slave al-Ḥusain *'Araq al-Maut* 'Death's sweat'[43] and his secretary Aḥmad b. Muḥammad *Jarāda* 'Locust'. When al-'Abbās b. al-Ḥasan was killed during the reign of al-Muqtadir, Ibn Bassām[44] said concerning him (metre *Madīd*)): *We have been delivered from a tribulation, and Karb* [46 *ad-Dawā' has gone. / In truth, by God, this man was a perpetual offence to intelligent people.* He also said concerning Jarāda (metre *Wāfir*): *Can any good thing be expected from Jarāda, seeing that the locust was created for destruction?*

Al-Mubarrad. This was Abū'l-'Abbās Muḥammad b. Yazīd, eminently renowned amongst those literary men and grammarians

[38] Cf. Barbier de Meynard, *op. cit.*, Vol. IX, 192-3, and above, pp.50-1.

[39] Sc. in 252/866 when al-Musta'īn, having lost general support in Baghdad, was persuaded to abdicate in favour of his cousin al-Mu'tazz, the candidate of the Turkish soldiery; cf. Muir, *The Caliphate*, 534-5.

[40] Cf. Barbier de Meynard, *op. cit.*, Vol. IX, 202, Vol. X, 55-6, 115-16. This section also occurs in the *Thimār al-qulūb*, 300, s.v. 'Ka'b al-Baqar'.

[41] Cf. *ibid.*, 551-2, s.v., and Barbier de Meynard, *op. cit.*, Vol. X, 112-14.

[42] Abū Aḥmad al-'Abbās b. al-Ḥasan b. Makhlad al-Jarjarā'ī was Vizier to al-Muktafī and al-Muqtadir 291-5/904-8; cf. Sourdel, *Le vizirat 'Abbāside*, I, 359-70, and *idem*, EI[2] Art. 'al-Djardjarā'ī'.

[43] Cf. Barbier de Meynard, *op. cit.*, Vol. IX, 237-8, Vol. X, 85-6. According to the *Thimār al-qulūb*, 548, *'Araq al-Maut* is proverbial for anything harsh and violent. The al-Ḥusain mentioned here was active in the latter part of al-Mutawakkil's reign, and at some stage in his career, was in charge of the *Barīd* in Egypt; cf. H. F. Amedroz, 'Tales of official life from the "Tadhkira" of Ibn Hamdun, etc.', JRAS (1908), 423, citing Ṭabarī, III, 1841.

[44] Abū'l-Ḥasan 'Alī b. Muḥammad al-Bassāmī, called Ibn Bassām, Abbasid poet especially famed for his satires; d. 302/914 (Mas'ūdī, *Murūj*, VIII, 257-72; Ibn Khallikān, tr. II, 301-4).

whose works are continually cited and quoted.[45] People give two accounts of how he got the name al-Mubarrad:

The first is that he merited what was said of him in the verses of a certain poet (metre *Basīṭ*): *Indeed, despite his learning, al-Mubarrad is cold and frigid* (dhū bard), *both when he is serious or, if you please, when he is being gay. / But it is rare that your eyes light upon a man whose character is not revealed, if you consider the matter, in his nickname.*

The second is that he was called this by antiphrasis, just as the proverbially sharp-sighted raven is called *al-aʿwar* 'the one-eyed', and just as al-Mutawakkil named the mother of his son al-Muʿtazz *Qabīḥa* 'the ugly one', whereas she was the most beautiful woman of her time; she had the nickname engraved on her ring, 'I am Qabīḥa, so simply reverse the epithet!' Likewise, Abu Nuwās named a slave boy *Samij* 'the hideous one' (metre *Basīṭ*): *His master named him 'the hideous one' because he considered him so handsome.*[46] [47

Al-Mubarrad used to say, 'No-one has ever played upon my nickname so cleverly as al-Warrāq, who was himself called *Sadhāb* "[the herb] rue".[47] I went past him one day when he was sitting at the door of his house. He got up and greeted me, and then, without pressing me in an embarassing way, offered me hospitality at his table. "What have you got just now?" I asked. He replied, "I've got you garnished with myself", that is, he had cold meat (*laḥm mubarrad*) dressed with chopped rue (*sadhāb muqaṭṭaʿ*). I burst out laughing and stopped to eat at his house.'

Nifṭawaih 'little naphtha-like or bitumen-like one'.[48] This was Abū ʿAbdallāh Ibrāhīm b. Muḥammad b. ʿArafa the grammarian, and in this nickname he was compared with naphtha because of his ugliness. The name was formed on the pattern of 'Sībawaih', because as a grammarian, Nifṭawaih was connected with him, followed his opinion and taught a commentary on his famous

[45] Al-Mubarrad (210-85/826-98), the great grammarian and philologist of Basra and then Baghdad; cf. Yāqūt, *Irshād*, VII, 137-44, Ibn Khallikān, tr. III, 31-7, and Brockelmann, EI¹ s.v. According to Yāqūt, *loc. cit.*, the form of his name should be 'al-Mubarrid' = *al-muthbit li'l-ḥaqq* 'He who affirms the truth', but his enemies of the Kufan school of philology changed it to 'al-Mubarrad' with the *a* vowel. Cf. also, Barbier de Meynard, *op. cit.*, Vol. X, 198-200.

[46] On antiphrasis in Arabic, see W. Marçais, 'L'euphemisme et l'antiphrase dans les dialectes arabes d'Algérie', *Orientalische Studien Th. Nöldeke gewidmet* (Giessen 1906), I, 431-8; A. Fischer, 'Arab. *baṣīr* "scharfsichtig" per antiphrasin = "blind" ', ZDMG, LXI (1907), 425-34, 751-4, for the Arabs' dislike of direct reference to the misfortune of blindness; and D. Cohen, '*Aḍdād* et ambiguité linguistique en Arabe', *Arabica*, VIII (1961), 12-14. Other examples of nicknames given by antiphrasis or euphemism are given in Caetani and Gabrieli, *op. cit.*, 171.

[47] The by-name *al-Warrāq* 'copyist, bookseller' was naturally a common one amongst scholars. The one intended here might be Abū Ḥafṣ al-Warrāq, rival and enemy of Ibn ar-Rūmī. It might also be Muḥammad b. al-Walīd at-Tamīmī, a contemporary and pupil of al-Mubarrad's, or his son Aḥmad, both of whom were called Ibn al-Warrāq, cf. Jalāl ad-Dīn Abū'l-Faḍl 'Abd ar-Raḥman as-Suyūṭī, *Bughyat al-wuʿāt fī ṭabaqāt al-lughawiyyīn wa'n-nuḥāt* (Cairo 1326/1908), 112, 169, and Jamāl ad-Dīn Abū'l-Ḥasan 'Alī al-Qifṭī, *Inbāh ar-ruwāt 'alā anbā' an-nuḥāt* (Cairo 1369-74/1950-5), III, 223 (I am grateful to Dr M. A. Ghul for these latter two suggestions and the references).

[48] Accepting Nöldeke's view that these Persian endings in *-ōe*, *-ōi* > Arabic *-waih*, are basically hypochoristic in effect ('Persische Studien. I Persische Koseformen', SBWAW, CXVI [1888], 387-417).

grammar book.[49] A poet said of him (metre *Sarī'*): *If* [48
God's revelation had come down on Nifṭawaih, that could have been a disaster for him; / God would have burnt him up with the first half of his name (nifṭ/nafṭ = *'naphtha'*), *and have made the second half a malediction on him* (waih = *'woe'*).[50] In one of his verses, Ibn Bassām vocalised the name as 'Nifṭūya' (metre *Sarī'*):

Once in a dream, I saw our father Adam, may God, the Bestower of Grace, grant him intercession;

He said to me, 'Go, announce to all my descendants, those living in the rugged places and those in the plains,

That I hereby divorce their mother Eve, if Nifṭūya is one of my progeny.[51]

[Miskawaih 'little musk-like one'.] Amongst those literary men and grammarians who were given nicknames formed on the same pattern as the preceding one, was Miskawaih, the treasurer of Ibn al-'Amīd.[52] He recited these verses as a greeting to his master when the latter had just moved into a new palace (metre *Basīṭ*): *Do not be over-impressed by the beauty of the palace in which you are living; the merit of the sun does not lie in the heavenly spheres in which it moves. / Even if the sun had a hundred more constellations, that would not augment its merits one little bit.*[53] [49

[Mabramān.[54]] In regard to the grammarian thus named, he is the one Ibn Langak al-Baṣrī[55] mentioned (metre *Wāfir*): *Your words only make our heads spin and ache; no hearer can make any sense of them. / Overweening pride, lies and slanders! O Mabramān, you have wearied us to death* (la-qad abramtanā)!

Jaḥẓa 'having protuberant eyeballs'. He was Abū'l-Ḥasan Aḥmad b. Ja'far b. Mūsā b. Yaḥyā b. Khālid al-Barmakī.[56] He was called thus because he had protuberant, staring eyes. In appearance, he was one of the ugliest men in God's creation, yet at the same time, one of the most versatile and well-endowed artistically. He was, indeed, just as he himself said in one of his witty poems (metre *Basīṭ*):

O you who have invited me and then recoiled from me, you have by God, plunged me into disappointment.

I would have been content with bread made from rice flour, a few

[49] Nöldeke, *op. cit.*, 389, stresses the normative example of Sībawaih's name in the adoption of these *-ōe/-waih* endings.

[50] According to Ibn Khallikān, tr. I, 27, the author of these two verses was 'Abdallāh Muḥammad b. Zaid al-Wāsiṭī, but according to Yāqūt, *Irshād*, II, 311-12, it was Ibn Duraid.

[51] These three verses occur in *Irshād*, II, 307. The form in *-ūya* corresponds more nearly to the Persian original, and must have been the one of everyday Arabic usage, the form in *-waih* being a grammarians' one; cf. Nöldeke, *op. cit.*, 389-93. For Nifṭawaih (244-323/858-935), who was a pupil of al-Mubarrad, see Yāqūt, *Irshād*, II, 307-15, Ibn Khallikān, tr. I, 26-7, who quotes the *Laṭā'if* on the origin of his name, and Barbier de Meynard, *op. cit.*, Vol. X, 245-6.

[52] On Abū 'Alī Aḥmad b. Muḥammad b. Ya'qūb, called Miskawaih (d. 421/1030), whose wide interests ranged from science and ethics to historical writing, see Yāqūt, *Irshād*, II, 88-96 and Margoliouth, *Lectures on Arabic historians*, 128ff. (the anonymous EI[1] Art. 'Ibn Miskawaih' is poor and uninformative).

[53] These two verses occur in the *Yatīmat ad-dahr* of Tha'ālibī, III, 163, in the subsection on Ibn al-'Amīd.

[54] Sc. Abū Bakr Muḥammad b. 'Alī al-'Askarī, called Mabramān (d. 345/956-7), cf. Yāqūt, *Irshād*, VII, 42-3, and Barbier de Meynard, *op. cit.*, Vol. X, 200-1. The meaning of the *laqab* is obscure, but it is perhaps to be connected with the colloquial Arabic *barrām* 'chatterbox, loquacious person'.

[55] Abū'l-Ḥasan Muḥammad b. Muḥammad, called Ibn Langak ('son of the little lame one'), poet and grammarian of Basra who flourished in the 4th/10th century; cf. *Yatīmat ad-dahr*, II, 348-59, and *Irshād*, VII, 77-81.

[56] On Jaḥẓa, philologist, poet and musician, descendant of the Barmakī Viziers (d. 324/936), see Pellat, EI[2] Art. 'Djaḥẓa'; cf. also Barbier de Meynard, *op. cit.*, Vol. IX, 236-7.

hors d'oeuvres in a spiced, vinegar sauce (kāmakh)[57] *and a morsel of fish pickled in brine* (binn),[58]
Together with a skin of wine made from date-syrup, [*wine*] *which has stood for a long time at the bottom of an earthenware jar.*
A story-teller, poet or singer would not be too dear for this [50
[*little*] *which we have mentioned.*

If it were possible to extend the last line to include 'a secretary . . .', then it could well apply to him, for he was a very fluent stylist and had a delightful skill as a secretary. However, poetry and singing were his two principal accomplishments, though he further had a most extensive knowledge of history and the other arts which give polish and interest to a man. One of his neatest achievements is his well-known line (metre *Wāfir*): *The heavens became clear and bright, until people said, 'There must be a reconciliatory remonstrance between Jaḥẓa and time.'*[59]

Jaḥẓa used often to repeat the lines which Ibn ar-Rūmī said about him, and he would wonder in delight at the accuracy of his words (metre *Kāmil*)[60]: *They tell me that Jaḥẓa has borrowed those staring eyes of his from the elephant of the chess-board*[61] *or from the crab. / Let us commiserate with his companions! They endure the punishment of looking at him in return for the pleasures of hearing him!*

Al-'Aṭawānī 'devotee of al-'Aṭawī'. He was Abū Aḥmad b. Abī Bakr the secretary, the noted wit of Bukhārā and poet of Transoxania in the early years of the Sāmānid dynasty.[62] His father was Ismā'īl b. Aḥmad's Vizier. During Naṣr b. Aḥmad's reign, Abū Aḥmad became puffed up and thought himself above the service of al-Jaihanī and al-Bal'amī; he composed satires against them, [51
emulating Ibn Bassām's satires against the Viziers. They reacted and turned on him,[63] so that everything went wrong for him and he was plunged into ruin. He was a great admirer of al-'Aṭawī's verse, and he used to consider it superior to all the other poetry of the recent Islamic poets (*ash'ār al-muḥdathīn*).[64] He knew it all by heart and he used to praise it at great length, until he acquired the nickname of al-'Aṭawānī 'devotee of al-'Aṭawī'. Abū Manṣūr al-'Abdūnī has said about him (metre *Ṭawīl*)[65]:

57 *Kāmakh* < Persian *kāma*, older form *kāmak* = sour and piquant hors d'œuvres used to stimulate the appetite (Fleischer, 'Studien über Dozy's *Supplément* . . . ', in *Kleinere Schriften* [Leipzig 1885-8], II, 773); cf. some verses by Ibn al-Mu'tazz describing the various types of *kawāmikh* in Mas'ūdī, *Murūj*, VIII, 392-4.

58 On the *binnī/bunnī* fish, a kind of carp found in all the great rivers of the Fertile Crescent, see M. Streck, 'Bemerkungen zu einigen arabischen Fischnamen', ZDMG, LXI (1907), 635-8; from the fish's name, *binnī/binn* comes also to mean the brine in which the fish is pickled (cf. Dozy, s.v.). Abyārī and Ṣairafī, however, interpret *binn* in their notes as 'a morsel of fat'.

59 This line became quoted proverbially; cf. Tha'ālibī, *Thimār al-qulūb*, 183, s.v. ''Itāb Jaḥẓa'.

60 Jaḥẓa and Ibn ar-Rūmī were close friends at the Caliphal court; cf. R. Guest, *Life and works of Ibn er Rûmî*, 18.

61 Elephant (*fīl*) = the modern Bishop. Cf. H. J. R. Murray, *A history of chess* (Oxford 1913), 159, 220ff.

62 On 'Aṭawānī, see his biography in *Yatīmat ad-dahr*, IV, 64-9, on which this present section is based; and cf. also, Barbier de Meynard, *op. cit.*, Vol. X, 86-8.

63 Following AS's emendation of *fa-anḥayā*.

64 Muḥammad b. 'Abd ar-Raḥmān al-'Aṭawī flourished in the middle years of the 3rd/9th century under the patronage of the Mu'tazilī chief Qāḍī, Aḥmad b. Abī Du'ād al-Iyādī, head of the *Miḥna* or Inquisition under al-Mu'taṣim and al-Wāthiq; cf. *Aghānī* (Beirut 1956-7), XX, 143-50.

65 For Abū Manṣūr Aḥmad b. 'Abdūn, poet and secretary in Bukhārā, see the biography in *Yatīmat ad-dahr*, IV, 76-8, cf. 65.

O Abū Aḥmad, through your unreasoning folly you have spoilt all the benefits which were heaped on you by official patronage and by your parents.

You have become exposed to derision from all sides, and everyone now calls you 'al-'Aṭawānī'.

Your attitude in this dashing of your fortunes is an attitude which you must have picked up and been taught in imitation of the retrograde motion of the crab.

Abū Aḥmad was the author of the following line (metre *Basīṭ*): *From Āmul, I crossed the desert* (al-mafāza), *hoping* [52 *thereby for better fortune* (āmulu 'l-mafāza).

A section which includes various nicknames

[Ṭimās.] Aḥmad b. 'Abdallāh the secretary, nephew of Ibrāhīm b. al-'Abbās aṣ-Ṣūlī,[66] used to be called Ṭimās, because he was one-eyed.[67] Al-Buḥturī mentioned him in his line (metre *Ṭawīl*): *A moonless* [*night*], *with only the dying flicker of a setting moon,*[68] *like the eye of Ṭimās, drooping with sleep.* Al-Mutawakkil was once shown a list containing the names of secretaries whom he was to nominate to various official posts, and amongst them was the name of Ṭimās. He jabbed his finger at it and exclaimed, 'He weeps at the prospect of being cupped, and he calls the sun an enemy, the snake "the long one" and the Jinn "inhabitants of the house"!'

[Kharrā' Nakhl 'the one who defecates on a palm tree'.[69]] There was in Baghdad a shaikh of Hāshimite lineage who had this nickname, and Ibn ar-Rūmī said of him (metre *Mujtathth*):

Indeed, the person who called you Kharrā' Nakhl must [53 *have been a dotard out of his senses,*

Since excrement is good for palm trees, and the dates can be eaten,

But in my opinion, you yourself are nothing but a mixture of pus and the bitter cococynth.

[Liḥyat at-Tais 'goat's beard'.] A certain singer in Baghdad had this nickname.[70] His favourite measure was *Qifā nabki*, hence Ibn Bassām said of him (metre *Sarī'*): *I say, when his singing distresses me,*[71] *'Make it shorter, O Liḥyat at-Tais! / Give up* Qifā nabki *and its familiarity* ('irfānahā)! *May God not have mercy on Imru'ul-Qais!'*[72]

It is said that no-one has such a great array of nicknames to show as have the general populations of Baghdad and Nīshāpūr, for these people are famous, and always have been famous, for their facility in giving nicknames.

[66] Ibrāhīm b. al-'Abbās (d. 243/857) was the grandfather of the author Abū Bakr Muḥammad b. Yaḥyā aṣ-Ṣūlī, on whom see below, p. 71, n. 12. Ibrāhīm was celebrated as a secretary and as a poet; his verses were later collected together by Abū Bakr Muḥammad, cf. *Aghānī* (Beirut), IX, 38-65 = (Cairo, Dār al-Kutub 1346-/1927-) X, 43-67, and Yāqūt, *Irshād*, I, 260-77. According to *Aghānī*, IX, 50-1 = X, 54-5, Ibrāhīm used to find his nephew Ṭimās a great bore.

[67] Apparently the *laqab* is to be connected with *ṭamīs* 'obliterated, blind', *aṭmasa 'l-'ain* 'to blind'; cf. also, Barbier de Meynard, *op. cit.*, Vol. X, 75.

[68] Following AS's emendation of J's *ghābir* to *ghā'ir*.

[69] Cf. Barbier de Meynard, *op. cit.*, IX, 371-2.

[70] *Liḥyat at-tais* is also the name popularly given to the shrub *Cistosus villosus* L., one of the *Cistaceae* family from which the opiate laudanum was obtained; see the anonymous *Tuḥfat al-ahbāb*, ed. and tr. H. P. J. Renaud and G. S. Colin (Paris 1934), 108, No. 241, and P. Guigues, 'Les noms arabes dans Sérapion, «Liber de simplicii medicina»', JA, Ser. 10, Vol. V (Jan.-June 1905), 540, 544, Nos. 282, 299.

[71] Following AS's emendation of J's *iḥtawā* to *ajtawī*.

[72] Referring both to the *Mu'allaqa* of Imru'ul-Qais and to his ode with a similar beginning of *Qifā nabki min dhikrā ḥabībin wa 'irfāni wa-rasmin 'afat āyātuhu mundhu azmāni*, cf. W. Ahlwardt, *The divans of six ancient Arabian poets* (London 1870), Arabic text 160.

The nicknames of the people of Baghdad include: *Harīsat al-Hāshimī*[73] 'the Hāshimite's *harīsa*'; *Bādhinjānat al-Kātib* 'the secretary's aubergine'; *Manārat al-Khādim* 'the eunuch's column'; *Rijl at-Ṭā'ūs* 'the peacock's leg'; *Raiḥān al-Kanīf* 'sweet-smelling herbs of the privy'; [54 *al-Qufl al-'Aṣir* 'the stiff lock', applied to [the Caliph] al-Mu'tamid 'alā 'llāh; and *Lail ash-Shitā'*, 'winter's night', applied to a tall and gloomy individual.

Those of the people of Nīshāpūr include: *Kulyat al-Jamal* 'camel's kidney'; *Sarāwīl al-Ba'īr* 'camel's drawers'; *Ṣūf al-Kalb* 'dog's wool'[74]; *Niqāb al-'Anz* 'goat's belly'; *Mahd al-Baqara* 'cow's cradle'; *Lijām ash-Shaiṭān* 'Satan's bridle'; *Kusb al-Fujl* 'waste pulp left when radishes are squeezed'; *Busr al-Ijjāṣ* 'unripe plums'; and *Duhn ar-Rībās* 'oil of rhubarb'.

[73] *Harīsa* = cooked wheat and minced meat kneaded together into a pâté. A detailed account of how it should be prepared and served is given in some verses in Mas'ūdī, *Murūj*, VIII, 402-3, where it is said to have been a favourite dish of the Sāsānid emperors.

[74] Cf. Tha'ālibī, *Thimār al-qulūb*, 316-17, s.v., where this is said to be proverbial for something difficult to obtain.

Chapter Four.

Concerning the secretaries of former ages.[1]

Idrīs (? Enoch), peace be upon him, was the first to write with a pen. Yūsuf (sc. Joseph), peace be upon him, used to act as secretary for the Mighty One of Egypt. Hārūn (sc. Aaron) and Yūsha‘ b. Nūn (sc. Joshua son of Nun, *sic*) used to act as secretaries for Moses, peace be upon him. Sulaimān (sc. Solomon), peace be upon him, used to act as secretary for his father David, peace be upon him. God Most High has mentioned his rôle as a secretary, and has given a clear exposition of his eloquence and powers of concision in His words 'It (sc. Bilqīs's letter) is from Solomon, and it runs, "In the name of God, the Merciful, the Compassionate. Do not act proudly against me, but come to me submissively." '[2] Āṣaf b. Barakhyā[3] used to act as secretary for Solomon.

The secretaries at the time of the coming of Islam. When Islam first arose, the men who could write in Arabic numbered ten-odd: 'Umar, 'Uthmān, 'Alī, Ṭalḥa, Khālid[4] and Abāna, [56 the two sons of Sa'īd [b. al-'Āṣ b. Umayya], Abū Ḥudhaifa b. 'Utba b. Rabī'a, Abū Sufyān b. Ḥarb and his two sons Yazīd and Mu'āwiya, Ḥāṭib b. 'Amr b. 'Abd Shams, al-'Alā' b. al-Ḥaḍramī, Abū Salama b. 'Abd al-Asad,[5] 'Abdallāh b. [Sa'd b.] Abī Ṣarḥ and Ḥuwaiṭib b. 'Abd al-'Uzzā.

The secretaries of the Messenger of God, God's prayers and peace be upon him.[6] 'Uthman and 'Alī, may God be pleased with them, used to write down the revelations directly in the presence of the Messenger of God, God's prayers and peace be upon him, and when they were absent, Ubayy b. Ka'b and Zaid b. Thābit, may God be pleased with them, acted in their place. When none of these was present, the rest of the secretaries undertook the task. Khālid b. Sa'īd b. al-'Āṣ and Mu'āwiya b. Abī Sufyān used to record, in Muḥammad's presence, his day-to-day needs [57

[1] Much of Tha'ālibī's material in this chapter may also be found in Jahshiyārī's *Kitāb al-wuzarā' wa'l-kuttāb*, in the long section on secretaryship and official correspondence in Ibn 'Abd Rabbihi's *al-'Iqd al-farīd* (Cairo 1367-8/1948-9), IV, 155ff. and in books on the *awā'il* such as that of Abū Hilāl al-'Askarī (see above, Introduction, p. 19).

[2] Qur'ān, xxvii, 30-1.

[3] The alleged Vizier and confidant of Solomon; cf. Wensinck, EI² s.v.

[4] This name emended by AS from the ' 'Uthmān' of J.

[5] This name emended by AS from the ' 'Abd al-Ashhal' of J.

[6] This section occurs in Jahshiyārī, *op. cit.*, 9ff.; cf. also the list in Mas'ūdī, *Tanbīh*, 283-4, tr. 371-2.

and affairs, and when they were away, al-Mughīra b. Shu'ba acted in their stead.

'Abdallāh b. al-Arqam and al-'Alā' b. 'Uqba used to act as scribes for the general body of believers, writing for them in their tribal territories and at their watering places; they also acted as scribes in the houses of the men and women of the Anṣār. Not infrequently, Ibn al-Arqam would write out the letters which the Prophet, God's prayers and peace be upon him, addressed to neighbouring rulers. Ḥudhaifa b. al-Yamān used to write down the estimated yield of the Ḥijāz date harvest. Zaid b. Thābit, may God be pleased with him, in addition to his rôle as one of those who wrote down the Prophet's revelations, used also to write to the neighbouring rulers.[7] Mu'aiqīb b. Abī Fāṭima a confederate of the Banū Asad, was specially appointed by the Messenger of God to record the Prophet's shares in the plunder. [58

Ḥanẓala b. ar-Rabī' b. [al-Muraqqa' b.] Ṣaifī, the nephew of Aktham [b. Ṣaifī al-Usayyidī], was the official deputy for the whole body of the secretaries of the Prophet, God's prayers and peace be upon him, standing in whenever one of them was away; hence he too gradually acquired the designation of secretary. The Prophet used to deposit his ring with him. 'Abdallāh b. [Sa'd b.] Abī Sarḥ used to act as one of the Prophet's secretaries, but then he apostatised and joined the polytheists, proclaiming that Muḥammad simply had written down [as alleged revelations] whatever had come into his head.[8] On the day that Mecca was conquered, 'Uthmān, who had a foster-relationship with 'Abdallāh, brought him forward and asked the Prophet to free him as a favour to 'Uthmān; the Prophet agreed to this.

The secretaries who became Caliphs. 'Alī b. Abī Ṭālib, may God be pleased with him, used to act as one of secretaries of the Prophet, God's prayers and peace be upon him, and later became Caliph; 'Uthmān, may God be pleased with him, used to act as secretary to the Prophet and to Abū Bakr, may God be pleased with him,[9] and later became Caliph; Mu'āwiya used to act [59 as one of the Prophet's secretaries, and later became Caliph; Marwān b. al-Ḥakam was 'Uthmān's secretary and then later became Caliph; 'Abd al-Malik b. Marwān was secretary in charge of the Dīwān at Medina, and later became Caliph.

Other outstanding figures amongst the secretaries. 'Abdallāh b. Aus al-Ghassānī, leader of the Arabs in Syria, used to act as Mu'āwiya's secretary. Sa'īd b. Nimrān al-Hamdānī, the tribal chief of [the Banū] Hamdān, used to act as secretary to 'Alī, may

7 According to the '*Iqd*, IV, 161, Zaid learnt Persian from the envoy of the Sāsānid emperor, and Greek, Ethiopic and Coptic from various servants in the Prophet's household. Zaid is further said to have known Hebrew; cf. Wensinck, EI¹ s.v.

8 Some commentators identify Ibn Abī Sarḥ as the person concerning whom the revelation came down, 'Who does greater wrong than the one who invents falsehood about God, or who says, "A divine revelation has been sent down to me", when no revelation has been sent down at all' (Qur'ān, vi, 93). The Caliph 'Uthmān later appointed in 26/647 his foster-brother to replace 'Amr b. al-'Āṣ as governor of Egypt, and thus attracted to himself considerable obloquy (cf. Muir, *The Caliphate*, 203-4).

9 AS inserts the phrase '. . . and to Abū Bakr, may God be pleased with him', omitted from J.

God be pleased with him, as did 'Abdallāh b. Ja'far and 'Ubaidallāh
b. Abī Rāfi'. 'Abdallāh b. Khalaf al-Khuzā'ī, the father of the
famous Ṭalḥa (*Ṭalḥa aṭ-Ṭalaḥāt*), was the secretary in charge of
the Dīwān of Basra during the reigns of 'Umar and 'Uthmān,
may God be pleased with them. Ziyād [b. Abīhi] was suc- [60
cessively secretary for al-Mughīra, Abū Mūsā [al-Ash'arī],
'Abdallāh b. 'Āmir b. Kuraiz and Ibn 'Abbās, and then finally
became governor of the two Iraqs. Khārija b. Zaid b. Thābit, may
God be pleased with him, was in charge of the Dīwān at Medina
before 'Abd al-Malik had the job; then, after 'Abd al-Malik, there
came 'Amr b. Sa'īd [b. al-'Āṣ] and 'Uthmān b. 'Anbasa b. Abī
Sufyān. All these tenures of office fell within a single reign, that
of Mu'āwiya, may God be pleased with him.

'Āmir ash-Sha'bī was 'Abdallāh b. al-Muṭī''s secretary, and
then he acted likewise for 'Abdallāh b. Yazīd, the governor appointed by Ibn az-Zubair over Kufa. Sa'īd b. Jubair, may God
have mercy on him, was in turn secretary to 'Abdallāh b. 'Utba
b. Mas'ūd, and then to Abū Burda b. Abī Mūsā [al- [61
Ash'arī], the Qāḍī appointed by al-Ḥajjāj to succeed Shuraiḥ.
Al-Ḥasan b. Abī'l-Ḥasan al-Baṣrī was ar-Rabī' b. Ziyād's secretary
in Khurāsān. Muḥammad b. Sīrīn was secretary to Anas b.
Mālik, may God be pleased with him, in Fārs. Maimūn b. Mihrān
was 'Umar b. 'Abd al-'Azīz's secretary. Rauḥ b. Zinbā' used to
act as 'Abd al-Malik b. Marwān's secretary; 'Abd al-Malik once
said concerning him, 'Abū Zur'a is a veritable Syrian for obedience,
an 'Irāqī for his calligraphic skill, an Ḥijāzī for his knowledge of
law and a Persian in his knowledge of secretaryship.'[10]

Yazīd b. Abī Muslim used to be al-Ḥajjāj's secretary, since he
was the latter's foster-brother.[11] Al-Ḥajjāj used to allot him as
salary 300 dirhams per month. Of this, he gave his wife 50 dirhams; 45 went on buying meat; and the rest was used for buying
flour and for other expenses. If there was anything left [62
over, he would purchase with it water and give it to the poor, or
else he might get some fresh fruit and divide it out amongst them.
Despite this, al-Ḥajjāj regarded him as a tiresome person. It is
related that al-Ḥajjāj once visited him on some occasion when he
was ill. He found Yazīd sitting round a fire-clay stove and an
earthenware lamp. He exclaimed, 'O Abu'l-'Alā'! I see that your
allowance must be inadequate!' The latter replied, 'O Amīr! if
300 dirhams aren't enough for me, then 30,000 wouldn't suffice!'

These people are those who acted as secretaries during the
early years of Islam; various authors have written books dealing

[10] Rauḥ b. Zinbā' was chief of the tribe of Judhām in Syria during the time of Mu'āwiya, Yazīd and 'Abd al-Malik, and one of the leaders of the South Arab or Kalb group, dying in 84/703; cf. Lammens, *Études sur le règne du Calife Omaiyade Mo'âwia Ier*, 214, n. 7 on his *dahā'*, shrewdness, and also below, p. 119.

[11] Cf. Jahshiyārī, *op. cit.*, 26, with this anecdote about Yazīd b. Abī Muslim, and on Yazīd's fate after al-Ḥajjāj's death, see Mas'ūdī, *Murūj*, v, 404–6.

with the secretaries of more recent times, including the *Akhbar al-wuzarā'* 'Accounts of the Viziers' of al-Jahshiyārī, aṣ-Ṣūlī's *Kitāb al-wuzarā'* 'Book of Viziers',[12] and the *Yatīmat ad-dahr* 'The unique pearl of the age' of the present author.

[12] Sc. of Abū Bakr Muḥammad b. Yaḥyā aṣ-Ṣūlī (d. 335/946-7 or 336/947-8), chess-player, historian, littérateur and boon-companion of the Caliphs; cf. I. Kratschkovsky, EI[1] s.v.

Chapter Five.

Concerning those with the longest family traditions of possessing certain qualities or of exercising certain functions, and concerning those who could trace back the longest unbroken lines of descent in regard to various functions or qualities.

The prophet with the longest unbroken prophetic pedigree. This was Joseph the Veracious One, son of Jacob or Israel, son of Isaac, the One intended for sacrifice, the son of Abraham the Friend of God, God's prayers be upon them all. Apart from this, no other case is known of a prophet who was the son of a prophet who was the son of a prophet who was the son of a prophet.

The Persian emperor with the longest unbroken kingly pedigree. This was Shīrūya b. Aparwīz b. Hurmuz b. Anūshirwān b. Qubādh b. Fīrūz b. Yazdajird b. Bahrām Gūr b. Yazdajird b. Bahrām b. Shāpūr b. Hurmuz b. Narsī b. Bahrām b. Bahrām b. Shāpūr b. Ardashīr b. Bābak.[1]

The Caliph with the longest unbroken line of direct ancestors who held that office. This was al-Muntaṣir b. al-Mutawakkil b. al-Muʻtaṣim b. ar-Rashīd b. al-Mahdī b. al-Manṣūr; his [64
brother al-Muʻtazz also had the same lineage.

It is a curious fact that the Persian emperor with the longest unbroken kingly pedigree, Shīrūya, killed his own father Aparwīz and seized his kingdom, yet only survived himself for a further six months; and likewise, the Caliph with the longest unbroken Caliphal pedigree, al-Muntaṣir, killed his father al-Mutawakkil and proclaimed himself Caliph, yet only lived for six months after that.[2]

The King of the Arabs with the longest unbroken chain of ancestors exercising kingship. This was the Lakhmid an-Nuʻmān

[1] The complete series of Sāsānid emperors is enumerated in Muḥammad b. Ḥabīb's *Muḥabbar*, 361-3, and in Ibn Qutaiba's *Maʻārif*, 652-67, the latter in great detail; Thaʻālibī's curt list presents discrepancies from both, but is nearer to the latter than to the former.

[2] Thaʻālibī also notes this curious fact in his *Ghurar as-siyar*, 730, and in his *Bard al-akbād*, in *Khams rasā'il*, 111 (omitted from Rescher's translation).

b. al-Mundhir b. al-Mundhir[3] b. Imru'ul-Qais b. an-Nu'mān b. Imru'ul-Qais b. 'Amr b. 'Adī.[4]

The man with the longest unbroken chain of ancestors on both sides of his parentage who were kings or Caliphs. This was Yazīd b. al-Walīd b. 'Abd al-Malik b. Marwān. He was a Caliph, and his father, grandfather, great-grandfather and paternal uncles were all Caliphs. His mother was Shāh-Āfrīd bint Fīrūz b. Yazdajird b. Shahriyār, and her mother was one of the daughters of Shīrūya b. Aparwīz. Shīrūya's mother was Maryam, daughter of the Byzantine emperor, and Fīrūz's mother was the daughter of the Khāqān, ruler of the Turks. It was Yazīd who boasted (metre [65
Rajaz): *I am the descendant of the Persian emperor, my forefather was Marwān, and both the Emperor of Byzantium and the Khāqān of the Turks were my ancestors.*[5]

The Viziers with the longest unbroken chain of ancestors holding that same office. These were Abū 'Alī al-Ḥusain b. al-Qāsim b. 'Ubaidallāh b. Sulaimān b. Wahb, and his brother Abū Ja'far Muḥammad b. al-Qāsim.[6] Abū 'Alī al-Ḥusain was al-Muqtadir's Vizier; Abū Ja'far Muḥammad was al-Qāhir's Vizier; their father al-Qāsim was Vizier to al-Mu'taḍid and then to al-Muktafī; 'Ubaidallāh was al-Mu'taḍid's Vizier; and Sulaimān was Vizier to al-Muhtadī and then to al-Mu'tamid. Thus both al- [66
Ḥusain and Muḥammad were Viziers sons of a Vizier son of a Vizier [son of a Vizier]. A poet said of one of the two of them (metre *Ramal*): *O Vizier, son of a Vizier, son of a Vizier, son of a Vizier, / In an unbroken descent, like pearls strung in a necklace for going round a woman's throat.*

The man with the longest chain of ancestors, all of whom could claim to be Companions of the Messenger of God, God's prayers and peace be upon him.[7] This was Muḥammad b. 'Abd ar-Raḥmān b. Abī Bakr b. Quḥāfa, for all four of these actually saw the Prophet, and were therefore accounted amongst his Companions.

The man of noble family with the longest chain of ancestors, all of whom were afflicted by blindness.[8] This was 'Abdallāh b. al-'Abbās b. 'Abd al-Muṭṭalib, for all three of them became blind towards the end of their life.

The man with the longest chain of ancestors, all of whom met violent deaths.[9] This was 'Umāra b. Ḥamza b. Muṣ'ab b. az-Zubair b. 'Awwām b. Khuwailid; only here in the house of az-Zubair, amongst all the Arabs and Persians, is known an unbroken series of six men who died violently. 'Umāra and [67

[3] This second 'b. al-Mundhir' is in J but omitted from A S.

[4] Again, *Muḥabbar*, 358-60, and *Ma'ārif*, 645-50, enumerate the series of the kings of al-Ḥīra, and again, Tha'ālibī's list is closer to Ibn Qutaiba's.

[5] Cf. *Muḥabbar*, 31. Yazīd III was, in fact, the first Umayyad Caliph whose mother was not a free-born Arab woman; only a generation or less before, the fact of having a slave mother had prevented the supremely-capable Maslama b. 'Abd al-Malik from sharing in the succession. Ṭabarī, II, 1874, calls Yazīd's mother an *umm walad* = concubine, and Mas'ūdī, *Murūj*, VI, 31, explicitly says that he was the first son of a concubine to become Caliph. This connection of hers with the Sāsānids was therefore probably an invention to ameliorate this taint of slave blood; cf. M. Sprengling, 'From Persian to Arabic', AJSL, LVI (1939), 214-20.

[6] Sc. the Banū Wahb, a family originally of Nestorian Christian origin from the region of Wāsiṭ. They had been secretaries under the Umayyads; Wahb had been secretary to Ja'far b. Yaḥyā al-Barmakī and then to al-Faḍl b. Sahl. Abū 'Alī al-Ḥusain, called *'Amīd ad-Daula*, was Vizier to al-Muqtadir 319-20/931-2; cf. Sourdel, *Le vizirat 'Abbāside*, I, 312-13.

[7] Cf. Ibn Qutaiba, *Ma'ārif*, 591, and Ibn Rusta, *al-A'lāq an-nafīsa*, ed. de Goeje (Leiden 1892), 228, tr. G. Wiet (Cairo 1955), 274.

[8] Cf. *Ma'ārif*, 589; Ibn Rusta, 227, tr. 273.

[9] Cf. *Ma'ārif*, 221-4 (from al-Wāqidī), 589; Ibn Rusta, 227, tr. 272-3.

Ḥamza were both killed at the battle of Qudaid in warfare against the Ibāḍiyya [sect of the Khawārij][10]; Muṣ'ab was killed at Dair al-Jāthalīq in the war between him and 'Abd al-Malik b. Marwān[11]; az-Zubair was killed at the Wādī 's-Sibā' during the battle of the Camel; al-'Awwām was killed during the war of al-Fijār; and Khuwailid was killed in warfare with the tribe of Khuzā'a.

The Qāḍī with the longest unbroken chain of ancestors who held that office.[12] This was Bilāl b. Abī Burda b. Abī Mūsā al-Ash'arī. He himself was qāḍī of Basra; his father Abū Burda was qāḍī of Kufa; and his grandfather Abū Mūsā acted as qāḍī for 'Umar b. al-Khaṭṭāb before he was made a governor and became active in the work of conquest.[13] There was also Sawwār [68 b. 'Abdallāh b. Sawwār, who was qāḍī of Basra and Kufa for al-Mahdī, and his [grand] father Sawwār b. Qudāma was a qāḍī under al-Manṣūr.[14]

The man with the longest unbroken chain of ancestors who were outstanding in religious law (*fiqh*). This was Ismā'īl b. Ḥammād b. Abī Ḥanīfa. He was a faqīh, and his father Ḥammād was a faqīh, though not of the same rank as his own father Abū Ḥanīfa, who was unsurpassed in his skill at devising legal fictions and expedients (*ḥiyal*) and has not been equalled in it to this day.

The Chamberlain (*Ḥājib*) to the Caliphs with the longest unbroken chain of ancestors who held that office. This was al-'Abbās b. al-Faḍl b. ar-Rabī'. Al-'Abbās was chamberlain to al-Amīn; al-Faḍl was first chamberlain and then Vizier to ar-Rashīd; and ar-Rabī' was chamberlain to al-Manṣūr and al-Mahdī.[15] Abū Nuwās said of them (metre *Kāmil*):

Three of them in succession have outshone their monarchs in glory; all of them, if they are to be summed up, are mighty, overpowering characters.

Ar-Rabī' was an outstanding leader, and likewise al-Faḍl, who came after him, and with al-'Abbās, the noble one, branches from this same growth have sprung forth.

Al-'Abbās is a grim-faced lion (('abbās) *when the battle* [69 *waxes fierce, al-Faḍl is munificence itself* (faḍl) *and ar-Rabī' is the life-giving spring* (rabī').

The man with the longest unbroken line of ancestors famous for their liberality.[16] This was 'Amr b. 'Abdallāh b. Ṣafwān b. Umayya b. Khalaf; all of these were successively noted for their liberality.

The man with the longest unbroken line of ancestors notorious for their treacherousness.[17] This was 'Abd ar-Raḥmān b. Muḥam-

[10] Sc. the battle which took place at Qudaid near Mecca in 130/747 between the people of Medina and the Khārijī leader Abū Ḥamza; cf. Ṭabarī, II, 2006-7, and Bakri, *Mu'jam mā 'sta'jam* (Cairo 1364-71/1945-51), III, 1054-5.

[11] I.e. in 72/691; the 'Monastery of the Catholicos' lay near Ḥarbā, to the south of Sāmarrā; cf. Wellhausen, *The Arab Kingdom*, 192ff., and Sachau, 'Vom Klosterbuch des Šâbuštî', APAW (1919), No. 10, pp. 9, 23.

[12] *Ma'ārif*, 266; Ibn Rusta, 227, tr. 272.

[13] Cf. EI[2] Arts. 'Abū Burda al-Ash'arī' (J. Schacht) and 'Abū Mūsā al-Ash'arī' (L. Veccia Vaglieri).

[14] As de Jong points out, the text here is disturbed and apparently defective.

[15] On al-Faḍl and his family, see Zetterstéen, EI[1] s.v.

[16] Cf. *Muḥabbar*, 140-1, in greater detail than here.

[17] This section, together with additional detail, in *ibid.*, 244-6, and substantially the same in Ibn Rusta, 229, tr. 275-6.

mad b. al-Ash'ath b. Qais b. Ma'dīkarib. 'Abd ar-Raḥmān himself acted treacherously towards al-Ḥajjāj b. Yūsuf when the latter appointed him as a provincial governor and he rebelled against al-Ḥajjāj, clashing with him in some eighty engagements, the last of which brought about his end.[18] Muḥammad b. al-Ash'ath acted treacherously towards the people of Ṭabaristān. 'Ubaidallāh b. Ziyād had appointed him governor there, and he made a treaty of peace with them. But then he turned on them, so the people held the mountain passes against him and killed his son Abū Bakr, treating him ignominiously.[19] Al-Ash'ath acted treacher- [70
ously towards the Banū'l-Ḥārith b. Ka'b. He led a raid against them, but they took him captive. He ransomed himself for two hundred camels and gave them an immediate payment of one hundred; the other hundred camels remained owing to them, but he never handed them over. Then Islam came along and all obligations contracted during the Jāhiliyya were annulled.[20] There was a peace treaty made between Qais b. Ma'dīkarib and the Banū Murād, to be valid for a fixed period, and on the last day of this term, which happened to be a Friday, Qais launched a raid on them. He was a Judaist by religion, and he alleged that it would be unlawful for him to make war on the following day since it was the Sabbath. So he attacked the Banū Murād, but they killed him and scattered his forces. As for Ma'dīkarib, he acted treacherously towards the people of Mahra, with whom he had a peace treaty; he broke the agreement and raided them, so they killed him and slit open his belly, filling the cavity with pebbles.

The poets with the longest poetic pedigrees. According to al-Mubarrad, it used to be stated that the family of Ḥassān [b. Thābit] were the most poetic of families, for six of their number, in an unbroken series, were all accounted poets, sc. Sa'īd b. 'Abd ar-Raḥmān b. Ḥassān b. Thābit b. al-Mundhir b. Ḥarām and his five ancestors enumerated there. But then the family of Abū Ḥafṣa came along, and the poetic gift passed by inheritance and was handed down from father to son for ten generations. They all recited verse before the Caliphs and received handsome rewards for it.

The first was Abū Ḥafṣa, one of 'Uthmān's freedmen and a poet.[21] It was he who said (metre *Ṭawīl*): *I did not say to the people on the day when 'Uthmān's palace was besieged* (yaum ad-dār), *'Make terms!'; indeed not, nor did I say, 'Choose life in preference to death!' / But I said to them 'Fight on with your* [71
swords drawn, until [authority] is restored to the old man.'

[18] See above, p. 59.

[19] Muḥammad was appointed when 'Ubaidallāh was governor of Khurāsān 53-6/673-6 (Balādhurī, *Futūḥ al-buldān*, 330-1; H. L. Rabino di Borgomale, 'Les préfets du Califat au Ṭabaristān de 18 à 328/639 à 939-40', JA, CCXXXI [1939], 241-2). Muḥammad was himself killed by 'Ubaidallāh during his son 'Abd ar-Raḥmān's rebellion in Iraq (*Muḥabbar*, 245-6).

[20] H. Reckendorff notes, EI² Art. 'al-Ash'ath', that the designation of al-Ash'ath and all his house as inveterate traitors stems from his rebellious attitude during the Ridda and also from his part in the negotiations during the battle of Ṣiffīn in 37/657; according to pro-Shī'ī tradition, he forced 'Alī to accept the principle of arbitration and to take Abū Mūsā al-Ash'arī as his negotiator.

[21] The family of Abū Ḥafṣa asserted that they came from a Persian captured at the fall of Iṣṭakhr in Fārs and then sold to 'Uthmān; opponents of the family seem to have alleged that they were of Jewish origin, converted through the agency of Marwān b. al-Ḥakam (*Aghānī* [Beirut], IX, 68 = [Dār al-Kutub], X, 71, cf. Goldziher, *Muhammedanische Studien*, I, 204-5; there is also an article on the family in Ibn Khallikān, tr. III, 343-8, s.v. 'Marwān b. Abī Ḥafṣa').

He was also the one who said at the battle of the Camel, where he had been fighting at Marwān b. al-Ḥakam's side (metre *Rajaz*): *I am the one who comes repeatedly to the watering-places of strife, returning for charge after charge.*

Then came Yaḥyā b. Abī Ḥafṣa, who said (metre *Basīṭ*): *O would that the joys of youth would return! But alas, that is something that cannot be brought back. / How many a cunning and resourceful man, whose striking power the other cunning men fear, and who protects his own savage territories, have I left chopped to pieces!*[22]

Then came Sulaimān b. Yaḥyā b. Abī Ḥafṣa, who said (metre *Ṭawīl*): *How many a woman has said to me in reproach, 'How is it that you are poor and indigent, when everyone else's riches are multiplying?' / I replied to her, 'I bestow lavishly all that my hands possess, whereas some of the other folk are not open-handed.'* [72

Then came Marwān b. Sulaimān b. Yaḥyā b. Abī Ḥafṣa, who said (metre *Kāmil*): *How can the inheritance of the paternal uncles* (sc. of al-'Abbās, the Prophet's uncle) *pass to the daughters' children* (sc. the children of 'Alī and his wife Fāṭima, the Prophet's daughter)? *Such a thing is impossible!*[23] / *God has diverted away from them shares [in the inheritance], but then they have tried to get hold of it without being entitled to shares.*[24]

Then came Abū'l-Janūb b. Marwān b. Sulaimān b. Yaḥyā b. Abī Ḥafṣa. It was he who spoke these lines about Mūsā al-Hādī and ar-Rashīd. Mūsā endeavoured to seize him, until he had to flee from Iraq into the desert (metre *Wāfir*):

At the moment, Mūsā is Commander of the Faithful, but you will be Commander of the Faithful tomorrow;

We will make the choice[25] *of Caliph after Mūsā, even though those who envy us will be abased in the process* (literally, *'the noses of those who envy us will be rubbed in the dust'*).

I see that it was your father who has handed on the Caliphate to his sons (sc. al-Mahdī settled the succession on his two sons al-Hādī and then ar-Rashīd), *and in the same way, you will bequeath it to your sons.*

Then came Marwān b. Abī'l-Janūb b. Marwān b. Sulaimān b. Yaḥyā b. Abī Ḥafṣa, who said to al-Ma'mūn (metre *Ṭawīl*): *If any peak of glory higher than the Caliphate were known, and it could be reached in this life through nobility of character, he would attain it.*

And to al-Mu'taṣim (metre *Basīṭ*): *When first I entered the presence of the Caliph of God, the spotless one* (ma'ṣūm) *of his community, he drew me nearer and heaped riches on me, / With* [73
gifts like those which his father, who was like a father to me, once

[22] Following the emendations of AS to this line.

[23] The argument is that the Abbasids, as descendants of the Prophet's paternal uncle, are in the position of agnates (*'aṣabāt*) in the Islamic law of inheritance, given the greater share in the inheritance because they were originally the male members who defended and fought for the family or tribe; whereas the Alids, descended only from the Prophet's daughter, are in the less favoured position of cognates (*dhawū'l-arḥām*).

[24] The strongly anti-Alid feeling of the Abū Ḥafṣa family is clearly illustrated in these well-known lines, and above all in the verses given below of Abū's-Simṭ Marwān b. Yaḥyā. Hence in *Aghānī* (Beirut), IX, 91 = (Dār al-Kutub), X, 94, citing these two verses of Marwān b. Sulaimān, a pro-Shī'ī writer uses after the poet's name the formula *la'anahu Allāh* 'May God curse him!'

[25] Following AS's emendation of *sa-nakhtāru*. The reference in these lines is to al-Hādī's attempt to set aside ar-Rashīd's; claim to the succession after him and to substitute his own young son Ja'far as *walī al-'ahd*; cf. Mas'ūdī, *Murūj*, VI, 280-2, on al-Hādī's intentions here.

lavished, and which his grandfather, the Chosen One, al-Mahdī, once gave me.

Then came Yaḥyā b. Marwān b. Abī'l-Janūb b. Marwān b. Sulaimān b. Yaḥyā b. Abī Ḥafṣa, who wrote the following line, which al-Jāḥiẓ recited (metre *Basīṭ*): *Say to those ones, 'They have their eyes fixed on me continuously; do not set me up as a target in defence of your honours.'*

Then came Abū's-Simṭ Marwān b. Yaḥyā b. Marwān b. Abī'l-Janūb b. Marwān b. Sulaimān, al-Mutawakkil's poet. He was one of the most favoured of men and one of the most highly-rewarded of poets. He began one of his odes as follows (metre *Ṭawīl*): *Greetings upon Juml, hurrah for Juml, bravo for Juml, even though [saying this] may mean estrangement for me* (literally, *'the breaking of my connection'*).

And further on in the poem, he continued,

Your forefather 'Alī was more excellent than you; [nevertheless,] the electors of the Shūrā rejected him, although they were just and fair men.

He offended the Messenger of God when he offended his daughter (sc. Fāṭima), *in that he sought the hand in marriage of the accursed one Abū Jahl's daughter.*[26]

Accordingly, the Messenger of God denounced the marriage plans of your forefather, speaking against them from the pulpit decisively and trenchantly.[27]

At the side of his marriage with the Prophet's daughter, he wanted to become linked with the daughter of God's enemy! O what an appalling deed!

Your forefather appointed two men as arbiters in the affair, who repudiated him just as a man casts off his sandal.[28]

His son al-Ḥasan later sold the Caliphate (sc. to Mu'āwiya) *so the two of them* (sc. 'Alī and al-Ḥasan) *have invalidated your threadbare claim.*

You abandoned it (sc. the Caliphate) *when it belonged to those who did not deserve it* (sc. the Umayyads), *and then you claimed it after it had gone back to its rightful source* (sc. to the children of al-'Abbās). [74

Then came Maḥmūd b. Marwān, who said to al-Muntaṣir (metre *Ṭawīl*): *It is long since I saw the Imām Muḥammad* (sc. al-Muntaṣir), *and I had not feared that I would be so long away from him; / But I became estranged [from him], even though my residence is close by him; how strange that my house should be so near, yet I should be so remote from his favour!*

[26] It seems that 'Alī, although the son-in-law of the Prophet, was also eager for an alliance with the Meccan clan of Makhzūm, still rich and powerful despite their losses at Badr. Some other sources make the intended bride a daughter of Muḥammad's uncle and enemy Abū Lahab – possibly this is a confusion of the similar nicknames of the two most celebrated of the Prophet's opponents in Mecca. In the event, 'Alī took no other wife during Fāṭima's lifetime, but the proposed alliance was difficult for the Shī'a to explain later, when they had to stress 'Alī's closeness and obedience to Muḥammad. As a result of the affair, later authorities deduced that monogamy was one of the *khaṣā'is*, special virtues of Fāṭima. Cf. Lammens, *Fāṭima et les filles de Mahomet* (Rome 1912), 50-2.

[27] A S unaccountably misses out this line of the poem, supplied here from J.

[28] Referring to the refusal of allegiance to 'Alī on the part of az-Zubair and Ṭalḥa before the battle of the Camel. The strongly anti-Alid atmosphere of the whole poem reflects the atmosphere of orthodoxy and Sunnī reaction during the reign of Abū's-Simṭ Marwān's patron al-Mutawakkil, when the Mu'tazilī and pro-Shī'ī trends of the previous three reigns were reversed.

Then came Mutawwaj b. Maḥmūd b. Marwān. Aṣ-Ṣūlī relates that he was with Ibn al-Mu'tazz one day, and some of Mutawwaj's poetry was recited in his public audience.[29] It was wretched stuff, and was not worth the paper it was written on. Ibn al-Mu'tazz remarked, 'Shall I give you an appropriate comparison for the poetry of the Abū Ḥafṣa family and its increasing badness with each generation of the line?' We replied, 'If it please the Amīr.' So he began, 'It is like water heated up in a cooking-pot for a sick person but then found to be no longer required. In Marwān's time it was at its original hotness; then it came down to Abū 'l-Janūb with some of its heat lost. When it came down to the second Marwān it had become tepid; with Yaḥyā, its tepidity increased; with Abū's-Simṭ it was really cold; and with Maḥmūd it began to freeze. Finally, by the time it reached this man Mutawwaj, it had frozen up completely. Now it can't possibly get any worse!'

[29] This story occurs in fact in Ṣūlī's *Ash'ār aulād al-khulafā' wa-akhbāruhum*, ed. J. Heyworth-Dunne (London 1936), 116-17.

Chapter Six.

Concerning outstanding levels of achievement or character reached by various classes of people.

The most handsome man-and-wife couple in Islam. Firstly, there was ‘Uthmān b. ‘Affān, may God be pleased with him, and Ruqayya, daughter of the Prophet, God’s prayers and peace be upon him. It is related that the Prophet once sent a man with a present of some morsels of food[1] to ‘Uthmān, and the man was held up. When he got back, the Prophet said to him, ‘If you like, I will tell you what has delayed you.’ The man replied, ‘Yes, do, O Messenger of God.’ The latter explained, ‘You were looking at ‘Uthmān and Ruqayya and marvelling at what a fine couple they are, weren’t you?’ The man had to agree that this was so.

Then there was also al-Walīd b. ‘Utba b. Abī Sufyān[2] and Lubāba bint ‘Abdallāh b. al-‘Abbās, may God be pleased with him. She used to comment, ‘I have never looked at my face in the mirror at the side of someone else’s without feeling pity for them, except when al-Walīd has been there. When I see my own face at the side of his, its handsomeness makes me feel pity on my own face.’

Finally, there was Muṣ‘ab b. az-Zubair and ‘Ā’isha bint Ṭalḥa. People used to say that if anyone wishes to see the sun and the moon together, let him look at this pair. [76

The men with the most noble lineage. These were al-Ḥasan and al-Ḥusain, for ‘Alī was their father, Fāṭima their mother, the Messenger of God their grandfather, the Messenger of God’s son al-Qāsim[3] their maternal uncle, Ja‘far aṭ-Ṭayyār their paternal uncle and Khadīja, the first lady amongst all the women of the worlds, was their grandmother.

The woman with the most noble lineage. This was Fāṭima,

[1] *Laṭaf*, either from *laṭaf* pl. *alṭāf* ‘present’ or *laṭafa* pl. *laṭaf* ‘tasty morsel of food’ (Dozy); I have tried to combine both meanings in my translation.

[2] Nephew of Mu‘āwiya, governor of Medina 57-60/677-80 and 61-2/681-2; died of plague in 64/683-4, according to Mas‘ūdī, *Murūj*, v, 170, whilst reciting the prayers at Mu‘āwiya II b. Yazīd’s funeral.

[3] Sc. Muhammad’s son by Khadīja, from whom he derived his own *kunya* of ‘Abū’l-Qāsim’, and who died in infancy.

because her father was the lord of mankind, Muḥammad, God's prayers and peace be upon him; her mother was Khadīja, the mother of the faithful; her husband was the lord of all those entrusted with the prophetic charge (*sayyid al-auṣiyā'*), 'Alī, may God be pleased with him; and her two sons (sc. al-Ḥasan and al-Ḥusain) were the lords of all the noble youths in the garden of Paradise.

The person with the most penetrating vision into the future (*afras an-nās*). 'Abdallāh b. Mas'ūd, may God be pleased with him, said that there were three persons sharing this honour: the Mighty One [of Egypt] when he made a prediction in regard to Joseph, peace be upon him, and said to his wife, 'Give him an honourable dwelling; perhaps he may be of use to us or we may adopt him as a son'[4]; Ṣafūrā, the daughter of Shu'aib,[5] [77
peace be upon him, when she said, 'O my father, hire him (sc. Moses), indeed, the best one that you can hire is the strong and faithful one'[6]; and Abū Bakr the Veracious, may God be pleased with him, when he appointed 'Umar as his successor over the community of Muslims.

The woman with the most noble group of sons-in-law. Az-Zubair b. Bakkār related from Muḥammad b. Sallām from Muḥammad b. al-Faḍl al-Hāshimī[7] and Abān b. 'Uthmān, that this was Hind bint Ḥamāṭa, the old woman of the Banū Jurash, who had four daughters. The first, Maimūna bint al-Ḥārith al- [78
Hilāliyya, was the wife of the Messenger of God, God's prayers and peace be upon him; the second, Lubāba bint al-Ḥārith, called Umm al-Faḍl, was al-'Abbās b. 'Abd al-Muṭṭalib's wife; the third, Salmā bint 'Umais al-Khath'amiyya, was Ḥamza b. 'Abd al-Muṭṭalib's wife; and the fourth, Asmā' bint 'Umais, was successively the wife of Ja'far b. Abī Ṭālib, of Abū Bakr and of 'Alī, may God be pleased with him.[8]

A man who became father-in-law to four Caliphs.[9] This was 'Abdallāh b. 'Amr b. 'Uthmān b. 'Affān, may God be pleased with him: of his daughters, 'Abda married al-Walīd b. 'Abd al-Malik; 'Ā'isha married Sulaimān b. 'Abd al-Malik; Umm Sa'īd married Yazīd b. 'Abd al-Malik; and Ruqayya married Hishām b. 'Abd al-Malik. Previous to 'Abdallāh, there was no-one known who had four sons-in-law who were all brothers and Caliphs, and no-one has been known since. [79

The most noble of men in regard to the wives they took. [Firstly there was] Muṣ'ab b. az-Zubair, because he took as his wives Sukaina bint al-Ḥusain b. 'Alī b. Abī Ṭālib; 'Ā'isha bint

[4] Qur'ān, xii, 21.

[5] Sc. the Qur'ānic prophet, sent to the unbelieving people of Midian. According to F. Buhl, EI[1] s.v., it is only the later commentators who identify Shu'aib with Jethro, the father-in-law of Moses, who lived in Midian; there is no evidence in the Qur'ān for this identification.

[6] Qur'ān, xxviii, 26.

[7] Corrected by AS from the 'al-Jumaḥī' of J.

[8] Cf. W. Montgomery Watt, *Muhammad at Medina* (Oxford 1956), 380-1, 394-5, 397, on this group of women and the life of at least three of them in what seems to have been a matrilineally-organised group in Mecca under al-'Abbās.

[9] The same list in *Muḥabbar*, 243, and Ibn Rusta, 204, tr. 238.

Ṭalḥa b. ʻUbaidallāh; Amat al-Ḥamīd bint ʻAbdallāh b. ʻĀmir b. Kuraiz; and Qulāba[10] bint Rayyān, son of Unaif al-Kalbī, the lord of the Arabs. Muṣʻab used to say that he grew impassioned over nobility of lineage just as other men grew impassioned over beauty. The dowries of both Sukaina and ʻĀ'isha amounted to a million dirhams [each]; concerning this fact, a certain poet once recited to ʻAbdallāh b. az-Zubair (metre *Kāmil*): *Convey to the Commander of the Faithful a message from one who desires to give him good counsel and intends no treachery; / He has married a maiden with a bride-price amounting to a whole million, yet the leaders of the army remain starving.*[11] [80

[Secondly, there was] Khālid b. Yazīd b. Muʻāwiya, who married Umm Kulthūm bint ʻAbdallāh b. Jaʻfar b. Abī Ṭālib, Āmina bint Saʻīd b. al-ʻĀṣ and Ramla bint az-Zubair. Concerning these marriages, a certain poet[12] incited ʻAbd al-Malik against him with these words (metre *Ṭawīl*): *O Commander of the Faithful, beware of Khālid, for he is hostile to your interests; / When we look at the wives he has married, we realise what he intends and where he is heading for.*[13]

Three women in Islamic times, with no comparable fourth one. Each one of these three gave birth to two Caliphs; two of these women were amongst the Marwānids and one of them amongst the Abbasids. The two amongst the Marwānids were Wallāda bint al-ʻAbbās al-ʻAbsiyya, wife of ʻAbd al-Malik b. Marwān, to whom she bore al-Walīd and Sulaimān, both of whom became Caliphs; and then Shāh-Āfrīd bint Fīrūz b. Yazdajird b. Shahriyār, who bore al-Walīd b. ʻAbd al-Malik the sons Yazīd and Ibrāhīm, both of whom became Caliphs. The one from the Abbasids [81 was al-Khaizurān al-Jurashiyya, who bore al-Mahdī the sons Mūsā al-Hādī and Hārūn ar-Rashīd. With reference to her, Ibn Abī Ḥafṣa said (metre *Kāmil*): *O Khaizurān, may greeting on greeting be upon you! Your two sons will surely rule over the people.*

A woman with twelve male relatives, all of them Caliphs.[14] This was ʻĀtika bint Yazīd b. Muʻāwiya: her father was Yazīd; her grandfather was Muʻāwiya; her brother was Muʻāwiya b. Yazīd; her husband was ʻAbd al-Malik b. Marwān; her father-in-law was Marwān b. al-Ḥakam; her son was Yazīd b. ʻAbd al-Malik; her grandson was al-Walīd b. Yazīd; al-Walīd, Sulaimān and Hishām were her step-sons (sc. ʻAbd al-Malik's sons by other wives, the first two by Wallāda, see above); and Yazīd and Ibrāhīm, al-Walīd's two sons, were her step-grandsons.

The nearest approach to this amongst the Abbasids was Umm

[10] AS supplies this name from parallel sources in place of the 'Fulāna' of J.

[11] These lines are cited in *Aghānī* (Beirut), III, 238 = (Dār al-Kutub), III, 361, with the poet's name given as Anas b. Zunaim [ad-Du'alī] al-Laithī, and in Balādhurī, *Ansāb al-ashrāf*, V, 282-3, and Ibn Qutaiba, *Kitāb ash-shiʻr wa'sh-shuʻarā'*, 461-2, with the name Anas b. Abī Unās b. Zunaim ad-Du'alī al-Kinānī.

[12] Identified in *Aghānī* (Beirut), XVI, 176 = (Dār al-Kutub), XVI, 90-1, as Shadīd b. Shaddād b. ʻĀmir b. Laqīṭ b. Jābir.

[13] When Muʻāwiya II died childless, Khālid, as the dead man's brother, had an obvious claim to the succession. However, he was set aside in favour of Marwān b. al-Ḥakam, with the promise that he would succeed Marwān when he was himself an adult. In fact, Marwān ousted Khālid from the position of *walī al-ʻahd*, married Khālid's mother and generally treated him with contempt. Concerning Khālid's marriage here mentioned, according to the story in the *Aghānī*, Khālid sought Ramla's hand during ʻAbd al-Malik's reign and after the killing of ʻAbdallāh b. az-Zubair. Al-Ḥajjāj sent a message to him reproaching him for seeking an alliance with the Umayyads' enemies, and complaining that Khālid should have consulted him first; but Khālid brusquely rejected this. See the section on Khālid and Ramla in *Aghānī* (Beirut), XVI, 171-81.

[14] This section, the first paragraph almost verbatim, in *Muḥabbar*, 404-5.

Ja'far [Zubaida] bint Ja'far b. Abī Ja'far al-Manṣūr: her grandfather was al-Manṣūr; her paternal uncle was al-Mahdī; her husband was ar-Rashīd; her own son was al-Amīn; and al-Ma'mūn and al-Mu'taṣim were her step-sons (sc. by slave wives of ar-Rashīd). Abū'l-'Ainā'[15] used to say, *If Umm Ja'far were* [82 *to unbraid her plaits, they would be bound to touch some Caliph or heir to the Caliphate.*

A woman who performed the Pilgrimage with a magnanimity of character such as no king or queen had ever displayed before. This was Jamīla bint Nāṣir ad-Daula Abī Muḥammad al-Ḥasan b. 'Abdallāh b. Ḥamdān, the sister of Abū Taghlib. She made the Pilgrimage in the year 366 [/976-7], and this particular Pilgrimage year became proverbially famous and a memorable date. She displayed great magnanimity of character, distributed a large amount of wealth, did many pious deeds and performed many acts of liberality – all these to an extent that the charitable works done in the course of the Pilgrimage by Zubaida and other daughters of Caliphs and kings, and even by Caliphs and kings themselves, only partially equalled.

Certain trustworthy authorities have told me that she provided all the people present at the Pilgrimage that year with *sawīq* made from loaf-sugar and snow. In addition to many other things, she brought with her, loaded on camels, fresh green vegetables contained in earthenware crocks. She commissioned 500 mounts for those pilgrims who were limbless; she bestowed 10,000 dinars on the Ka'ba; she provided for use in the Ka'ba during her stay in Mecca candles made from ambergris; she freed 300 slaves [83 and 200 slave girls; she gave handsome subsidies to all those who had come as an act of piety to reside in Mecca (*al-mujāwirīn*); and she provided 50,000 fine robes for the generality of population there. She had with her 400 litters (*'ammāriyya*),[16] each lined with satin, so that it was never known in which one she herself was.[17]

Her subsequent fate was as follows. When she returned to her native land of Mosul, time brought one of its reverses of fortune, and 'Aḍud ad-Daula Fanā-Khusrau seized her possessions, her strongholds and her ancestral territories.[18] Circumstances reduced her to every sort of deprivation and humiliation, and she was exposed to crushing poverty. Fanā-Khusrau sought her hand in marriage, but out of pride and scorn she rejected his proposal, and he therefore became filled with hatred for her. When she fell into his hands, his passion for her had cooled, and he persistently

[15] Abū'l-'Ainā' Muḥammad b. al-Qāsim al-Hāshimī, the well-known philologist and poet of Basra, blind in the latter part of his life, d. 283/896 (cf. Brockelmann, EI² s.v.).

[16] On this term, see Dozy, s.v.; the meaning is confirmed by its use in Mas'ūdī, *Murūj*, VII, 111, in Shābushtī, *Kitāb ad-diyārāt*, cf. Sachau, APAW (1919), No. 10, p. 24, and in 'Arīb b. Sa'd al-Qurṭubī, *Ṣilat ta'rīkh aṭ-Ṭabarī* (Cairo 1328/1910), 30, s.v. 303 A.H.

[17] Jamīla's magnificence is noted in Ibn al-Jauzī's mention of the Pilgrimage of 366, *al-Muntaẓam* (Hyderabad 1357-9/1938-41), VII, 84.

[18] On these events, see Miskawaih, in *Eclipse of the 'Abbasid Caliphate*, ed. and tr. Margoliouth and Amedroz (Oxford 1921-2), II, 378-96, 401-4, tr. V, 415-34, 439-43; Ibn al-Athīr, VIII, 508-10, 511-12, 513-15; M. Canard, *Histoire de la dynastie des H'amdânides de Jazîra et de Syrie* (Paris 1953), I, 561-77.

ill-treated her, even stripping her of her clothing and veil, and then offering her the choice of two alternatives: either to hand over the whole amount remaining of the money stipulated in the peace treaty she had made with him, or else to repair to a brothel and there earn enough to pay him the sum demanded of her. In the end, she could see no way out, and she realised that her final dishonouring and shame were near, so she took advantage of her guards' negligence and drowned herself in the Tigris – may God have mercy on her![19]

A ruler of our own time who got possession of the kingdoms of nine powerful rulers, either by conquest or through inheritance; according to Abū Manṣūr al-Barīdī,[20] no parallel to this is known in Islam. This was 'Aḍud ad-Daula Abū Shujā' Fanā-Khusrau, and the nine rulers were: [84

[Firstly,] Abū 'Alī Muḥammad b. Ilyās, ruler of the province of Kirmān.[21]

[Secondly,] Yūsuf b. al-Wajīh, ruler of the region of 'Umān.[22]

[Thirdly,] [Mu'izz ad-Daula] Abū'l-Ḥusain b. Būya, ruler of Iraq and the province of al-Ahwāz.[23]

[Fourthly,] Nāṣir ad-Daula Abū Muḥammad b. Ḥamdān, ruler of Mosul, Diyār Rabī'a, Diyār Bakr and the adjoining regions.[24]

[Fifthly,] [Ẓahīr ad-Daula] Abū Ṭāhir Wushmagīr b. Ziyār, ruler of Gurgān and Ṭabaristān.[25]

[Sixthly,] [Rukn ad-Daula] Abū 'Alī b. Būya, ruler of Ray, Iṣfahān, Abhar, Zanjān, Qum, Qāshān and the whole of the province of Jibāl.[26]

[Seventhly.] ['Imād ad-Daula] 'Alī b. Būya, ruler of the province of Fārs.[27]

[Eighthly,] the ruler over al-Aḥsā' and the Qarāmiṭa, ruler of

19 Miskawaih merely says that Jamīla surrendered to the general Abū'l-Wafā' Ṭāhir, and was incarcerated at Baghdad in 'Aḍud ad-Daula's harem; both Mez, *The renaissance of Islam*, tr. 24, n. 9, and F. Rosenthal, 'On suicide in Islam', JAOS, LXVI (1946), 257, consider that the story of Jamīla's dishonouring and suicide is an unlikely one.

20 Abū Manṣūr Sa'īd b. Aḥmad al-Barīdī is mentioned by Tha'ālibī in *Yatīma*, II, 243, in the section on Abū Isḥāq Ibrāhīm aṣ-Ṣābi', where Tha'ālibī says that he met Abū Manṣūr Sa'īd in Bukhārā. He was thus one of the five sons of Abū 'Abdallāh Aḥmad al-Barīdī, of the well-known Barīdī family influential in Basra and Ahwāz in the second quarter of the 4th/10th century; cf. Sourdel, EI² s.v.

21 For a chronological account of 'Aḍud ad-Daula's conquests, see H. Bowen, EI² s.v.; on the conquest of Kirmān, Ibn al-Athīr, VIII, 432-4.

22 According to *ibid.*, VIII, 474-5, 'Umān was conquered in 363/973 by 'Aḍud ad-Daula's Vizier Abū'l-Qāsim al-Muṭahhar b. Muḥammad; but according to Zambaur, *Manuel de généalogie et de chronologie*, 127, Yūsuf b. Wajīh, the first of a short line of Wajīhids, died in 322/934 and the line ended *c.* 340/951-2. Yūsuf b. Wajīh is not mentioned in Ibn al-Athīr's account of the Būyid conquest.

23 These regions came to 'Aḍud ad-Daula on his uncle's death in 356/967.

24 'Uddat ad-Daula Abū Taghlib b. Nāṣir ad-Daula was defeated by 'Aḍud ad-Daula in 367/978 and driven out of the eastern territories of the Ḥamdānids.

25 AS erroneously has 'Ziyād' for the 'Ziyār' of J. The Ziyārid ruler Qābūs b. Wushmagīr was driven out of his lands by 'Aḍud ad-Daula's brother Mu'ayyid ad-Daula Abū Manṣūr in 371/981, and never regained them till after 'Aḍud ad-Daula's death.

26 The overlordship of these territories fell to 'Aḍud ad-Daula on his father's death in 366/976-7.

27 'Aḍud ad-Daula succeeded here in 338/944 whilst still a child, his uncle being sonless.

the Arabian peninsula and the mountains held by the Khawārij (*Jibāl ash-Shurāt*).[28]

[Ninthly,] the ruler of the [Persian Gulf] waters, ruler of the fortress of Huzū. Before Fanā-Khusrau, no-one had ever conquered it; it is the fortress concerning whose owner God Most High has said, 'And behind them was a king, who was taking every ship by force.'[29]

[28] This can only have been the extension of Būyid influence or suzerainty, and not outright conquest. According to de Goeje, *Mémoire sur les Carmathes du Bahraïn et les Fatimides* (Leiden 1886), 192-3, the Qarāmiṭa of al-Aḥsā' enjoyed good relations with 'Aḍud ad-Daula, and maintained an official representative at Baghdad, the general Abū Bakr b. Shāhūya; relations only deteriorated after 'Aḍud ad-Daula's death in 372/983, when his son Ṣamṣām ad-Daula arrested this general and provoked a Qarmaṭī attack on Kufa (Ibn al-Athīr, IX, 29-30). The Jibāl ash-Shurāt are presumably the Jabal Akhḍar in the interior of 'Umān (Mas'ūdī, *Murūj*, v, 440, lists the Jibāl 'Umān as one of the haunts of the Khawārij), although the anonymous *Ḥudūd al-'ālam*, tr. Minorsky (London 1937), 67, 151, 415, mentions that the Jabal ash-Shurāt is also the name of that part of the Syrian mountain chain running between Sinai and Zughar to the south of Damascus.

[29] Qur'ān, xviii, 78. For Huzū, see Yāqūt, *Mu'jam al-buldān* (Beirut 1374-6/1955-7), v, 406: a fortress on the Persian coast opposite the island of Kīsh. Yāqūt quotes Ibrāhīm b. Hilāl aṣ-Ṣābi' on 'Aḍud ad-Daula's conquest of it from the Arabs of the Banū 'Umāra; he saw the ruins of it, and thought the descriptions of its impregnability much exaggerated. Cf. also, G. Le Strange, *The lands of the eastern Caliphate* (Cambridge 1905), 257.

Chapter Seven.

Concerning curious coincidences and patterns in names and patronymics.

Five prophets, peace be upon them, each one known by two different names. Muḥammad and Aḥmad; ʿĪsā (sc. Jesus) and al-Masīḥ; Dhū'l-Kifl[1] and Ilyasaʿ; Yaʿqūb and Isrā'īl[2]; and Yūnus (sc. Jonas) and Dhū'n-Nūn.

A story about the filiation of ʿAlī b. Abī Ṭālib, may God be pleased with him. Hishām b. al-Kalbī[3] related: 'One day I was with a group of people at ⌈al-Walīd⌉ ash-Sharqī al-Quṭāmī's house, when he said, "Do any of you know ʿAlī b. ʿAbd Manāf b. Shaiba b. ʿAmr b. al-Mughīra b. Zaid, one of the noblest of mankind after the Messenger of God, God's prayers and peace be upon him?" Those present averred that they knew nothing about this man, but Hishām said, "This is in fact ʿAlī b. Abī Ṭālib, because Abū Ṭālib's name was ʿAbd Manāf, ʿAbd al-Muṭṭalib's name was Shaiba, Hāshim's name was ʿAmr, ʿAbd Manāf's name was al-Mughīra, and Quṣayy's name was Zaid." '

⌊86

Series of names repeated in the lines of kings and chiefs. Al-Jāḥiẓ says[4] that one only finds names repeated in series amongst rulers and chiefs: consider, for instance, Bahrām b. Bahrām b. Bahrām amongst the kings of Persia, al-Ḥārith b. al-Ḥārith b. al-Ḥārith amongst the Ghassānids, and al-Ḥasan b. al-Ḥasan b.

[1] On this mysterious personage, twice mentioned in the Qur'ān but not definitely identifiable with Elijah or Elisha or any other Biblical character, see G. Vajda, EI[2] s.v.

[2] Cf. Wensinck, EI[1] Art. 'Isrā'īl'; Muḥammad at first apparently considered Jacob as a son of Abraham, see Qur'ān, xi, 74/71.

[3] Sc. the famous historian and antiquary, authority on the genealogies of the early Arabs and author of the *Kitāb al-aṣnām* 'Book of idols' on the gods of the pre-Islamic Arabs; d. 204/819-20.

[4] Jāḥiẓ mentions in *al-Bayān wa't-tabyīn*, I, 34, that he had written a special work on this topic, *Kitāb al-asmā' wa'l-kunā wa'l-alqāb wa'l-anbāz* 'Book of names, patronymics, nicknames and insulting epithets', but no trace of this is extant; cf. Pellat, 'Ǧāḥiẓiana III. Essai d'inventaire de l'œuvre ǧāḥiẓienne', *Arabica*, III (1956), 152, No. 25. On the repetition of names within families, see Caetani and Gabrieli, *Onomasticon arabicum*, I, 67, 137.

al-Ḥasan amongst the great men of Islam.[5] The present writer says: one day, I discussed these names with the Khwārazm-Shāh Abū'l-'Abbās Ma'mūn b. Ma'mūn, and he cited the case of his own son Ma'mūn, at that time in Sīstān, who was called Ma'mūn b. Ma'mūn b. Ma'mūn.[6]

Three cousins, all contemporaries, all called 'Alī, and each one a prominent man, a scholar in law and in theology, a pious believer and quite capable of acting as an Imām or leader. These were 'Alī b. 'Abdallāh b. al-'Abbās b. 'Abd al-Muṭṭalib; 'Alī b. al-Ḥusain b. 'Alī b. Abī Ṭālib b. 'Abd al-Muṭṭalib; and 'Alī b. 'Abdallāh b. Ja'far b. Abī Ṭālib b. 'Abd al-Muṭṭalib.

Each of these three had a son called Muḥammad, the sons being cousins of each other, and each being a prominent man, a scholar in law and in theology, a pious believer and quite capable of acting as an Imām or leader. These were Muḥammad b. 'Alī b. 'Abdallāh b. al-'Abbās b. 'Abd al-Muṭṭalib; Muḥammad b. 'Alī b. al-Ḥusain b. 'Alī b. Abī Ṭālib b. 'Abd al-Muṭṭalib; and Muḥammad b. 'Alī b. 'Abdallāh b. Ja'far b. Abī Ṭālib b. 'Abd al-Muṭṭalib. [87

According to al-Jāḥiẓ, this is one of the strangest things which has ever befallen in the world or ever happened in the course of time; it is an excellence which no-one else has ever shared with them.

Two wielders of power in the Islamic period, whose names both began with *'ain*, who each killed three other wielders of power whose names all began with *'ain*. The first was 'Abd al-Malik b. Marwān, who killed 'Abdallāh b. az-Zubair, 'Amr b. Sa'īd b. al-'Āṣ and 'Abd ar-Raḥmān b. Muḥammad b. al-Ash'ath. The second was Abū Ja'far al-Manṣūr, whose name was 'Abdallāh b. Muḥammad, who killed Abū Muslim 'Abd ar-Raḥmān b. Muḥammad, his own paternal uncle 'Abdallāh b. 'Alī and the governor of Khurāsān 'Abd al-Jabbār b. 'Abd ar-Raḥmān.[7]

A case where *'ain* son of *'ain* son of *'ain* killed *mīm* son of *mīm* son of *mīm*. Marwān b. Muḥammad b. Marwān, the last of the Marwānid rulers, used to say, 'We find in our books that *'ain* son of *'ain* son of *'ain* will kill *mīm* son of *mīm* son of *mīm*, and I believe that 'Abdallāh b. 'Umar b. 'Abd al-'Azīz will kill me in the end, because I am Marwān b. Muḥammad b. Marwān.' This came to 'Abdallāh b. 'Alī (sc. the uncle of the Abbasid Caliphs as-Saffāḥ and al-Manṣūr), and he commented, 'Abū 'Abd al-Malik is mistaken: I have more *'ains* in my name than 'Abdallāh b. 'Umar b. 'Abd al-'Azīz, because I am 'Abdallāh b. 'Alī b.

[5] This item of information also in Ibn Qutaiba, *Ma'ārif*, 590, Ibn Rusta, 228, tr. 273, and Tha'ālibī, *Bard al-akbād*, in *Khams rasā'il*, 122.

[6] The whole of this paragraph further appears in Tha'ālibī's *Ghurar as-siyar*, in the portion not printed by Zotenberg. The latter suggested that the mention of the Shāh's son as being in Sīstān probably refers to the period after the Ghaznavid conquest of Khwārazm, when members of the Ma'mūnid family were carried off into captivity in various provinces of the Ghaznavid empire (Preface, vii-viii, xvii); but Abū'l-'Abbās Ma'mūn himself was killed in the civil strife in Khwārazm which preceded the Ghaznavid invasion.

[7] This information recorded in Mas'ūdī, *Murūj*, VI, 217-18, in a conversation between al-Manṣūr and 'Abdallāh b. 'Ayyāsh.

'Abdallāh b. al-'Abbās b. 'Abd al-Muṭṭalib b. Hāshim, and Hāshim's [original] name was 'Amr b. 'Abd Manāf.' It was [88
indeed, he who killed Marwān.[8]

A remarkable thing. The only two people with the name Ja'far
who became Caliphs were al-Mutawakkil and al-Muqtadir, and
both of them were murdered, each moreover on a Tuesday night.[9]

Prominent leaders who had two or three patronymics, and
towns with two different names. It used to be said that only the
most outstanding of leaders were known by two or three patronymics,[10] and the only towns known by two names are those
which are provincial capitals. Consider, for instance, 'Uthmān b.
'Affān, who had the patronymics Abū 'Abdallāh, Abū 'Amr and
Abū Lailā; 'Abdallāh b. az-Zubair, called Abū Bakr, Abū Khubaib
and Abū 'Abd ar-Raḥmān; Ṣakhr b. Ḥarb, called Abū Ḥanẓala and
Abū Sufyān; 'Abd al-'Uzzā b. 'Abd al-Muṭṭalib, called Abū Lahab
and Abū 'Utba; Qaṭarī b. al-Fujā'a, called Abū Muḥammad [89
and Abū Na'āma; and Hārūn ar-Rashīd, called Abū Ja'far and
Abū Muhammad.[11]

As for the towns with two names, these include Mecca and
Ṣalāḥ; Medina and Yathrib; Miṣr and al-Fusṭāṭ; Bait al-Maqdis
and Īlyā'; Baghdad and Madinat as-Salām; Ray and al-Muḥammadiyya; Iṣfahān and Jayy; Nīshāpūr and Abarshahr; Balkh and
Bāmiyān (*sic*); Sīstān and Zaranj; and Khwārazm and Kāth. [90

Two of the rulers of Khurāsān, each called Nūḥ, and each
troubled by a commander-in-chief whose patronymic was Abū
'Alī. The first was Nūḥ b. Naṣr, whose commander-in-chief Abū
'Alī aṣ-Ṣaghānī rebelled against him and made war on him; and
the second was Nūḥ b. Manṣūr, whose commander-in-chief Abū
'Alī b. Sīmjūr rebelled against him and attacked him.[12]

[8] A similar anecdote in *ibid.*, VI, 108-9. Predictions concerning the downfall of the Umayyads seem to have been current in the first half of the 2nd/8th century, especially amongst Alid circles; cf. van Vloten, *Recherches sur la domination arabe.* In this predictional *Jafr* literature, a large part was played by interpretation of the numerical value of letters, the occult value of letters and numbers and the use of them, as here, to conceal people's names; cf. Ibn Khaldūn, *Muqaddima*, tr. Rosenthal, II, 209ff., and T. Fahd, EI[2] Art. 'D̲jafr'.

[9] In 247/861 and 320/932 respectively.

[10] Cf. on the subject of multiple *kunyas*, Caetani and Gabrieli, *op. cit.*, I, 108-10, and Goldziher, *Muhammedanische Studien*, I, 267, who also notes from Jāḥiẓ, *al-Bayān wa't-tabyīn*, that warriors used different patronymics in battle from those used in time of peace.

[11] This list substantially the same in *Ma'ārif*, 600.

[12] For these events, see Barthold, *Turkestan*, 246ff.

Chapter Eight.

Concerning diverse items of curious and striking information about the Prophet, Quraish and the rulers of the Arabs.

Those who closely resembled the Messenger of God, God's prayers and peace be upon him.[1] These were: [firstly,] Ja'far b. Abī Ṭālib. It is related from the Prophet that he told Ja'far, 'You resemble me both in outward appearance and in character.' [Secondly,] al-Ḥasan b. 'Alī b. Abī Ṭālib. When his mother Fāṭima dandled him up and down on her knee in babyhood, she used to croon (metre *Rajaz*): *By my father,*[2] *the spitten image of my own father* (sc. Muḥammad), *and not at all like 'Ali.*

[Thirdly,] Qutham b. al-'Abbās, who was killed in battle at Samarqand. [Fourthly,] Abū Sufyān b. al-Ḥārith b. 'Abd al-Muṭṭalib. [Fifthly,] Muslim b. Mu'attib[2] b. Abī Lahab. [92
[Sixthly,] Kābis[2] b. Rabī'a b. 'Adī. Mu'āwiya was told that Kābis b. Rabī'a, then at Basra, resembled the Prophet, God's prayers and peace be upon him, very closely, so he wrote to 'Abdallāh b. 'Āmir b. Kuraiz to send Kābis along to him. When the latter arrived, and Mu'āwiya saw him coming in through the doorway of the palace, he rose from his couch; he went forward to meet him and kissed him on his forehead between the eyes, gave him rich presents and granted him the district of Marghāb.[3]

Those who ill-treated the Messenger of God, God's prayers and peace be upon him.[4] These were Abū Lahab 'Abd al-'Uzzā b. 'Abd al-Muṭṭalib; al-Ḥakam b. Abī'l-'Āṣ b. Umayya; 'Uqba b. Abī Mu'aiṭ; and 'Amr b. aṭ-Ṭulāṭila al-Khuzā'ī. None of [93
these became Muslims, with the exception of al-Ḥakam b. Abī'l-

[1] Parallel lists in Balādhurī, *Ansāb al-ashrāf*, I, 539; Muḥammad b. Ḥabib, *Muḥabbar*, 46-7; and Ibn Rusta, 200-1, tr. 234-5, quoting Ibn as-Sikkīt.

[2] Following the emendations from parallel sources made by AS.

[3] According to Yāqūt, *Mu'jam al-buldān*, v, 108, Marghāb is a river or channel in the Basra district.

[4] Essentially the same list in *Muḥabbar*, 157-8. The matter in this and the next section appears within the long section on those who opposed and mocked at the Prophet, in Balādhurī, *Ansāb al-ashrāf*, I, 123-56. Balādhurī also gives, in greater or less degrees of detail, the explanatory stories about the violent deaths of the mockers and scoffers, given in Tha'ālibī's next section. Muḥammad b. Ḥabīb, in *Muḥabbar*, 158-60, omits the explanatory stories, but they are cited in the Hyderabad text from the same author's *Kitāb al-munammaq*, (now edited by Kh. A. Fāriq [Hyderabad 1384/1964]), 484-7.

'Āṣ, and his faith was suspect; he was the one who was called *aṭ-Ṭarīd* 'the Banished One'.[5]

Those amongst Quraish who mocked and scoffed. Abū 'Ubaida Ma'mar b. al-Muthannā at-Taimī[6] says: 'Abd ar-Raḥmān b. Salib b. Shaiba related to us concerning God Most High's words to his Prophet, God's prayers and peace be upon him, 'Indeed, We have relieved you of the mockers',[7] i.e. Display your mission openly, for We have removed from you those who used to mock you and ill-treat you. These scoffers of Quraish were five in number, and they all died at Mecca on the same day. They were al-Walīd b. al-Mughīra al-Makhzūmī; al-'Āṣ b. Wā'il as-Sahmī, [94 the father of 'Amr b. al-'Āṣ; al-Ḥārith b. Qais as-Sahmī; Abū Habbār al-Aswad b. al-Muṭṭalib; and al-Aswad b. 'Abd Yaghūth az-Zuhrī, the son of the Prophet's maternal uncle, Āmina's brother. God brought about the destruction of all of these in a single day.

As regards al-Walīd, he went past a man of Khuzā'a who was feathering some arrows. He trod on one of the arrows, a sliver of wood flew up and severed his sciatic vein, and he died.[8]

With reference to al-'Āṣ, it happened thus. It rained during the night at Mecca, and the next morning al-'Āṣ went forth and told his son, 'Saddle my camel for me so that I may ride in the ravines surrounding the town and enjoy the freshness.' His son did this, and al-'Āṣ rode off till he came to one of the ravines round Mecca. He got his camel to kneel, but at this point, a snake bit his leg. The limb swelled up until it became as thick as a camel's neck, and he cried out, 'Muḥammad's Lord has killed me!' They looked for the snake but were unable to find it. They had to carry him home on a litter, his leg by now having gone black, but he died the same day.[9]

Concerning al-Ḥārith b. Qais, he ate some salted fish during the night, and was overcome with a violent thirst. He [95 started gulping down water, but his thirst could not be assuaged. In his pauses for breath, he gasped out, 'Muḥammad's Lord has killed me!' He kept on drinking till his belly burst and he died.[10]

As for Abū Habbār, he went out to meet his son Zam'a, who was returning from Syria. He remarked to his slave boy, 'Look, can you see anything?' The boy replied that he saw nothing. Then he said, 'Look again, and if you see a dark point in the distance, it will be my son Zam'a.' The boy said, 'I can see a dark mass now', so Abū Habbār said, 'Let us go out and meet him.' But then, an acacia tree loomed up before them, and when they

5 Sc. the father of the Umayyad Caliph Marwān, called *aṭ-Ṭarīd* because the Prophet banished him to the region of Ṭā'if, and he was not allowed to return to public life till the reign of 'Uthmān (Ibn Qutaiba, *Ma'ārif*, 353).

6 See on him, below, p. 91, n. 16.

7 Qur'ān, xv, 95.

8 Cf. *Ansāb al-ashrāf*, I, 134-5.

9 Cf. *ibid.*, I, 138-9. According to tradition, it was al-'Āṣ who taunted Muḥammad with being sonless (*abtar*, literally 'cut off'), a supreme source of shame amongst the Arabs; consequently, Qur'ān, cviii, 3, 'Indeed, the one who hates you will find himself sonless', was revealed in reference to him.

10 Cf. *Ansāb al-ashrāf*, I, 132. Tradition makes al-Ḥārith the person denounced in Qur'ān, xlv, 22/23, 'Have you considered the one who has taken as his god his own desire?'

reached it, Jibrīl (sc. the Archangel Gabriel) swooped down on him and beat him in the face with the tree's branches. Abū Habbār was meanwhile shouting to the boy, 'What are you doing? Come and help me, for Muḥammad's Lord is attacking me in the face!'[11] The boy replied, 'I can't see anyone attacking you, you are only hitting yourself!' He kept on hitting away until he killed himself. At this very moment, his son Zam'a came into sight from Syria.[12]

Finally, al-Aswad b. 'Abd Yaghūth, the Prophet's own cousin on the maternal side. He went to one of the Banū Kināna's watering-places and began to harangue them, warning them about Muḥammad in these terms: 'If you say that Muḥammad is a mere sorcerer, you are quite right, and if you say that he is mad, you are not far wrong either.' He then guaranteed to them various things if they would assassinate Muḥammad. He then returned to his family, but by this time, God had twisted and distorted his face and body and they had gone black; his family failed to recognise him and shut the door in his face. He started to expostulate, 'This is my house, and I'm al-Aswad b. 'Abd Yaghūth!' They retorted, 'You're lying, you're just a thief', and then threw him out. He was reduced to wandering through the ravines of Mecca, raving deliriously and crying, 'Muḥammad's Lord has killed me!', and very soon he was dead.[13]

God Most High then sent down the revelation, 'Indeed, We have relieved you of the mockers, Those who set up another deity alongside the One God; in the end they will know', i.e. they will know My punishment in the next world just as they are experiencing it in the present world. [96

Those whose hearts were won over (*al-Mu'allafa qulūbuhum*).[14] From Quraish: Abū Sufyān b. Ḥarb, Suhail b. 'Amr, Ḥuwaitib b. 'Abd al-'Uzzā, Habbār b. al-Aswad, al-Ḥārith b. Hishām, Ḥakīm b. Ḥizām, Ṣafwān b. Umayya and Qais b. 'Adī. [97

From Banū Fazāra: 'Uyaina b. Ḥiṣn al-Fazārī, known as 'the one lacking in judgement' and 'the one demanding unconditional obedience (*al-muṭā'*)'.[15]

From Banū Tamīm: al-Aqra' b. Ḥābis.

From Banū Naṣr: Mālik b. 'Auf.

From Banū Mālik: 'Abd ar-Raḥmān b. Yarbū'.

From Banū Sulaim: al-'Abbās b. Mirdās.

From Banū Thaqīf: al-'Alā' b. al-Ḥārith. [98

If these men had sincerely accepted the faith, the Messenger of God, God's prayers and peace be upon him, would not have had to conciliate them with gifts of camels and sheep.

11 Following the *yaḍribu wajhī* of J.

12 Cf. *Ansāb al-ashrāf*, I, 148-9.

13 Cf. *ibid.*, I, 131-2.

14 These were the leaders of the Meccans and of the surrounding Bedouin tribes to whom presents of camels were given from the immense booty taken at Ḥunain in 8/630, when the Hawāzin confederation and the men of Ṭā'if were defeated; lists of those given presents occur in the *Sīras* of Ibn Isḥāq and Wāqidī, in *Muḥabbar*, in Ṭabarī, etc. The idea that these gifts were specifically meant to win over the recipients to Islam, and the widening of the term *al-Mu'allafa qulūbuhum*, originally used with a restricted applicability, to include all the persons originally allotted gifts at al-Ji'rāna, seems to arise from tendentious stories circulated by the anti-Umayyad 'pious opposition' at Medina (Watt, *Muhammad at Medina*, 73-5, 348-53).

15 According to Lammens, *Le berceau de l'Islam, l'Arabie occidentale à la veille de l'Hégire. I Le climat—les Bédouins* (Rome 1914), 268ff., the epithet *muṭā'*, literally 'he who is obeyed', was only applied to those forceful tribal chiefs who had succeeded in raising themselves above the normal position of *primi inter pares* to a more despotic level.

Those who were notorious sodomites. These included: Abū Lahab 'Abd al-'Uzzā b. 'Abd al-Muṭṭalib; Umayya b. Khalaf; Munabbih b. al-Ḥajjāj; al-Akhnas b. Sharīq ath-Thaqafī; Sa'īd b. al-'Āṣ; Kuraiz b. Rabī'a, the grandfather of 'Abdallāh b. 'Āmir; Ḥāṭib b. 'Amr; and Hishām b. Shu'ba.

Those who were notorious for acting as the passive partners in sodomy. These included: Abū Jahl b. Hishām; 'Uqba b. Abī Mu'aiṭ; Shaiba b. Rabī'a; al-Ḥakam b. Abī'l-'Āṣ; Abū [99
Umayya b. al-Mughīra; 'Affān b. Abī'l-'Āṣ; Habbār b. al-Aswad; Hishām b. al-Walīd b. al-Mughīra; and an-Naḍr b. al-Ḥārith.

There is a story connected with each one of these, given by Abū 'Ubaida in his enumeration of the discreditable deeds and characteristics (*mathālib*) [of the Arabs].[16] He asserts that one of these, Habbār b. al-Aswad, was denounced to Abū Bakr the Veracious, may God be pleased with him, as having been the passive partner in anal intercourse. Abū Bakr enquired, 'What is the most exemplary punishment known amongst the Arabs?' They told him, 'Death by burning', so he ordered Habbār to be burnt alive. 'Abd ar-Raḥmān b. Ḥassān [b. Thābit] recited this line, alluding insultingly to one of his sons (metre *Ṭawīl*): *It was not my grandfather or father whom the Veracious One had burnt alive, when obscene practices had diverted the man from his wives.*

Those members of Quraish notorious as fornicators.[17] These included: Abū Sufyān; 'Abd ar-Raḥmān b. al-Ḥakam; 'Abd ar-Raḥmān b. Abī Bakr; Abū Shaḥma b. 'Umar; 'Utba b. [100
Abī Sufyān; 'Abdallāh b. Ubayy [b.] Khalaf; al-Mughīra b. Shu'ba, actually from the tribe of Thaqīf[18]; Sa'd b. Hishām b. 'Abd al-Malik; and Ibrāhīm b. Muḥammad b. Sa'd b. Abī Waqqāṣ.

The notorious liars of Quraish. Abū 'Ubaida says, al-Haitham [b. 'Adī] related to me from Ibn 'Ayyāsh that Hishām b. 'Abd al-Malik used to say that the notorious liars of Quraish were as follows: Ayyūb b. Salama; 'Abdallāh b. al-Ḥasan b. al-Ḥasan; 'Abdallāh b. 'Anbasa b. Sa'īd b. al-'Āṣ; Ibrāhīm b. 'Abd- [101
allāh b. Muṭī' al-'Adawī; and 'Āṣim b. 'Ubaidallāh b. 'Āṣim b. 'Umar b. al-Khaṭṭāb. Hishām also used to say that Anti-Christ

[16] Abū 'Ubaida Ma'mar b. al-Muthannā (d. 209/824-5) was taken by Goldziher to be the most learned and trenchant of the anti-Arab polemicists in the Shu'ūbiyya controversies ('Die Su'ûbijja and ihre Bekundung in der Wissenschaft', in *Muhammedanische Studien*, I, 194ff.). It is true that Ibn Qutaiba accuses him of being 'the most active investigator of people's disreputable deeds, and the most persistent exposer of the *mathālib* of the Arabs' (*Kitāb al-'Arab au ar-Radd 'alā 'sh-Shu'ūbiyya*, in M. Kurd 'Alī, *Rasā'il al-bulaghā'*[4] [Cairo 1374/1954], 346), and amongst Abū 'Ubaida's many works there is certainly mentioned a *Kitāb al-mathālib* 'in which he discusses the genealogies of the Arabs and the defects in them, and accuses the Arabs of things which people find painful to mention' (Mas'ūdī, *Murūj*, VII, 80; Ibn an-Nadīm, *Fihrist*, 79-80; cf. Goldziher, *op. cit.*, I, 190-4). But Sir Hamilton Gibb has recently denied that Abū 'Ubaida was so violently anti-Arab, and has asserted that the later Persophile partisans of the Shu'ūbiyya utilised parts of Abū 'Ubaida's researches on the Arabs' past expressly to discredit their opponents ('The social significance of the Shu'ūbīya', in *Studia orientalia J. Pedersen dicata* [Copenhagen 1953], 105-14 = *Studies in the civilization of Islam* [London 1962], 62-73; EI² Art. 'Abū 'Ubayda').

[17] The Arabic *zunāt* is here given the approximate translation of 'fornicators'. The abstract term *zinā* has a wider meaning than fornication in our sense, being applied to any act of copulation with a woman not linked to one either by the marriage bond or by the relationship of slave concubinage; cf. G.-H. Bousquet, *La morale de l'Islam et son ethique sexuelle* (Paris 1953), 47ff.

[18] Presumably included because of the traditionally close connection of Thaqīf of Ṭā'if with Quraish, and because of al-Mughīra's close association with the aristocracy of Quraish in the ruling of the conquered lands under the early Caliphs.

(*ad-Dajjāl*) would not appear whilst any one of these remained alive.

Those members of Quraish known for their lack of discretion and judgement (*al-ḥamqā*).[19] These were: 'Āmir b. Kuraiz b. Rabī'a; Mu'āwiya b. Marwān b. al-Ḥakam; Bakkār b. 'Abd al-Malik b. Marwān; al-'Āṣ b. Hishām; 'Abdallāh b. Mu'āwiya b. Abī Sufyān; 'Utba b. Abī Sufyān; Sahl b. 'Amr, the brother of Suhail[20]; and al-'Āṣ b. Sa'īd b. al-'Āṣ. [102

Those members of Quraish suspected of unorthodox beliefs (*az-zanādiqa*).[21] These were: Abū Sufyān; 'Uqba b. Abī Mu'aiṭ; Ubayy b. Khalaf; an-Naḍr b. al-Ḥārith b. Kalada; Munabbih and Nubaih, sons of al-Ḥajjāj and from the clan of Sahm; al-'Āṣ b. Wā'il as-Sahmī; and al-Walīd b. al-Mughīra. All these learnt their heterodoxy from the Christians of al-Ḥīra, and apart from Abū Sufyān, none of them became Muslims.[22]

Those of Quraish famous for their shrewdness.[23] These were: Mu'āwiya b. Abī Sufyān; Ziyād b. Abīhi; 'Amr b. al-'Āṣ; al-Mughīra b. Shu'ba; Qais b. Sa'd b. 'Ubāda; and 'Abdallāh [103 b. Budail b. Warqā' al-Khuzā'ī.

Defects found amongst prominent chiefs. Abū 'Amr b. al-'Alā'[24] has said: 'There is no defect which [theoretically] debars a man from leadership which we do not in fact find in one or other of the great chiefs.'[25]

The first defect is youthfulness, but Abū Jahl became chief of Quraish before his moustache had grown, and he took his place in the council chamber before his beard had started to spread.

[The second defect is] niggardliness, but Abū Sufyān, who was notorious for his avarice, became a chief.

[The third defect is that] a fornicator should not be a chief, but 'Āmir b. aṭ-Ṭufail became a chief, and he was more libidinous than a monkey.

[The fourth is that] a violent and tyrannical person should not be a chief, but Kulaib of Wā'il and Ḥudhaifa b. Badr became chiefs, and they were more violent than a serpent.

[19] This list is an abridgement of the one in *Muḥabbar*, 379-80.

[20] Sc. the Suhail b. 'Amr al-'Āmirī who acted as negotiator for Quraish in the drawing-up of the Treaty of Ḥudaibiyya in 6/628 between Muḥammad and the Meccans (cf. Ibn Duraid, *Kitāb al-ishtiqāq*, 69).

[21] The same list in *Muḥabbar*, 161. Since the term *zindīq* pl. *zanādiqa* only comes into use in early Abbasid times, when it is primarily applied to Manichaean and dualist heretics and to scoffing freethinkers, it is difficult to imagine what sense it can have as applied to contemporaries of Muḥammad. It seems, indeed, to be a mere term of abuse, for those mentioned in the list – and many of those mentioned in the other lists in this chapter of defects and vices – are well-known opponents of the Prophet.

[22] Ibn Rusta, 217, tr. 258, likewise says that certain members of Quraish brought back *zandaqa* from al-Ḥīra. The Lakhmid capital in central Iraq was notable at this time for its Christian population, members of the Eastern Syrian Church, amongst whom there was a high degree of literacy; wide-spread Arab traditions locate the source of writing in the Arabic script at al-Ḥīra. It is possible that there were some dualist and Manichaean elements there, but as was emphasised in the previous note, there is no evidence that these beliefs ever reached as far as the Hijaz.

[23] The same list in *Muḥabbar*, 184. On the significance attached to *dahā'*, shrewdness, at Mecca and Ṭā'if, see Lammens, *La cité arabe de Ṭāif à la veille de l'Hégire* (Beirut 1922), 138-9.

[24] One of the most prominent of the early Basran scholars (d. *c.* 154/770), being an expert on the 'readings' of the Qur'ān and on the poetry and history of the early Arabs; he seems to have handed down his lore orally, and his work is known from the notes taken by his pupils or from later citations of these (R. Blachère, EI² s.v.).

[25] The qualifications required by the tribal chief or *sayyid* for leadership are set forth by Lammens in *Le berceau de l'Islam*, 211ff.

[The fifth is that] a man lacking in discretion and judgement should not be a chief, but 'Uyaina b. Ḥiṣn, well-known for his lack of self-control, became a chief; the Prophet, God's prayers and peace be upon him, said of him, 'This is the one who is impulsive and poor in judgement, yet unchallenged in his power.' [104

[The sixth is that] a poor man should not be a chief, but Abū Ṭālib and 'Utba b. Rabī'a both became chiefs, being both poor, yet accorded great honour and respect.

However, it is unknown amongst either the Arabs or Persians for a notorious liar to become a chief. The Arabs say that one never finds a courageous hero who is not also generous, but 'Abdallāh b. az-Zubair gives the lie to that, because he was one of the bravest of men yet also one of the most niggardly. Similarly, the Arabs say that one never finds a poet who is not also a coward, but 'Antara b. Shaddād al-'Absī shows up the falsity of that, for he was one of the most poetically-talented of men yet also one of the bravest.

The persons with physical defects and disabilities.[26] Amongst rulers, al-Iskandar (sc. Alexander) had a twisted foot; Anūshirwān was one-eyed; Yazdajird was lame, as was also al-Ḥārith al-Aṣghar the Ghassānid king; Jadhīma al-Waḍḍāḥ was a leper; an-Nu'mān b. al-Mundhir had reddish eyes and hair; 'Abd al-Malik b. Marwān was foul-breathed; Yazīd b. 'Abd al-Malik had protuberant upper teeth and an apognathous jaw; Hishām [105 b. 'Abd al-Malik had a squint; and Marwān al-Ḥimār was fair and ruddy in complexion with blue eyes.[27]

[26] Lists of persons with physical defects occur e.g. in *Muḥabbar*, 296-305, 379-82, *Ma'ārif*, 578-95, and Ibn Rusta, 221-6, tr. 264-71; and there is mentioned a special *Kitāb dhawī'l-'āhāt* 'Book of those with physical defects' by Jāḥiẓ, not apparently extant (Pellat, *Arabica*, III [1956], 150, No. 12).

Amongst the nobles of Quraish, Abū Ṭālib was lame; Abū Jahl b. Hishām, Abū Lahab, Ziyād [b. Abīhi] and 'Adī b. Zaid all squinted; al-Aḥnaf b. Qais had a twisted foot (*kāna aḥnaf*), had teeth impacted together, had a disproportionately small head and scraggy neck, and had an assymetrical chin; Aqra' b. Ḥābis was bald (*aqra'*), hence his name; and Anas b. Mālik, may God be pleased with him, was leprous. Various people tell the story that 'Alī b. Abī Ṭālib, may God make his face noble, asked Anas about the words of the Prophet, God's prayers and peace be upon him,

[27] On the term *azraq* 'blue-eyed' and its implication of an ill omen, see Jāḥiẓ, *Ḥayawān*, v, 331, 332-3, and Fleischer, 'Studien über Dozy's *Supplément*...', in *Kleinere Schriften*, II, 554, who notes that its range of meaning includes those of 'hypocritical, deceitful', perhaps<the meaning 'sharp-sighted'. The term's pejorative meaning was probably also influenced by Qur'ān, xx, 102, 'On the day when the trumpet shall be blown, and We shall assemble the sinners on that day, bleary-eyed (?: *zurqan*)'. See now a discussion of the symbolic value of blue in Arabic by A. Morabia in SI, XXI (1964), 78, 92-4.

'O God, give aid to whomsoever aids him, and show hostility towards his enemies',[28] but Anas said, 'I have grown old [106
now and have forgotten.' 'Alī replied, 'If you are lying, may God bring down on you a hoariness that your turban will not be able to hide (sc. a hoariness which will not be merely confined to the hair)!' Hence Anas became afflicted with leprosy.

[Amongst poets and scholars,] ar-Rabī' b. Ziyād, al-Ḥārith b. Ḥilliza, Aiman b. Khuraim and al-Ḥasan b. Qaḥṭaba were leprous; 'Ubaida as-Salmānī, Ibn Sīrīn and the poet al-Kumait were deaf; and 'Ammār b. Yāsir and al-Muraqqish the Elder had the [107
ends of their noses cut off.

One of the Kufans criticised the legal scholars of Basra, alleging that al-Ḥasan [al-Baṣrī] was blue-eyed; that Qatāda [b. Du'āma] was blind; that Wāṣil [b. 'Aṭā'] was hump-backed; that 'Abd al-Wārith [b. Sa'īd] was a leper; and that Yaḥyā b. Sa'īd had a squint. Whereupon one of the Basrans riposted that 'Alqama [b. Qais] was lame; that Ibrāhīm an-Nakha'ī was one-eyed; that al-Mughīra [b. Shu'ba] became blind; that Sulaimān [b. Mihrān] had poor sight; that Masrūq [b. al-Ajda'] was gap-toothed; and that Shuraiḥ [b. al-Ḥārith] had no beard growing. Some [108
one else has said that 'Aṭā' b. Abī Rabāḥ, the Meccan legal scholar and traditionist, had a swarthy complexion, was flat-nosed, had a withered hand, was lame and one-eyed, and in the end, became totally blind.

Those who were one-eyed[29] include Abū Sufyān, who lost an eye at the siege of Ṭā'if; al-Ash'ath b. Qais, al-Mughīra b. Shu'ba and al-Ashtar an-Nakha'ī, all of whom lost an eye at the battle of the Yarmūk; Jarīr b. 'Abdallāh al-Bajalī, who lost an eye at Hamadhān whilst acting as governor there for 'Uthmān; 'Adī b. Ḥātim aṭ-Ṭā'ī and 'Utba b. Abī Sufyān, who each lost an eye at the battle of the Camel; al-Mukhtār b. Abī 'Ubaid, whom [109
'Ubaidallāh b. Ziyād hit in the face with a whip and put out one of his eyes; and the poets Ibn Aḥmar and Ibn Muqbil and [the philologist] al-Khalīl b. Aḥmad.

The great commanders who were one-eyed include al-Aḥnaf b. Qais, al-Mughīra b. Shu'ba, al-Muhallab b. Abī Ṣufra, Ṭāhir b. al-Ḥusain and 'Amr b. al-Laith. [110

Those who became blind in both eyes[30] include Abū Quḥāfa, the father of Abū Bakr the Veracious, may God be pleased with him; Abū Sufyān b. al-Ḥārith b. 'Abd al-Muṭṭalib; al-Barā' b. 'Āzib; Jābir b. 'Abdallāh al-Anṣārī, may God be pleased with him; Ḥassān b. Thābit al-Anṣārī; Abū Sufyān b. Ḥarb; 'Aqīl b.

[28] A reference to the Prophet's alleged words at Ghadīr Khumm, outside Medina, on his return from the Farewell Pilgrimage of 10/632, when, according to the Shī'a, Muḥammad linked 'Alī to himself in brotherhood; the words here quoted are adduced to show 'Alī's especially close relationship to the Prophet, and the day in question (13th Dhū'l-Ḥijja) is still an important Shī'ī festival. The actual tradition is quoted several times in Aḥmad b. Ḥanbal's *Musnad* and also in Ibn Māja's *Sunan*; cf. D. M. Donaldson, *The Shi'ite religion* (London 1933), 1ff. (I am grateful for this information to Emeritus Professor James Robson.)

[29] Cf. *Ma'ārif*, 586-7, Ibn Rusta, 224, tr. 268. Two works by Ṣalāḥ ad-Dīn al-Khalīl b. Aibak aṣ-Ṣafadī are extant, the first on the one-eyed, the *Kitāb ash-shu'ūr bi'l-'ūr*, and the second on the fully-blind, the *Nakt al-himyān fī nukat al-'umyān*; see on them, Goldziher (who first attributed them correctly to their author), 'Beiträge zur Geschichte der Sprachgelehrsamkeit bei den Arabern. I' SBWAW, LXVII (1871), 233ff., and Brockelmann, GAL, II, 40, Suppl. II, 28.

[30] Cf. *Ma'ārif*, 587-9, Ibn Rusta, 224, tr. 269. The frequency of ophthalmia and blindness amongst Quraish (probably from the dry and dusty conditions in Mecca), and especially amongst the house of al-'Abbās, was such that it became regarded as a sign of noble lineage cf. Lammens, *Le Califat de Yazîd Ier*, 228, and *idem*, *Le berceau de l'Islam*, 201.

Abī Ṭālib; al-ʿAbbās b. ʿAbd al-Muṭṭalib and his son ʿAbdallāh; Abū Bakr b. ʿAbd ar-Raḥmān b. al-Ḥārith b. Hishām; al- [111 Qāsim b. Muḥammad b. Abī Bakr aṣ-Ṣiddīq and Saʿd b. Abī Waqqāṣ, who both lost their sight towards the end of their lives; and Bashshār b. Burd al-Muraʿʿath.

Those rulers who had their eyes put out include Hurmuz b. Anūshirwān; [the Caliphs] al-Qāhir, al-Muttaqī and al-Mustakfī; Ṣamṣām ad-Daula Abū Kālījār b. Fanā-Khusrau; and Abū'l-Ḥārith Manṣūr b. Nūḥ b. Manṣūr b. Nūḥ.

Those who were inordinately tall[31] include ʿUmar b. al-Khaṭṭāb, may God be pleased with him, who gave the appearance of being mounted with the rest of the people walking by his side; ʿAdī b. Ḥātim and Jarīr b. ʿAbdallāh al-Bajalī, whose feet, when they rode, almost slithered along the ground; Qais b. Saʿd b. ʿUbāda [112 who was extremely tall and corpulent; and ʿUbaidallāh b. Ziyād, may God curse him, for whenever people saw him walking, they thought because of his tallness that he must be mounted. ʿAlī b. ʿAbdallāh b. al-ʿAbbās was tall and handsome to such a degree that many people marvelled at his height. In this connection, an old man once remarked, 'Glory to God! How small people are getting these days! I have in the past seen al-ʿAbbās circumambulating the Kaʿba as if he were a white-coloured tent!' This was repeated to ʿAlī, who commented, 'I come up to my father's shoulders, and he came up to my grandfather's shoulder.' It is further related that the Ghassānid king Jabala b. al-Aiham was twelve spans in height.

Those who were especially short[32] include ʿAbdallāh b. Masʿūd, may God be pleased with him, who was so short that people sitting down almost came up to the same height as him standing. Also, Ibrāhīm b. ʿAbd ar-Raḥmān b. ʿAuf, who was short and stumpy; he married Sukaina bint al-Ḥusain b. ʿAlī, but she did not like him, so got the marriage annulled. Al-Ḥasan al- [113 Baṣrī,[33] may God be pleased with him, is reputed to have said that Pharaoh was only a cubit in height. [Amongst the poets,] al-Ḥuṭaiʾa was exceedingly short, hence his nickname *al-Ḥuṭaiʾa* 'the dwarf',[34] and Dhū'r-Rumma and Kuthayyir were also very short. Thābit b. Sinān [aṣ-Ṣābiʾ][35] records in his *History* that because the Vizier Abū Jaʿfar Muḥammad b. al-Qāsim was so short, they were obliged to reduce the height of the Caliphal throne by the span of four fingers' breadth. The Vizier al-Abbās b. al-Ḥasan [al-Jarjarāʾī][36] was extremely short, and it was said of him (metre *Basīṭ*): *Do not look at al-ʿAbbās with his* [114

[31] Cf. the section in *Muḥabbar*, 233-4, 'Those who used to ride on stout horses but whose toes nevertheless trailed on the ground'; *Maʿārif*, 592-3; and Ibn Rusta, 225-6, tr. 269-70. Much of Thaʿālibī's section appears also in Masʿūdī, *Murūj*, VIII, 324.

[32] Cf. *Maʿārif*, 594, Ibn Rusta, 226, tr. 271.

[33] Al-Ḥasan b. Abī'l-Ḥasan al-Baṣrī, by origin a *maulā* from Lower Iraq, was famed as a traditionist, ascetic and proto-Ṣūfī; d. 110/728.

[34] Cf. Barbier de Meynard, 'Surnoms et sobriquets dans la littérature arabe', JA, Ser. 10, Vol. IX, 366-7, and on al-Ḥuṭaiʾa's notorious ugliness, Goldziher, EI[1] s.v.

[35] Thābit b. Sinān, uncle of Hilāl b. al-Muḥassin and author of a history dealing with the years between the accession of al-Muqtadir in 295/908 and his own death in 365/976; this work is no longer extant, but was extensively utilised by Miskawaih for his own chronicle, the *Tajārib al-umam* (cf. Margoliouth, *Lectures on Arabic historians*, 136).

[36] Sc. the Vizier of al-Muktafī nicknamed *Karb ad-Dawā*', see above, p. 62.

short stature in mind, but consider the excellence and nobility which he has raised up![37] | *Indeed, the smallest of the stars of the night appears to the beholder as the highest and most remote in the sky.*

Those who were carried in their mothers' wombs longer than the normal gestation period[38] include aḍ-Ḍaḥḥāk b. Muzāḥim, who was born after sixteen months; Shu'ba [b. al-Ḥajjāj b. Ward], born after two years; Harim b. Ḥayyān, carried in the womb for four years, hence his name Harim 'the aged one'; Muḥammad b. 'Ajlān, in the womb for more than three years, as was also Mālik b. Anas. Al-Wāqidī relates that he heard the women of the family of al-Jaḥḥāf, the descendants of Zaid b. al-Khaṭṭāb, saying that none of them ever carried a child for less than thirty months. [115

[Those who were born prematurely][39] include 'Abd al-Malik b. Marwān, ['Āmir b. 'Abdallāh] ash-Sha'bī and Jarīr, all born at seven months.

The Caliphs who were bald[40] include 'Umar, 'Uthmān, 'Alī, Marwān and 'Umar b. 'Abd al-'Azīz; but after him, baldness did not occur amongst the Caliphs.

An unparalleled case of five brothers whose graves lay as far apart from each other as they could possibly be. These were al-'Abbās b. 'Abd al-Muṭṭalib's children: 'Abdallāh was buried at Ṭā'if, 'Ubaidallāh at Medina, al-Faḍl in Syria, Qutham at Samarqand[41] and Ma'bad in Ifrīqiyya. No other case is [116 known of two Caliphs, father and son, whose graves were as far apart as those of ar-Rashīd and al-Ma'mūn, buried at Ṭūs and Tarsus respectively. It was said concerning them (metre *Khafīf*): *They left him in the two open spaces at Tarsus, just as they had left his father at Ṭūs.*[42]

The dominant traits of the Umayyad rulers and the curious fact that their subjects imitated their rulers' inclinations.[43] Al-Haitham b. 'Adī related:

'Abd al-Malik b. Marwān's dominant trait was a love of poetry, and during his reign, people used to recite poetry to each other, used to instruct each other in the stories of the poets and used to be much occupied with poetry.

[37] Reading with AS, *shādā*, for the *sādā* of J. The author of the lines is al-Buḥturī.

[38] Cf. *Ma'ārif*, 594-5, and Ibn Rusta, 226-7, tr. 271-2.

[39] Cf. *Ma'ārif*, 595, and Ibn Rusta, 227, tr. 272.

[40] Cf. *Ma'ārif*, 585, and Ibn Rusta, 223, tr. 267. As with blindness, the frequency of baldness amongst the early Caliphs became regarded as a sign of nobility; see Lammens, *Le Califat de Yazîd Ier*, 43.

[41] According to Balādhurī, *Futūḥ al-buldān*, 402, 'Abdallāh b. al-'Abbās exclaimed when he heard the news of his brother's death in remote Central Asia, 'How great a distance between his birthplace (sc. in the Ḥijāz) and his grave!' In the time of the traveller Ibn Baṭṭūṭa (8th/14th century), Qutham's tomb at Samarqand still had as its custodian (*nāẓir*) an Abbasid, the great-great-grandson of the penultimate Baghdad Caliph, al-Mustanṣir (*Riḥla*, ed. Defrémery and Sanguinetti [Paris 1853-9], III, 54).

[42] According to Mas'ūdī, *Murūj*, VII, 101-2, the poet was Abū Sa'īd al-Makhzūmī.

[43] Enumerations and discussions of these traits appear in several works; see, for example, Ibn Tiqtaqā, *Kitāb al-Fakhrī* (Cairo 1317/1899), 114, tr. C. E. J. Whitting (London 1947), 123. One of the earliest extant discussions is in a brief work by the historian and geographer Ibn Wāḍiḥ or al-Ya'qūbī (d. ?292/905), called *Mushākalat an-nās li-zamānihim* 'The adaptation of men to their time', ed. W. Millward (Beirut 1962), where the Umayyads are dealt with on pp. 16-21. Furthermore, Ya'qūbī in his *Ta'rīkh* shows a considerable interest in the question of the adaptation of people to the interests of their rulers, and Millward also notes that in the *Mushākala* (see his Introd., 5) he appears as an early writer with an interest in the *awā'il*. Ya'qūbī names no sources in the *Mushākala*, but his information goes back, as does that of Tha'ālibī's here, to the Iraqi historian al-Haitham b. 'Adī (d. 193/807), amongst whose works is enumerated a *Ta'rīkh al-'Ajam wa Banī Umayya*.

Al-Walīd b. 'Abd al-Malik's dominant trait was a love of building, the construction of irrigation works and other projects, and the acquisition of estates. During his reign, people used to talk at length about the techniques of building, used to urge others to lay down foundations and get buildings erected, and used avidly to amass estates and properties.

Sulaimān b. 'Abd al-Malik's dominant trait was a love of food and women, and in his time people used to describe various fancy dishes of food and discuss the choicest and rarest ones. They would recount with eagerness and profuseness stories about women, and would ask each other about their marriage relations with their free wives and the sexual enjoyment which they derived from their slave concubines, and would vie with each other in sexual indulgence. [117

'Umar b. 'Abd al-'Azīz's dominant trait was a love of the Qur'ān, of the ritual prayers and of fasting. In his time, friends used to meet each other and ask, 'What portion of the Qur'ān are you reading tonight?' or 'How much of the Qur'ān do you know by heart? And when will you finish it?' or 'How many times did you pray yesterday, and did you pray more frequently in the mosque than at home?' or 'Are you fasting just now? And how much of the month are you fasting for?'

Yazīd b. 'Abd al-Malik used to love horses and singing girls. People used to vie with each other in picking out the best of these, and they would seek to ingratiate themselves with the Caliph by selecting the finest horses or the most beautiful singing girls and presenting them to him.

Hishām b. 'Abd al-Malik used to love clothes and delicate fabrics. Hence people used to compete with each other in trafficking in these garments; they would seek to acquire in trade the various types of fabrics and would describe to each other the different varieties of them.

Al-Walīd b. Yazīd was a devotee of pleasure, wine and music; during his reign, people used to busy themselves with objects of sport and pleasure, they would indulge themselves with date wine and would chant and sing poetry.

The person who remarked that people follow the religion of their rulers and that the ruling authority is like a market to which everything that has a sale is brought, spoke very truly.[44]

The Abbasid Caliphs and the wealth which they amassed.[45] It is said that amongst the Abbasids, there was one who was the opening of the dynasty, another who was the mid-point and a

[44] This aphorism occurs also in Ghazālī's *Naṣīḥat al-mulūk*, tr. F. R. C. Bagley, *Ghazālī's book of counsel for kings* (London 1964), 61.

[45] There is considerable detail on the wealth left by the Caliphs in Qāḍī Ibn az-Zubair's *Kitāb adh-dhakhā'ir wa't-tuḥaf*, ed. M. Ḥamīdallāh (Kuwait 1959), 213ff., section on outstanding inheritances.

third who was the closing one, these being al-Manṣūr, al-Ma'mūn and al-Mu'taḍid respectively. It used also to be said that [118
the wealth amassed by as-Saffāḥ, al-Manṣūr, al-Mahdī and ar-Rashīd was scattered by al-Amīn; that the wealth amassed by al-Ma'mūn, al-Mu'taṣim and al-Wāthiq was scattered by al-Mutawakkil; and that the wealth amassed by al-Muntaṣir, al-Mu'tazz, al-Muhtadī, al-Mu'tamid, al-Mu'taḍid and al-Muktafī was scattered by al-Muqtadir.

Al-Manṣūr is said to have left at his death 950 million dirhams. Aṣ-Ṣūlī relates in his *Kitāb al-aurāq* 'Book of the written sheets' that ar-Rashīd left 100 million dinars.[46] Others, however, say that he left behind him such an amount as had never before in the history of this world been known, in that his estate comprised furnishings and furniture, gold and silver coins, jewels and riding beasts, as well as estates and immovable property, amounting in all to 125 million dinars.

According to Ibrāhīm b. Nūḥ,[47] al-Muktafī left, out of what his predecessor al-Mu'taḍid had amassed, 100 million dinars. This comprised 20 million dinars' worth of gold and silver coinage and vessels made from precious metals; 20 million dinars' worth of jewels, perfumes, aromatic substances, etc.; 20 million dinars' worth of clothing, carpets and hangings; 20 million dinars' worth of horses, weapons and military slaves; and 20 million dinars' worth of estates, immovables and properties. [119

Included in the property left behind by al-Muktafī[48] and added up for valuation, were 63,000 Khurāsānī, Marvazī and Shu'aibī[49] garments; 8,000 pieces of cloth for wrapping round the body as garments; 13,000 Marvazī turbans; four million garments of bleached linen, not counting the white cotton ones; 1,800 sets of robes of particoloured Yemenī and other types of cloth woven with gold thread; and 18,000 canes' full of the superfine muslin used as lining material, which is imported from Kirmān inside the hollow tubes of the Giant Reed,[50] the like of which alone was considered suitable for this purpose. (When these tubes came to be sold[51] during Ibn Muqla's Vizierate, at a time when the treasury was completely empty, they were found thrown aside in one of the store rooms. Financial necessity was now so pressing that even these had to be sold, and they were brought out and disposed of. Each tube fetched two dinars, yielding a total of 36,000 dinars.) Furthermore, when the large-sized Armenian under-carpets and the medium-sized ones were counted up in the carpet storehouse, it was found that there were 18,000 under-

[46] According to Abyārī and Ṣairafī, this item of information does not occur in the three fragments of the *Kitāb al-aurāq* published by Heyworth-Dunne.

[47] I have not been able to trace this man.

[48] Both J and AS have here 'al-Mustakfī (reigned 333-4/944-6), but the remainder of the section only makes sense chronologically if we read here 'al-Muktafī'. This section therefore follows on from the previous one and describes in more detail the wealth left by al-Muktafī (d. 289/902), and the passage on the sale of the tubes is a parenthesis relating to the ensuing reign of al-Muqtadir, when the Caliphate fell into dire financial difficulties. Ibn Muqla served as al-Muqtadir's Vizier 316-18/928-31.

[49] Dozy, *Supplément*, s.v. corrects the *Sha'bī* of the texts to *Shu'aibī*.

[50] *Qaṣab fārisī* = *Arundo donax*.

[51] Reading with AS *bī'at* for the *yub'ath* of J.

carpets all told. It is said that all this lot was either sold or stolen or used up, until the moment arrived when, towards the end of al-Muqtadir's reign, a mattress or such-like was sought for the Caliph to sit down on, but none could be found. [120

Two feasts given in Islamic times and unrivalled for their splendour and magnificence.[52] The feast given by al-Ḥasan b. Sahl when al-Ma'mūn consummated his marriage with al-Ḥasan's daughter Būrān, acquired the title of 'the feast *par excellence* of Islamic times', until the time of the feast at Buzurgvār came along, when people said that it equalled al-Ḥasan's one. Indeed, some people aver that the feast at Buzurgvār was *the* feast of Islamic times, and that there were none before or after it to equal it, except for what was reported of the celebration when al-Ma'mūn consummated his marriage with Būrān.

The dazzling splendour, height of nobility and munificent scale which al-Ḥasan attained in this feast reached such a peak that he entertained al-Ma'mūn and all his military commanders and courtiers at Fam aṣ-Ṣilḥ[53] for forty days, and he provided a spectacle of an unusualness and lavishness never before seen. [121

Al-Mubarrad relates that he heard al-Ḥasan b. Rajā'[54] say: 'We used to have on our pay-roll at the time of al-Ma'mūn's stay with al-Ḥasan b. Sahl, 36,000 boatmen. One day, we ran out of wood for the fires, so we lit under the cooking-pots canvas soaked in olive oil.'

When the night appointed for the consummation approached and Būrān was for the first time brought face-to-face with her husband, they laid down in readiness for the celebrations a mat embroidered with gold, and they brought in a wickerwork basket encrusted with jewels and containing large pearls. These pearls were scattered amongst the women present, who included Zubaida and ar-Rashīd's daughter, Ḥamdūna, but none of the ladies moved forward to touch any of the pearls. Hence al-Ma'mūn called out, 'Show your respect and your regard[55] to Abū Muḥammad (sc. al-Ḥasan b. Sahl)!' So they all stretched forth their hands and took a pearl, leaving the rest of them gleaming on the gold-embroidered mat. Al-Ma'mūn exclaimed, 'What a fine poet is al-Ḥasan b. Hāni' (sc. Abū Nuwās)! It is just as if he were present at this very moment when he said (metre *Basīṭ*): *As if its bubbles, great and small, were a gravel of pearls dashed on an earth of gold.*

In the hall appointed for the celebration were set candles of ambergris, amounting to 200 *riṭl*s in weight. Al-Ma'mūn cried

[52] Tha'ālibī's information on these two feasts appears also in a similar form in his *Thimār al-qulūb*, 130-1, s.v. 'Da'wat al-Islām'.

[53] Yāqūt, *Mu'jam al-buldān*, IV, 276, describes Fam aṣ-Ṣilḥ as a river channel above Wāsiṭ, where al-Ḥasan had his palace; it was formerly a populous district, but in Yāqūt's time was largely depopulated. According to Ṭabarī, III, 1081, al-Ḥasan's *mu'askar* (=military base, encampment) was there.

[54] Al-Ḥasan b. Rajā' b. Abī'ḍ-Ḍaḥḥāk, famous as a secretary in the time of al-Ma'mūn, was the brother-in-law of al-Faḍl b. Sahl; see his biography (said to be derived from aṣ-Ṣūlī's *Kitāb al-akhbār al-manthūra*) in Ibn al-Abbār, *I'tāb al-kuttāb*, 168-70.

[55] Following the emendation to the texts proposed by Defrémery of *akrimnahu* for *akrimnahā* (JA, Ser. 6, Vol. x [July-Dec. 1867], 347).

out in discomfort at the smoke from them, so they brought in for him an ordinary tallow candle, and the whole of the nights, as long as he stayed with al-Ḥasan, were in this way made as bright as day. When it was the turn of al-Ma'mūn's military commanders to be entertained, pieces of paper, each with the name of an estate written on it, were scattered amongst them. Whoever got hold of one of these papers, al-Ḥasan transferred to him the ownership of the estate in question.

Altogether, al-Ḥasan is said to have spent four million dinars on this celebration. When al-Ma'mūn decided to depart, [122
he presented al-Ḥasan with a million dinars and granted him the fiscal rights over aṣ-Ṣilḥ; he also reproached him for expending so much effort and trouble and for incurring so much expense. Al-Ḥasan replied, 'O Commander of the Faithful, do you think that all this comes out of Sahl's money? By God, it is just your own money which is now being given back to you; I only wanted God to grant you outstanding prosperity for the rest of your days and to grant you outstanding happiness in your marriage, just as He has given you a superior position over all mankind.'[56]

The second great feast was that of Buzurgvār[57] when al-Mutawakkil celebrated the circumcision of his son al-Mu'tazz.

One of the episodes in the course of this was that after the great commanders and nobles had finished eating, al-Mutawakkil sat down, and he caused to be set down in front of himself jewel-encrusted golden stands on which were heaped pieces of ambergris, amber and musk moulded into shapes and figures, and these stands were placed stretched out in a row. The great commanders, courtiers and holders of high official positions were gathered round. There were placed before them large trays of gold set with all kinds of jewels on both surfaces. Between the two rows was a space. The attendants brought in palm-leaf baskets covered over with leather sheets and filled with dirhams and dinars in equal proportions; these were now poured into the space until they became piled high above the level of the trays. Those present were told to drink, and then those who had drunk were each to draw out three handfuls, with their fists gripping as much as they could, from the coins poured from the baskets. Whenever one place became empty, more coins were poured out of the baskets to refill it just as it was before. Slave boys stood at the end of the [123
assembled gathering, crying out, 'The Commander of the Faithful bids all of you to take as much as you like!' So everyone there stretched forth his hands and took some of the money. They

56 This feast is described in several sources as the ultimate in magnificence, e.g. in Ṭabarī, III, 1081-5, year 210/825-6; in Shābushtī, *Kitāb ad-diyārāt*, tr. in Sachau, APAW (1919), No. 10, pp. 32-4; in Qāḍī Ibn az-Zubair's *Kitāb adh-dhakhā'ir wa't-tuḥaf*, 98-101; and in Niẓāmī 'Arūḍī Samarqandī, *Chahār maqāla*, ed. Qazwīnī and Mu'īn (Tehran 1333/1954), 32-6, E. G. Browne's revised translation (London 1921), 21-3.

57 The exact form of this name is uncertain. Yāqūt, *Mu'jam al-buldān*, I, 410, vocalises it as Bazkuwār and says that it was a building forming part of al-Mutawakkil's palace at Sāmarrā. This identification has been confirmed by the excavations of Herzfeld at Manqūr, three miles to the south of Sāmarrā; cf. K. A. C. Creswell, *Early Muslim architecture: Umayyads, early 'Abbāsids and Ṭūlūnids* (Oxford 1932-40), II, 265-70, who vocalises the name as Balkuwārā.

became weighted down with all that they had taken, so would go out and pass the money over to their slave boys and then return to their places. When the entertainment came to an end, 1,000 robes of honour were distributed amongst those present; they were given 1,000 mounts to depart on, each with gold and silver trappings; and 1,000 slaves were freed.[58] [124

Sons born of slave mothers. Al-Jāḥiẓ says that at one time, people had no great liking for slave concubines, but when they saw al-Qāsim b. Muḥammad b. Abī Bakr, Sālim b. 'Abdallāh b. 'Umar and 'Alī b. al-Ḥusain b. 'Alī, who were the sons of slave mothers and yet had no peers either in Medina or in the Ḥijāz or in Iraq or anywhere in the world, they became enthusiastic about concubines.[59] Mu'āwiya used to say that if it were not for the fact that he had already exacted from the people an oath of allegiance to [his son] Yazīd, he would have left the choice to an electoral council (*shūrā*) of al-Qāsim and Muḥammad.[60] Amongst the youths of the Marwānid family, there was none comparable with 'Abd al-Malik b. 'Umar b. 'Abd al-'Azīz for ascetic piety, eloquence and love of righteousness, and he had a slave mother. Similarly, there was no Marwānid who was more courageous, better educated, possessed of sounder judgement, more gifted with all the virtues,[61] more successful as a military conqueror or having a more upright and faithful character than Maslama b. 'Abd al-Malik, and he had a slave mother.[62] But it is sufficient in this connection to cite Ishmael the son of Abraham, whose mother Hagar was a slave.

Al-Jāḥiẓ goes on to say that four of the Imāms descended from al-Ḥusain were born of slave mothers, sc. 'Alī [Zain al-'Ābidīn] b. al-Ḥusain, Mūsā [al-Kāẓim] b. Ja'far [aṣ-Ṣādiq], 'Alī [ar-Riḍā] b. Mūsā and Muḥammad [al-Jawād] b. 'Alī b. [125 Mūsā, and these are the equivalents of Caliphs to the Shī'a.[63] As for the Abbasids, who are the Caliphs of the Sunnī majority, most of them have been the sons of slave mothers.

The present author says: the only Abbasid Caliphs with free mothers were as-Saffāḥ, born of Raiṭa bint al-Ḥārith b. Ka'b; al-

[58] This feast is described by Shābushtī in Sachau, *op. cit.*, 30-2. Both this account and the one of al-Ḥasan b. Sahl's feast occur in Shābushtī's excursus to his section on the Dair as-Sūsī on the west bank of the Tigris in the district of al-Qādisiyya of Sāmarrā.

[59] These three are similarly cited in Mubarrad's section on 'Noble people born of slave mothers', in *al-Kāmil* (Cairo 1376/1956), II, 120.

[60] It is not clear which Muḥammad is meant. It is chronologically possible that Muḥammad b. 'Alī b. al-Ḥusain, called al-Bāqir, is meant, but according to Ibn Qutaiba, *Ma'ārif*, 215, this man's mother was a free woman, the daughter of al-Ḥasan b. 'Alī. The suggestion of Abyārī and Ṣairafī, that this was Muḥammad b. 'Alī b. Mūsā, called al-Jawād (text, 124 n. 2), is chronologically impossible.

[61] *Ajma'*, possibly with the meaning 'more assiduous in attendance at the congregational worship, *jamā'a*'.

[62] Amongst the Umayyads, all, with the possible exception of Mu'āwiya, seem to have had liaisons with slave concubines, but the offspring of these generally remained in the background, and not until the last days of the dynasty did one of them actually achieve the throne (see above, p. 73, n. 5). Here, therefore, lies the reason for the exclusion of Maslama from the succession in favour of his three less capable brothers and his cousin 'Umar b. 'Abd al-'Azīz. See the detailed discussion in Lammens, *Le Califat de Yazîd Ier*, 82-7.

[63] The descendants of 'Alī seem early to have contracted marriages with slaves and clients; see *ibid.*, 83-4.

Mahdī, born of Umm Mūsā bint Manṣūr b. 'Abdallāh; and
al-Amīn, born of Zubaida bint Ja'far b. Abī Ja'far. In regard to all
the rest, just note the following: al-Manṣūr's mother was a slave
called Salāma; the mother of Mūsā and Hārūn was a slave called
al-Khaizurān; al-Ma'mūn's mother was one called Marājil; al-
Mu'taṣim's, one called Mārida; al-Wāthiq's, one called Qarāṭīs;
al-Mutawakkil's, one called Shujā'; al-Muntaṣir's, one called
Ḥabashiyya; al-Mu'tazz's, one called Qabīḥa; al-Musta'īn's, one
called Mukhāriq; al-Muhtadī's, one called Farda; al- [126
Mu'tamid's, one called Qainān; al-Mu'taḍid's, one called Ḍirār;
al-Muktafī's, one called Jījak[64]; al-Muqtadir's, one called Shaghib;
al-Qāhir's, one called Qaina; ar-Rāḍī's, one called Ẓalūm; al-
Muttaqī's, one called Zuhra; al-Mustakfī's, one called Amlaḥ
an-Nās; al-Muṭī''s, one called Mash'ala; aṭ-Ṭā'i''s, one called
Hazār; and al-Qādir's, one called Dimna.[65] [127

The trades and crafts of prominent men.[66] Abū Ṭālib traded in
perfume; Abū Bakr, 'Uthmān, Ṭalḥa and 'Abd ar-Raḥmān b. 'Auf
traded in cotton and linen cloths; Sa'd b. Abī Waqqāṣ made
arrows; al-'Awwām, father of az-Zubair, dealt in wheat; az-
Zubair, 'Amr b. al-'Āṣ and 'Āmir b. Kuraiz were butchers; al-
Walīd b. al-Mughīra and Abū Jahl's brother al-'Āṣ b. Hishām
were blacksmiths; 'Uqba b. Abī Mu'aiṭ was a wine-seller; Abū
Sufyān traded in olive oil and hides; 'Utba b. Abī Waqqāṣ, [128
Sa'd's brother, was a carpenter; Umayya b. Khalaf dealt in stone
cooking-pots; 'Abdallāh b. Jud'ān was a slave-dealer, hiring out
slave girls as prostitutes and selling their children; al-'Āṣ b.
Wā'il treated sick horses and camels; and an-Naḍr b. al-Ḥārith
b. Kalada and Marwān's father al-Ḥakam b. Abī'l-'Āṣ played the
lute and sang.

According to al-Madā'inī,[67] Yazīd b. al-Muhallab laid out a garden at his residence in Merv, but when Qutaiba [b. Muslim] became governor there, he turned it over to his camels. The Marzbān of Merv remonstrated with him, saying that Yazīd used to have it as a garden, but he had reduced it to a pasture ground for his camels; Qutaiba retorted that it was because his own father had been a camel-driver, whereas Yazīd's father had been a gardener.

Muḥammad b. Sīrīn was a dealer in cotton and linen cloths;
Mujammi' az-Zāhid was a weaver; Ayyūb as-Sikhtiyānī [129
traded in tanned goatskins (*julūd as-sikhtiyān*), hence his name;
al-Musayyib, father of Sa'īd b. al-Musayyib, was an olive-oil
dealer; Abū Ḥanīfa dealt in silks; and Mālik b. Dīnār was a

[64] For this name, AS has the meaningless *J.n.j.k. Jījak* is of course Turkish *chichek* 'flower'.

[65] In the chronological list of the Abbasid Caliphs in *Muḥabbar*, 33-46, the mothers of the Caliphs and their ethnic origins are carefully detailed, in accordance with Muḥammad b. Ḥabīb's well-known interest in female line ancestry.

[66] There are similar sections in *Ma'ārif*, 575-7, and Ibn Rusta, 214-16, tr. 254-6. On Muslim attitudes towards the practitioners of trades and crafts, see R. Brunschvig, 'Métiers vils en Islam', SI, XVI (1962), 41-60; Lammens accordingly thought that the attribution to the members of noble Meccan families of such ignoble trades as those of butcher or blacksmith must be a later fabrication of the anti-Arab Shu'ūbiyya (*L'Arabie occidentale avant l'Hégire* [Beirut 1928], 28-9).

[67] Sc. the historian of Basra, d. 225/840, whose historical traditions and narratives were much used by later authors (cf. Margoliouth, *Lectures on Arabic historians*, 85-90).

copyist, who made his living by transcribing Qur'āns. Wāṣil b. 'Aṭā' was a spinner; it is said that he used to go to the premises of one of his freedmen and sit amongst the spinners in order to learn about the circumstances of women who were keeping up appearances but really living in poverty (*al-mastūrāt*),[68] and he used to give these women financial allowances.[69] It is also related that Abū Salama al-Khallāl used to frequent the company of the scabbard-makers (*al-khallālūn*) of Kufa, and thus acquired his name.[70]

[68] *Al-mastūrāt, ahl as-sitr* = those who are poor but conceal their poverty, i.e. something like our modern distressed gentlefolk; al-Mubarrad calls them *al-muta'affifāt* 'those who live restrained, modest lives'.

[69] It is for this second reason, his frequenting of the spinners' quarter, that Wāṣil got his name, according to Jāḥiẓ, *al-Bayān wa't-tabyīn*, I, 32-4, quoting his own *Kitāb al-asmā' wa'l-kunā*, and to al-Mubarrad, *al-Kāmil*, III, 192.

[70] Differing explanations are given for the name. According to Jahshiyārī, 55, Abū Salama had made scabbards (*khilal*); according to Ibn Khallikān, tr. I, 468, he had lived in the quarter of the vinegar-makers, *Khallālūn* (<*khall* 'vinegar'), and Sourdel, *Le vizirat 'Abbāside*, I, 65, n. 1, regards this as the more probable.

Chapter Nine.

Concerning interesting and entertaining pieces of information about various unusual happenings and strange coincidences.

A king who became ruler whilst still in his mother's womb. The only case known is that of Shāpūr Dhū'l-Aktāf. His father Hurmuz died without leaving any male heir to succeed him. The great officials and military commanders were perturbed about this, but they made enquiries about the dead ruler's wives and learnt that one of them was pregnant. They all rejoiced at this, and they laid the crown on that wife's abdomen, agreeing to raise to the throne whatever child was in her womb. They waited eagerly until she gave birth to a boy; he was named Shāpūr Dhū'l-Aktāf and his story is well known.[1]

A king of the Islamic period who reigned for forty years. The only king amongst the great rulers of the Islamic period who reigned this long was Mu'āwiya, who was for twenty years an Amīr and then a Caliph for a further twenty years. It is further said that Naṣr b. Aḥmad the Elder ruled in Bukhārā and the rest of Transoxania for forty years. Naṣr b. Aḥmad b. Ismā'īl [131 [the Younger] certainly ruled Khurāsān and Transoxania for thirty-one years.[2] I personally have been informed that Abū 'Abdallāh Muḥammad b. Aḥmad b. 'Irāq's tenure of power in Khwārazm exceeded fifty years.[3]

A Caliph who rode the horses of the postal and intelligence system (*Barīd*). No Caliph is known ever to have done this except for al-Hādī. He was away in Gurgān when al-Mahdī died at Māsapadhān. Ar-Rashīd wrote to him telling him the news and offering him his allegiance as successor to the throne, sending an envoy with [the Caliphal insignia of the Prophet's] ring, sceptre and cloak. The envoy took eight days to reach Gurgān, and Mūsā [al-Hādī] reached Baghdad by means of the *Barīd* just thirteen

[1] This unusual manner of succession is noted by Muḥammad b. Ḥabīb in *Muḥabbar*, 362, and the full story appears in Ibn Qutaiba, *Ma'ārif*, 656.

[2] These two Sāmānid Amīrs reigned 250-79/854-92 and 301-31/914-43 respectively.

[3] This ruler is listed by al-Bīrūnī as the last of the line of twenty-two Afrīghid Khwārazm-Shāhs of Kāth, who were overthrown in 385/995 by the Ma'mūnids of Gurgānj; cf. Sachau, 'Zur Geschichte und Chronologie von Khwârazm', SBWAW, LXXIII (1873), 500-3, LXXIV (1873), 291.

days after al-Mahdī's death. Salm b. 'Amr said[4] (metre *Sarī'*):
When the noblest of the house of Hāshim succeeded in Gurgān to the Vicegerency of God,
He flew across the land and traversed it with the speed of Solomon, the one who could command the wind.
The wind was brought under control for this very purpose, whilst he sped onwards on a swift, obedient mount. [132

A Caliph who was hailed on his accession by his paternal uncle, his father's paternal uncle and his grandfather's paternal uncle. This was ar-Rashīd, who was hailed by his paternal uncle, Sulaimān b. al-Manṣūr; then by al-'Abbās b. Muḥammad, his father al-Mahdī's paternal uncle; and then by 'Abd aṣ-Ṣamad b. 'Alī, the paternal uncle of his grandfather Abū Ja'far al-Manṣūr.

A Caliph who was hailed on his accession by seven of his relatives, all the sons of Caliphs. This was al-Mutawakkil, who was hailed by Muḥammad b. al-Wāthiq, Aḥmad b. al-Mu'taṣim, Mūsā b. al-Ma'mūn, 'Abdallāh b. al-Amīn, Abū Aḥmad b. ar-Rashīd, al-'Abbās b. al-Hādī and Manṣūr b. al-Mahdī.

A Caliph who kissed the hand of a Caliph in homage and then afterwards had his own hand kissed in homage by the latter. This was al-Mu'taṣim bi'llāh. He halted in the presence of Ibrāhīm b. al-Mahdī at one point during the latter's Caliphate,[5] dismounted and kissed his hand in homage. He brought forward his son Hārūn to kiss Ibrāhīm's hand and said, 'O commander of the Faithful, Hārūn, my son, is your servant!' At this, Ibrāhīm ordered a present of 10,000 dirhams to be given to Hārūn. Subsequently, al-Mu'taṣim was proclaimed Caliph, and Ibrāhīm halted before him, and at the very same spot went forward on foot and kissed al-Mu'taṣim's hand in homage. Exclaiming, 'O Commander of the Faithful, this is my son Hibatallāh' ', he pushed the latter forward to kiss al-Mu'taṣim's hand. At this, al-Mu'taṣim likewise ordered a present of 10,000 dirhams to be given to Hibatallāh.

Al-Mu'taṣim later recounted this incident to 'Alī b. al-Junaid,[6] who reproached him, saying, 'By God, you have acted unbecomingly here, O Commander of the Faithful!' Al-Mu'taṣim [133 protested, 'What do you mean? How is this?' 'Alī replied, 'Ibrāhīm bestowed 10,000 dirhams on Hārūn at a time when he had no territories in his possession other than the city of Baghdad, and you have the whole world under your control!' Al-Mu'taṣim admitted that he was right, and decreed that Hibatallāh should be given 10,000 dinars.

4 Poet of Basra and then of Baghdad in the reigns of al-Mahdī, al-Hādī and ar-Rashīd. He was a pupil of Bashshār b. Burd and was considered by Jāḥiẓ to be one of the naturally gifted *muwallad* poets; cf. *al-Bayān wa't-tabyīn*, I, 50, III, 251-2.

5 Ibrāhīm was proclaimed Caliph for a brief moment during al-Ma'mūn's absence from Baghdad in 201/816-17.

6 'Alī b. al-Junaid al-Iskāfī, described as a native of the Sawād of Iraq, appears in Mas'ūdī, *Murūj*, VII, 107-13, as one of the boon-companions and intimates of al-Mu'taṣim.

Aṣ-Ṣūlī states that no other case is known of one Caliph kissing the hand of another and then the positions being exactly reversed, except for this instance of Ibrāhīm and al-Mu'taṣim. He then continues: 'One of the most remarkable occurrences, personally witnessed and authenticated by myself, was that I went one Wednesday morning to the Vizier al-Qāsim b. 'Ubaidallāh's[7] house at a time when he was at death's door. I saw that al-Qāsim's two sons, Abū 'Alī al-Ḥusain and Abū Ja'far Muḥammad had just come out; those present all stood up out of respect, and al-'Abbās b. al-Ḥasan[8] came up to them and kissed their hands. Al-Qāsim died that day and al-'Abbās was appointed Vizier. Then I saw al-'Abbās ride to al-Qāsim's house to pay his condolences; the two sons of al-Qāsim, whose hands al-'Abbās had kissed that morning, now came out in the evening of the same day and kissed al-'Abbās's hands.' [134

A Caliph who successively belonged to five different categories of men. Ibrāhīm b. al-Mahdī was first of all numbered amongst the class of Caliphs' sons, then became a Caliph himself, then a boon-companion, then a singer, and finally, one of the elder members of the Hāshimite family.[9]

A Caliph who was deposed and imprisoned and then restored to the Caliphate. This was Muḥammad al-Amīn. Al-Ḥusain b. 'Alī b. 'Īsā b. Māhān brought him out in full view of the people dressed only in his robes and without a turban, paraded him and then deposed him from the Caliphate, imprisoning him for two days in the palace of the Green Dome (*al-Khaḍrā'*) in al-Manṣūr's Round City.[10] But at that point, the army mutinied against al-Ḥusain, and on the third day he fled. He was pursued by Tamīm, Abū Ja'far's freedman, and by Ghālib, with a group of soldiers, and they later brought back his head to Muḥammad. Meanwhile, they were releasing Muḥammad from prison; he was in a state of extreme thirst, and in their great haste, they gave him water from a vessel used for ablutions (i.e. one ritually polluted from the point of view of drinking), fearing that he was on the point of death. All this took place three years and fifteen days after he had first been hailed as Caliph.[11] Once reinstated in office, he spent the ensuing year and a half in a state of warfare and siege until his final fate overtook him.

Al-Muqtadir experienced a period of harsh treatment and then deliverance exactly like that which happened to al-Amīn. After the army commanders and leading court figures had conspired together, killed the Vizier al-'Abbās b. al-Ḥasan and deposed al-

[7] Abū'l-Ḥusain al-Qāsim b. 'Ubaidallāh, called *Walī ad-Daula*, was Vizier to al-Mu'taḍid and al-Muktafī 288-91/901-4; cf. Sourdel, *Le vizirat 'Abbāside*, I, 345-57.

[8] Sc. *Karb ad-Dawā'*, see above, p. 62.

[9] Because of his versatile and colourful career, the sources deal at considerable length with Ibrāhīm; much of this material has been gathered together by Barbier de Meynard in his 'Ibrahim fils de Mehdi, fragments historiques, scènes de la vie d'artiste au IIIe siècle de l'hégire (778-839 de notre ère)', JA, Ser. 6, Vol. XIII (Jan.-June 1869), 201-342.

[10] Sc. the great palace known as *al-Qubbat al-Khaḍrā'* or *Bāb adh-Dhahab*; the figure of a horseman which surmounted the dome was in later times credited with magical powers, that its lance would point in the direction from which the Caliph's enemies were about to appear. Cf. Le Strange, *Baghdad during the Abbasid Caliphate* (Oxford 1924), 31-2.

[11] Sc. in Rajab 196/March-April 812.

Muqtadir from the Caliphate – this being the first of the occasions on which he was deposed – they did homage to Ibn al-Mu'tazz and set about consolidating his position. However, Ibn al-Mu'tazz's position collapsed the next day, and the status quo under al-Muqtadir was restored.[12] [135

A Caliph who reigned for only a day and part of a day. This was Ibn al-Mu'tazz.[13] They did homage to him as Caliph after al-Muqtadir had been deposed. Next morning, Ibn al-Mu'tazz intended to go along to the Caliphal palace and seat of government, but there was a change of fortunes; with the support of the populace, al-Muqtadir's slave guards attacked his supporters and defeated them, so that they scattered and fled. Ibn al-Mu'tazz's personal position became precarious and he was forced to flee and go into hiding; he was, however, arrested and never seen again. Al-Muqtadir thus regained his throne, as has just been mentioned [in the previous section].

A Caliph whose affairs and fortunes all revolved round the number eight. This was al-Mu'taṣim bi'llāh. He was known as 'the one whose affairs are characterised by the number eight (*al-Muthamman*)', because God Most High ordained that all his affairs should be ordered according to that number. Thus he was the eighth generation of the progeny of al-'Abbās b. 'Abd al-Muṭṭalib, being the son of ar-Rashīd, son of al-Mahdī, son of al-Manṣūr, son of Muḥammad, son of 'Alī, son of 'Abdallāh, son of al-'Abbās. Furthermore, he was the eighth Abbasid Caliph, as-Saffāḥ being the first, al-Manṣūr the second, al-Mahdī the third, al-Hādī the fourth, ar-Rashīd the fifth, al-Amīn the sixth, al-Ma'mūn the seventh and al-Mu'taṣim himself the eighth. He was born in the year 178[/794]; he lived to the age of forty-eight; he was the eighth of ar-Rashīd's sons; he reigned for eight years, eight months and eight days; he left eight sons and eight [136
daughters; he left eight million dinars and eighteen million dirhams in coinage; he left 8,000 ghulāms and 18,000 horses; he made eight conquests; and he died on the eighth day before the end of the month Rabī' al-Awwal (sc. on the 22nd of that month in the year 227/9th January 842).[14]

A man who had ten sons, ten brothers and was the paternal uncle to ten of his nephews. This was Marwān b. al-Ḥakam. Mu'āwiya became apprehensive of him, and wrote to him in these terms: 'O Marwān, I bear witness that I once heard the Messenger of God, God's prayers and peace be upon him, say, "When al-Ḥakam b. Abī'l-'Āṣ's male offspring reach the number of thirty,

[12] This conspiracy took place in 296/908; cf. Sourdel, *op. cit.*, I, 370-5.

[13] Cf. Tha'ālibī, *Thimār al-qulūb*, 150-3, s.v. 'Khilāfat Ibn al-Mu'tazz', where this is said to be proverbial for anything short in duration.

[14] Cf. Ṭabarī, III, 1323-4, tr. Marin, *The reign of al-Mu'taṣim*, 127-8, giving most of this series of eights, but setting forth the date of the Caliph's death as 18th Rabī' al-Awwal, repeated thus by Mas'ūdī in *Murūj*, VII, 144.

they will seize God's money as personal spoils, they will introduce reprehensible practices into God's religion and they will reduce God's servants to the position of slaves." ' Marwān wrote back, 'In regard to what you have said, O Mu'āwiya, I am indeed the father of ten, the brother of ten and the paternal uncle of ten. Farewell!' The detailed interpretation of this is as follows. Marwān's own sons were 'Abd al-Malik, Mu'āwiya, 'Abd al-'Azīz, Bishr, 'Umar, Muḥammad, 'Ubaidallāh, 'Abdallāh, Ayyūb and Dā'ūd. His brothers were 'Uthmān the Elder, 'Uthmān the Younger, al-Ḥārith, 'Abd ar-Raḥmān, Ṣāliḥ, Abān, Yaḥyā, [137 Ḥabīb, 'Umar and Aus, all sons of al-Ḥakam. His brothers' sons were 'Abd al-Wāḥid, 'Abd al-Malik, 'Abd al-'Azīz and Sa'īd, their father being al-Ḥārith b. al-Ḥakam; Ḥarb, 'Uthmān and 'Umar, their father being 'Abd ar-Raḥmān b. al-Ḥakam; and Yūsuf, Sulaimān and Ḥabīb, their father being Yaḥyā b. al-Ḥakam.[15]

A father and son whose respective ages were remarkably close together. These were 'Amr b. al-'Āṣ and his son 'Abdallāh, between whom there was only thirteen years' difference; no other instance similar to this has been recorded.[16]

Two brothers whose respective ages were extremely far apart. These were Mūsā b. 'Ubaida, well-known as a narrator of traditions, and his brother 'Abdallāh, who was eighty years older than he was; no other instance similar to this has been recorded.

Four brothers, each one successively older than the next by ten years. These were Ṭālib, 'Aqīl, Ja'far and 'Alī, the sons of Abū Ṭālib. Ṭālib was ten years older than 'Aqīl, 'Aqīl ten [138 years older than Ja'far, and Ja'far ten years older than 'Alī.

Curious coincidences in ages. The Messenger of God, God's prayers and peace be upon him, Abū Bakr, may God be pleased with him, 'Umar, may God be pleased with him, 'Alī, may God be pleased with him, 'Abd al-Malik b. Marwān and al-Manṣūr all lived till the age of sixty-three; and al-Ma'mūn, al-Mu'taṣim, Ṭāhir b. al-Ḥusain, 'Abdallāh b. Ṭāhir, al-Ḥusain b. Ṭāhir, Ṭāhir b. 'Abdallāh, Muḥammad b. Ṭāhir, al-Muwaffaq, al-Mu'taḍid and Abū'ṣ-Ṣaqr [Ismā'īl b. Bulbul][17] all lived till the age of forty-eight.

Three [half-] brothers all born in the same year and all killed in the same year, being then forty-eight years old. These were Yazīd, Ziyād and Mudrik, the sons of al-Muhallab b. Abī Ṣufra, all of whom were killed at the battle of al-'Aqr.[18] Then [139 the eldest of al-Muhallab's sons was killed at Qandābīl in India,[19]

[15] To be father of ten and brother of ten involved a feat of family fecundity which gave enormous prestige in ancient Arabia, and it seems to have created a feeling that such a man was inevitably marked out for great power and authority (cf. Lammens, *Le Califat de Yazîd Ier*, 62). It was probably, in part at least, Mu'āwiya's fear of Marwān's political ambitions that drove him to the *istilḥāq*, adoption, of his father's alleged illegitimate son Ziyād b. Abīhi and to the unprecedented step of nominating during his own lifetime his son Yazīd as heir to the Caliphate.

[16] This item of information in *Ma'ārif*, 286.

[17] Vizier to al-Mu'tamid 265-77/879-90; despoiled of his wealth and killed 278/891.

[18] Sc. the 'Aqr ('gap of') Bābil near Karbalā'. In 102/720 Yazīd and others of the Muhallabīs rebelled against Yazīd II b. 'Abd al-Malik, raising the men of Lower Iraq, Ahwāz and Fārs, but were defeated by Maslama b. 'Abd al-Malik (Yāqūt, *Mu'jam al-buldān*, IV, 136). The remnants fled eastwards to Sind, where a general massacre of the Muhallabīs took place; cf. F. Gabrieli, 'La rivolta dei Muhallabiti nel 'Irāq e il nuovo Balāḏurī', RCAL, Ser. 6, Vol. XIV (1938), 199-236.

[19] Sc. in Quṣdār, in the north of modern Baluchistan, where a battle took place between the Muhallabīs and the Khārijī Hilāl b. Aḥwaz al-Māzinī; cf. Yāqūt, *op. cit.*, IV, 402.

and after this, for twenty years, all the children born to the house of al-Muhallab were males, and the only ones of it who died were females.

One of the Followers (*at-Tābi'ūn*)[20] who belonged to eight different categories of men. This was Abū'l-Aswad Ẓālim b. 'Amr b. Kināna ad-Du'alī, who was accounted amongst the categories of the eloquent ones, the learned ones, the poets, the Shī'a, the authorities on the Arabic language and its grammar, the misers, those with paralysed limbs and those who lived an exceptionally long time (*al-mu'ammarūn*).[21] No-one else is known to equal this record.

How Monday was the day in the life of the Prophet, God's prayers and peace be upon him, on which events significant for him took place. He was born on a Monday, began his prophetic mission on a Monday, migrated from Mecca to Medina on a Monday and died on a Monday.

How Ramaḍān was the month of 'Abd al-Malik b. Marwān's life in which events significant for him took place. 'Abd al-Malik used to say, 'I was born in Ramaḍān, I was weaned in Ramaḍān, I finished learning the Qur'ān by heart in Ramaḍān, I [140 reached the age of puberty in Ramaḍān, I was made a governor in Ramaḍān, I became Caliph in Ramaḍān, and I fear that I shall die in this month.' When Shawwāl (sc. the month following Ramaḍān) began, he felt safe, but it was in fact at this point that he died.[22]

A qāḍī who in the Islamic period exercised his legal office for seventy-five years. This was Shuraiḥ b. al-Ḥārith al-Kindī. 'Umar b. al-Khaṭṭāb, may God be pleased with him, appointed him qāḍī of Kufa, and he remained in office there for seventy-five years apart from three years during the civil war between Ibn az-Zubair and the Umayyads, when he was prevented from exercising his functions. In the end, he asked al-Ḥajjāj to relieve him of his duties as qāḍī, and at the age of a hundred and twenty, he was allowed to lay them down.[23]

Four men in the Islamic period each of whose loins brought forth a hundred children.[24] These were: Khalīfa b. Baww as-Sa'dī; Anas b. Mālik al-Anṣārī, may God be pleased with him; 'Abdallāh b. 'Umair al-Laithī; and Ja'far b. Sulaimān al-Hāshimī. [141 Al-Mutawakkil is said to have fathered fifty-odd male children and twenty-odd female ones.

A single night in which one Caliph was born, another Caliph died and a third Caliph was raised to office.[25] This was the night

[20] Sc. one of the generation which followed the Prophet's Companions, *aṣ-Ṣaḥāba*, those who had known Muḥammad personally.

[21] Abū'l-Aswad is regarded in Arabic sources as the proto-grammarian of the language (cf. J. A. Haywood, *Arabic lexicography* [Leiden 1960], 11-16); he does not, however, seem to be listed as a *mu'ammar* in the special works devoted to this class of men (cf. Goldziher, *Abhandlungen zur arabischen Philologie. II. Das Kitâb al-Mu'ammarîn des Abû Hâtim al-Siǵistânî* [Leiden 1899], Introd.).

[22] Sc. in Shawwāl 86/Sept.-Oct. 705.

[23] Sc. in 72/691-2. On Shuraiḥ, allegedly one of the Abnā', descendants of Persian soldiers settled in the Yemen, see Lammens, 'Ziād ibn Abīhi, Vice-roi de l'Iraq', in *Études sur le siècle des Omayyades*, 77-80.

[24] In *Muḥabbar*, 189, is a list, almost identical with that of Tha'ālibī here, of 'Four men of Basra, none of whom died until each saw a hundred offspring, these being his own children and grandchildren'; in *Ma'ārif*, 308, three such men are named.

[25] Cf. *Thimār al-qulūb*, 510 s.v. 'Lailat al-khilāfa'.

of Friday, the 16th of Rabī' al-Awwal of the year 170 [/15th September 786], during which al-Ma'mūn was born, al-Hādī died and ar-Rashīd was made Caliph. No instance similar to this is recorded.

A single day in which wealth was distributed on a scale never before known in the history of the world. On a single day, al-Ma'mūn allotted to his brother al-Mu'taṣim the western provinces of the Caliphate, together with a grant of 500,000 dinars; he entrusted the defences and strongpoints along the Arab-Byzantine frontier (*ath-thughūr wa'l-'awāṣim*) to his son al-'Abbās and likewise granted him 500,000 dinars; he appointed 'Abdallāh b. Ṭāhir governor of Jibāl with a commission to wage war on Bābak, and granted him 300,000 dinars; and finally, he granted a further 700,000 dinars to be shared between the remainder of his commanders. When 'Umar b. Nūḥ received his share of this wealth, he commented that this was the first day since the world began in which so much wealth was bestowed.

Four men in the Islamic period each of whom killed over a million men. These were: al-Ḥajjāj,[26] Abū Muslim, [142
Bābak[27] and al-Burqu'ī[28]; no fifth one ever equalled them in this.

A remarkable occurrence containing a moral example. Various authorities relate from 'Abd al-Malik b. 'Umair al-Lakhmī,[29] adducing varying chains of transmission, that he said: 'In this very same palace – he meant the governor's palace at Kufa – I saw the head of al-Ḥusain b. 'Alī b. Abī Ṭālib, may God be pleased with them, laid before 'Ubaidallāh b. Ziyād on a shield; later, I saw 'Ubaidallah b. Ziyād's head laid before al-Mukhtār b. Abī 'Ubaid on a shield; then I saw al-Mukhtār's head laid before Muṣ'ab [b. az-Zubair] on a shield; and finally, I saw Muṣ'ab's head laid before 'Abd al-Malik b. Marwān on a shield. I told this story to 'Abd al-Malik, but he regarded it as an ill omen and rose up abruptly from his place.' [143

A similar tale is related by aṣ-Ṣūlī, who said that al-Ḥusain b. Yaḥyā the secretary told him,[30] 'When al-Mu'tazz came to power, only a short period of time elapsed before the notables were assembled, the corpse of al-Mu'ayyad [b. al-Mutawakkil] was brought out, and those present were asked to testify that he had been summoned (sc. by the Angel of Death) and had answered the call and that there were no marks of violence on him. A few months later, they were again assembled, the corpse of al-Musta'īn was brought out and they were told, "Look, his predestined fate has overtaken him, and there are no marks on his body, so bear

[26] According to the hostile, pro-Shī'ī Mas'ūdī, al-Ḥajjāj condemned to death 120,000 men, apart from those killed in warfare (*Murūj*, v, 382, *Tanbīh*, 318, tr. 411).

[27] Sc. the head of the Neo-Mazdakite Khurramdīniyya sectaries, who led a revolt in Armenia and Azerbaijan against the Caliphate until he was killed in 223/838; cf. G. H. Sadighi, *Les mouvements religieux iraniens au IIième et au IIIième siècles de l'hégire* (Paris 1938), 229-80.

[28] It is suggested by Abyārī and Ṣairafī that this denotes Abū Ḥarb al-Yamanī, called *al-Mubarqa'* 'the Veiled One'; Abū Ḥarb claimed to be a Sufyānid Mahdī and rebelled in Palestine against al-Mu'taṣim in 227/841-2 (cf. Ṭabarī, III, 1319-22, tr. Marin, 124-6).

[29] AS corrects the *nisba* from the *al-Laithī* of J. Abū 'Amr 'Abd al-Malik al-Lakhmī or al-Qibṭī was qāḍī of Kufa in the time of al-Ḥajjāj; he died, a centenarian, in 136/753-4 (*Ma'ārif*, 473).

[30] The ensuing story refers to the events of 252/866 and shortly afterwards, when al-Musta'īn abdicated in favour of his cousin al-Mu'tazz, but was treacherously murdered by al-Mu'tazz, who similarly disposed of his own brother al-Mu'ayyad, the heir to the throne and favoured candidate of the Turkish guards (Ṭabarī, III, 1645ff., Muir, *The Caliphate*, 535-43).

witness to this." Then a little later, when al-Muhtadī had been made Caliph, al-Mu'tazz was brought out dead and they were asked to testify that he had died suddenly and naturally[31] and that there were no marks on him.[32] A year had not completely gone by before al-Mu'tamid succeeded to the Caliphate; al-Muhtadī's corpse was brought out and they were asked to testify that he had died from his wounds. Everyone marvelled at the rapid succession of these deaths in similar circumstances and in such a short space of time.'

Another remarkable occurrence rather similar to the preceding one. Al-Mu'taṣim sent Aitākh against al-Afshīn[33] and instructed him to tell al-Afshīn, 'O enemy of God! You have per- [144
petrated many vile deeds, but what do you think about what God is doing to you now?' Al-Afshīn replied to Aitākh,[34] 'O Abū Manṣūr! I once went with a message similar to this one of yours to 'Alī b. Hishām, and he said to me in turn, "O Abū'l-Ḥasan! I once went with a message like this to 'Ujaif b. 'Anbasa[35] and he said, 'Watch out for someone coming to you with a similar message!' " I tell you now likewise, watch out for someone coming to you!' And only a few more days passed before Aitākh himself was imprisoned and then killed.

Another example of a curious coincidence. The Barmakīs were a family celebrated for their nobility of character and their secretarial skill, and the Furātī family were similarly famous in their time for these qualities. It befell that ar-Rashīd brought ruin upon the Barmakī family in the seventeenth year of his Caliphate (sc. in 187/803), and in the same way, al-Muqtadir dealt a mortal blow to the Furātī family in the seventeenth year of his Caliphate (sc. in 312/924).[36]

Another instance. When al-Wāthiq's final illness grew severe, Aitākh went in to see whether the Caliph had died or not. But when he drew near, al-Wāthiq transfixed him with a glare from the outer corner of his eye; he trembled with fear, retreated hurriedly and fell on his sword till it broke, all because of the terror instilled into him by al-Wāthiq's state. An hour later, al-Wāthiq was dead, and his corpse was taken to a room to be washed. Along came a rat and gnawed away the eye which had transfixed Aitākh. Those who witnessed this were mightily astonished how a rat could eat out an eye whose look had [145
inspired such terror in Aitākh that his nerve had given way, and he had fallen on his sword so that it had broken; and all this happened in one short phase of the day.[37]

[31] Literally, 'had died the death of his nose', *māta ḥatfa anfihi*; this expression is said to have been first used by the Prophet, cf. at-Tibrīzī, commentary on the *Hamāsa* of Abū Tammām, ed. Freytag (Bonn 1828), 52 (poem of Samau'al b. 'Ādiyā'), and Mas'ūdī, *Murūj*, IV, 168-9.

[32] See Mez, *The renaissance of Islam*, 372, on the ways used for killing Caliphs which avoided the actual spilling of blood, a thing feared on religious grounds.

[33] On the fall of the Persian general al-Afshīn and Aitākh's part in it, see Ṭabarī, III, 1304ff., tr. Marin, 111ff.

[34] This anecdote, with reference to 'Alī b. Hishām, rebel governor of Jibāl, Iṣfahān and Azerbaijan and killed by al-Ma'mūn in 215/830-1, and to 'Ujaif, is alluded to by Ṭabarī, III, 1311, tr. 117, in his account of the trial and interrogation of al-Afshīn.

[35] 'Ujaif suppressed the Zuṭṭ revolt of 219-20/834-5 in Lower Iraq, but conspired against al-Mu'taṣim to raise al-'Abbās b. al-Ma'mūn to the throne, and both were killed by al-Afshīn (Ṭabarī, III, 1167-8, 1264-6, tr. 4-6, 82-3).

[36] Cf. Sourdel, *Le vizirat 'Abbāside*, II, 424-34, on Ibn al-Furāt's third and last Vizierate and his fall.

[37] There is an obvious lack of congruence between this story and the previous story but one, in which Aitākh is said to have been killed in the reign of al-Mu'taṣim; in fact, Aitākh was killed by al-Mutawakkil in 235/849-50 (Ṭabarī, III, 1384-6).

Another instance resembling the one above. After the head of Marwān b. Muḥammad [al-Ḥimār] had been brought before 'Abdallāh b. 'Alī,[38] he ordered it to be taken away. A cat came along, tore out the tongue and started chewing it. 'Abdallāh b. 'Alī, or someone else present at the time, commented, 'If fortune had never displayed to us any more of its wonders than Marwān's tongue in the mouth of a cat, this would have been example enough.' Before this, Marwān had reviewed 70,000 Arab troops outside al-Ḥīra, and then he had said, 'When one's time is up, powerful forces are of no avail.'[39]

Another instance. 'Ubaidallāh b. Ziyād, may God curse him, killed al-Ḥusain b. 'Alī, may God be pleased with him, on 'Āshūrā day (sc. the 10th Muḥarram 61/10th October 680), and God brought about his death on 'Āshūrā day of the next year.[40] [146

Another remarkable instance of how the Caliphs may be destitute of all requisites at the time of their deaths. Aḥmad b. Abī Du'ād[41] said: 'I have never seen anyone's manner of dying so desolate and unprovided for as the way certain Caliphs have died. I tied up the lower jaws of al-Ma'mūn, al-Mu'taṣim and al-Wāthiq after their deaths with my own hand, and on none of these occasions was there any cloth at hand suitable for tying up their jaws. In the end, I had to resort in each case to tearing up the woollen gown which I had on, in order to get a convenient piece of cloth.'

A similar instance. When al-Muktafī bi'llāh died, leaving behind him 100 million dinars, he was left for the remainder of that day, everyone being otherwise occupied with the succession of his brother al-Muqtadir. The Keeper of the Caliphal Wardrobe went past al-Muktafī's corpse; the dead Caliph had a linen cloak laid over his face, but the Keeper snatched it off, saying that he was accountable for it and that if it was missing, he feared he would have to make restitution for it. Later, one of al-Muktafī's slaves went by, and wept at seeing his dead master's face uncovered; he took a cloth which had been wrapped round his own head and spread it over the corpse.

When the corpse was borne away for washing and enshrouding, they were unable to find anywhere in the place a censer in which a few pieces of fragrant ambergris could be burnt. The person in charge of the preparation of the body had to send to his own house for something to serve as a censer; he ordered his slave girls to bring a red earthenware bowl, and they used this to perfume the room. Yet in the inheritance left behind by al-Muktafī, there were thousands of gold censers. [147

[38] Sc. the uncle of the first Abbasid Caliph as-Saffāḥ; imprisoned as a rebel by al-Manṣūr and died in prison in 147/764.

[39] This last pronouncement of Marwān's is also given in Ghazālī's *Naṣīḥat al-mulūk*, tr. Bagley, 98-9.

[40] 'Ubaidallāh was defeated and killed by Ibn al-Ashtar at the battle of the Zāb in Muḥarram 67/686. Cf. Ṭabarī, II, 707ff., not giving the exact date of the battle; this is given in Mas'ūdī, *Tanbīh*, 312, tr. 405, as 'Āshurā' day, 67 (unless this is a later, Shī'ī fabrication to point out a satisfying coincidence of dates).

[41] Chief Qāḍī under al-Mu'taṣim, al-Wāthiq and initially, under al-Mutawakkil, and leading spirit of the *Miḥna* or Inquisition under which Aḥmad b. Ḥanbal suffered; d. 240/854 (cf. Zettersteén-Pellat, EI² s.v.).

A curious fact about the deposition of every sixth Caliph. Aṣ-Ṣūlī remarks that people have observed that every sixth person made responsible for the welfare of the Islamic religion has right from its inception inevitably been deposed. In the first place, the care of the Muslim community was laid upon the lord of the progeny of Adam, the best of those who have ever walked on the face of the earth, the seal of the prophets, Muḥammad, God's prayers and peace be upon him. After him came Abū Bakr, 'Umar, 'Uthmān and 'Alī, may God be pleased with them, and then al-Ḥasan b. 'Alī, may God be pleased with him, who was deprived of his charge.

After this group came Mu'āwiya b. Abī Sufyān, Yazīd b. Mu'āwiya, Mu'āwiya b. Yazīd, Marwān b. al-Ḥakam, 'Abd al-Malik b. Marwān and then 'Abdallāh b. az-Zubair, who was deprived of his power and killed. After this group came al-Walīd b. 'Abd al-Malik, Sulaimān, 'Umar b. 'Abd al-'Azīz, Yazīd b. 'Abd al-Malik, Hishām and then al-Walīd [b. Yazīd], who was deposed and killed. The remaining members of the Umayyad family did not reach six in number.

The Abbasid dynasty now came to power, beginning with as-Saffāḥ, then al-Manṣūr, al-Mahdī, al-Hādi, ar-Rashīd and then al-Amīn, the sixth of the line, who was deposed and killed. Then there reigned al-Ma'mūn, al-Mu'taṣim, al-Wāthiq, al-Mutawakkil, al-Muntaṣir and al-Musta'īn, the sixth of this group, who was deposed and killed. Then there reigned al-Mu'tazz, al- [148
Muhtadī, al-Mu'tamid, al-Mu'taḍid, al-Muktafī and al-Muqtadir, again the sixth of the group, who was deposed at one point during Ibn al-Mu'tazz's *putsch*, restored to power but killed in the end.

The present author adds that al-Qāhir then became Caliph, followed by ar-Rāḍī, al-Muttaqī, al-Mustakfī, al-Muṭī' and aṭ-Ṭā'i', the sixth of the group, who was deposed.[42] This is indeed one of the strangest coincidences.

A further instance. 'Ubaidallāh b. 'Abdallāh b. Ṭāhir [al-Khuzā'ī][43] used to say: 'One of the most remarkable things which have ever happened in this world is that al-Mu'taḍid sent al-'Abbās b. 'Amr al-Ghanawī with 10,000 men to attack the leader of the Qarāmiṭa (sc. Abū Sa'īd al-Jannābī). In fact, the Qarmaṭī leader captured al-'Abbās in Hajar; he personally managed to escape, but the rest of his forces were all killed.[44] On the other hand, 'Amr b. al-Laith came with 50,000 troops to attack Ismā'īl b. Aḥmad, and 'Amr was the only one captured, all the rest of his soldiers escaping.'[45] [149

42 In his anxiety to complete the pattern down to his own time, Tha'ālibī omits to point out that of the five Caliphs preceding aṭ-Ṭā'i', all but one, sc. ar-Rāḍī, were also deposed.

43 Sc. the grandson of Ṭāhir Dhū'l-Yamīnain, governor of Khurāsān; 'Ubaidallāh, known as a poet and littérateur, was chief of the *Shurṭa* or guard in Baghdad in 253/867, and died in 300/912-13 (cf. Ibn Khallikān, tr. II, 79-81).

44 See on this campaign, Ṭabarī, III, 2192ff., year 287/900; Mas'ūdī, *Murūj*, VIII, 193-4; and de Goeje, *Mémoire sur les Carmathes du Bahraïn*, 37-43. According to Ṭabarī, 700 prisoners were taken with al-'Abbās; all these were executed and their corpses burnt, except that al-'Abbās was released to take a defiant message back to the Caliph. This release was generally regarded as a remarkable event; cf. also, Ibn Khallikān, tr. III, 417, IV, 331.

45 This is adduced as a remarkable fact in the *Siyāsat-nāma* of Niẓām al-Mulk, ch. iii, tr. Darke, *The book of government or rules for kings*, 20.

A remarkable concatenation of circumstances, sc. the successive deaths of nine rulers within a space of two years. These took place in the years 387 and 388 [997 and 998]; concerning them the present author has written as follows (metre *Ṭawīl*):

Have you not observed how, in the space of two years, a dread summoner has called the monarchs of our time to death and destruction?

Thus the hand of death has closed over Nūḥ b. Manṣūr,[46] *despite the sighs and regrets expressed in people's breasts.*[47]

Alas too for [Abū'l-Ḥārith] Manṣūr [b. Nūḥ],[48] *for on that day at Sarakhs, his kingdom was wrested from him and ruin enveloped him,*

With the putting out of his eyes, he lost everything, and went along, blind and a captive, overwhelmed by calamities.

The monarch of Egypt[49] *has travelled along his last road, and the slabs of the tomb have closed over the ruler of Jibāl.*[50]

One of death's emissaries has lain in wait to snatch away the ruler of Gurgānj[51] *from amongst his boon-companions;*

They used to hand round the cups of wine, but now they have drunk from the cups of death, and the tears of grief are flowing.

The face of his former prosperity has become twisted and [150
menacing (shāha) *for the Khwārazm-Shāh,*[52] *and a day of inauspiciousness has loomed up before him, in all its malevolence.*

Abū 'Alī [Sīmjūrī][53] *was formerly eminent in the land, trampling it beneath his feet, until dangerous courses lured him astray,*

And a sharp fang of evil, an intractable one, confronted him, whilst a bird of ill omen rose up before him, passing over to the left.

As for the ruler of Bust,[54] *that valiant lion, whose claws have laid open the ways to both east and west,*

A stout-chested camel, bearing a sudden stroke of misfortune, has pressed down on him, since what was pre-ordained had come to him,

And neither horses, swift-running as river torrents, nor elephants, towering up like mountains when they are pasturing,

Nor armies which, when they are more numerous than pebbles on the ground, make the plains and empty spaces seem cramped and crowded, have been of any avail to him.

Turns of evil fortune, themselves preceded by crushing calamities, came upon the Būyid Ṣamṣām ad-Daula.[55]

The ruler of Gūzgān[56] *has passed over the bridge of life, and death, the uncontrollable one, has fulfilled its last appointment with him.*

Fā'iq the eunuch (al-majbūb)[57] *has had his life cut short* [151
(jubba), *and there has been no-one on the earth to mourn his passing.*

[46] The Sāmānid Amīr, d. 387/997.

[47] Following the reading *al-jawāniḥ* of AS as stylistically preferable to J's *al-jawā'iḥ*.

[48] Son and successor of Amīr Nūḥ, deposed and blinded in 389/999, cf. Barthold, *Turkestan*, 264-6.

[49] The Fāṭimid Caliph al-'Azīz b. al-Mu'izz, d. 386/996.

[50] The Būyid Amīr Fakhr ad-Daula Abū'l-Ḥasan 'Alī, d. 387/997.

[51] The Ma'mūnid Khwārazm-Shāh Ma'mūn b. Muḥammad, assassinated 387/997, cf. Sachau, SBWAW, LXXIV (1873), 290ff.

[52] Abū 'Abdallāh Muḥammad, last of the Afrīghids of Kāth, deposed and jailed by Ma'mūn b. Muḥammad in 385/995; cf. Sachau, *loc. cit.*, and Barthold, *Turkestan*, 263.

[53] Rebel general of the Sāmānids, died in imprisonment 387/997 (*ibid.*, 264).

[54] Sebüktigin, nominally governor of Ghazna and Bust for the Sāmānids, d. 387/997.

[55] Ruler of Fārs, Ahwāz and Kirmān and son of 'Aḍud ad-Daula; blinded and deposed, and then killed in 388/998 (cf. Spuler, *Iran in früh-islamischer Zeit* [Wiesbaden 1952], 105).

[56] Probably the Farīghūnid Amīr Abū'l-Ḥārith Aḥmad b. Muḥammad, but the genealogy and chronology of this family are very confused and obscure; the problems involved are discussed by D. M. Dunlop in his EI² art. 'Farīghūnids'.

[57] Rebel slave general of the Sāmānids, d. 389/999; cf. Barthold, *Turkestan*, 266-7.

All these departed in the space of two years; the vulture of death has grasped them to itself, [a bird which] when it takes its ill-omened flight, other birds of prey drop down.

Is there not a useful moral example for you here? Yes, indeed, the way of heeding the example is clear.

Chapter Ten.

Concerning some examples of the specialities of the different lands, together with something about the excellences and imperfections of these places.

MECCA, MAY GOD PROTECT IT

Mecca is God Most High's sacred place (*ḥaram*), its inhabitants are God Most High's own people and the pilgrims visiting it are God Most High's own pilgrims; the house of God Most High (sc. the Ka'ba) is there, which He established as a place to which men might resort and as a place of security for all mankind.[1] It is there that the Friend [of God] (sc. Abraham) first laid out the ground for building the Ka'ba, there that the one intended for sacrifice (sc. Ishmael) halted and there that the Lord of Mankind and the Seal of the Prophets, Muḥammad, God's prayers and peace be upon him, was born.

One of the peculiarities of the *ḥaram* is that it is in a valley devoid of cultivation or trees, yet all the fruits of the earth can be found there.[2] [153

One of its special characteristics is that a wolf[3] may pursue a gazelle, or attack it and hunt it down, yet when it enters the *ḥaram*, it has to let its prey go.[4]

Also, no pigeon ever alights on the Ka'ba unless it is diseased; this can be proved by whoever examines it and investigates, for it will never alight there whilst it is hale and hearty.

Also, if a flock of birds fly over the Ka'ba, they diverge either to the right or left of it when they reach it, and never fly directly over it.

Also, if anyone sees it for the first time, he invariably either laughs or weeps (sc. from wonder and emotion at the sight).

[1] Allusion to Qur'ān, ii, 119/125.

[2] Cf. Qur'ān, ii, 120/126, xiv, 40/37, where Abraham prays to God that He will make the barren valley of Mecca fertile and fruitful, and also the story from Wahb b. Munabbih of Abraham's refoundation of the Ka'ba, in Ibn Rusta, 27, tr. 25-6. From the end of this sentence onwards, Tha'ālibī's section on Mecca follows Ibn Rusta's section on the *Khiṣāl al-Haram*, 57-8, tr. 60-2, which is in turn based on Jāḥiẓ's section of the same title in *Ḥayawān*, III, 139-42, and also on *ibid.*, 193-4.

[3] *Dhi'b*. In an Arabian context, according to Nöldeke, 'Fünf Mo'allaqāt. II. Die Mo'allaqāt 'Antara's und Labīd's', SBWAW, CXLII (1900), 78-9, *dhi'b* is more correctly the jackal-wolf, *Canis anthus, Canis lupaster*.

[4] This popular idea seems to be a conflation of the idea of the *ḥaram* as a sanctuary for wrongdoers and of the prohibition of the killing of wild animals within it, cf. M. Gaudefroy-Demombynes, *Le pèlerinage à la Mekke, étude d'histoire religieuse* (Paris 1923), 4-5, 10.

Also, if rain comes down on the door of the Ka'ba which faces towards Iraq, there will be fertility in Iraq during that year, and if it comes down on the door facing towards Syria,[5] there will be fertility in Syria during that year; but if all sides of the building get rained upon, there will be general fertility that year in all lands.

Also, stones have been thrown on the stoning-place[6] from the beginning of the institution of the pilgrimage right down to the present time, yet at this very moment, the pile is no bigger than if it were composed of stones thrown on just a single day. Were it not that this is a spot for miraculous signs, remarkable occurrences and wonders, that pile would have grown like a mountain; nor is this phenomenon to be explained by torrents sweeping the stones away or people carrying them off. [154

One of the customs in force at Mecca is that if any slave climbs up on to the Ka'ba, he becomes thereby free. No right of ownership is recognised over a person who scales it, for the exaltedness of its splendour and the abjectness of servitude are regarded as incompatible.[7]

There are certain pious men at Mecca who, out of respect for the Ka'ba, will never enter the building.

But who can possibly claim to encompass all the merits of Mecca? [155

MEDINA

It is the *ḥaram* of the Messenger of God, God's prayers and peace be upon him, the place to which he migrated for safety and his last resting-place.[8] Medina has acquired the alternative name of 'Ṭaiba' because its fragrance cancels out the unpleasantness of its situation; this fragrance diffuses itself into the vapours of the earth, into the odour of its soil and into the breezes of its air. The sweet scent found in its streets and gardens is an indication that when the city was made a *ḥaram*, it was also made into a miraculous sign. Perfumes, incense and aromatic substances have several degrees greater fragrance at Medina than the same products when found in other lands, even though the perfumes and incense in these latter places are more costly and highly-prized.

In many places, such as in the chief town of al-Ahwāz and in Antioch, perfume undergoes a change and its fragrance evaporates. Whereas in Medina, one can place on the head of a young black slave girl[9] a little bit of salt[10] and a little bit of some aromatic substance which, because it is so common there, is of

[5] In the reconstruction of the Ka'ba by 'Abdallāh b. az-Zubair, two doors were made instead of the former one, in restoration of the original, Abrahamic arrangement. The second door was opposite the first one, and at the side of the Yemenī angle; the sources say that it was to facilitate the movement of pilgrims, who would enter by one door and leave by another, but Gaudefroy-Demombynes surmises that there was a pre-Islamic *ṭawāf* or circumambulation round the two Yemenī angles containing the two holy stones (*op. cit.*, 38).

[6] I.e. the pile of stones at the *'aqaba* or slope down to the village of Minā, where the pilgrims hurl the stones they have previously gathered at Muzdalifa; according to a tradition of Ibn al-'Abbās, the angels carry off those stones whose presentation has been acceptable to God, thus keeping the pile at a constant, fixed height (cf. Gaudefroy-Demombynes, *op. cit.*, 268ff.).

[7] According to Gaudefroy-Demombynes, *op. cit.*, 4-5, Ibn Rusta, and following him here, Tha'ālibī, is the sole authority mentioning this tradition in regard to runaway slaves, but some general right of sanctuary in the *ḥaram* or at the Ka'ba probably dated from pre-Islamic times.

[8] The material in this section is based on Jāḥiẓ, *Ḥayawān*, III, 142-3, and Ibn Rusta, 59, tr. 62-3.

[9] The negro slave being considered the height of personal unpleasantness.

[10] I have followed Tha'ālibī in his *Thimār al-qulūb* and Ibn Rusta in reading *milḥ* 'salt'; the texts J and AS and Jāḥiẓ, *Ḥayawān*, III, 144, have *balaḥ* 'unripe dates'.

low value, and one then finds that it has acquired a sweet odour and fragrance which not even the bridal chamber of a woman of high rank can equal. Even soaked date stones, which the people of Iraq consider as having an excessively nasty smell when they are soaked for a long time, would be extremely sweet-smelling at Medina. [156

SYRIA

Its special characteristics include the fact that it is the homeland *par excellence* of the prophets, peace be upon them.[11] Right up to this present time, it has been the homeland of those religious devotees and ascetics who are called the *Abdāl*.[12] These are the persons concerning whom the historical traditions say that it is only through their prayers of intercession that God Most High has mercy on His creatures and pardons them. Their total number is always seventy, neither more nor less, and whenever one of them dies, another saint comes forward to take his place and keep the number up to seventy. The unique part of God's earth in which they dwell is on the mountains of al-Lukkām in Syria, the range which runs from Ḥimṣ to Damascus, where it becomes known as the Lebanon mountains.[13] The *Abdāl* are therefore sometimes described as living in the mountains of al-Lukkām and sometimes in those of Lebanon.[14]

The specialities of Syria include apples, whose excellence and wholesomeness are proverbial. Each year, the Caliphs used to have brought for them 30,000 apples in containers. It is said that they have a stronger fragrance when in Iraq than when they are in Syria.

Also, the purity and clarity of Syrian olive oil is proverbially famous. This is known as *rikābī* oil because it used to be [157
exported from Syria on the backs of camels (*rikāb* = 'riding-camel').[15] Syria has more olive trees than any other land, and the usefulness and wholesomeness of the olive tree needs no description.

Also, the thinness and translucence of Syrian glass are proverbially famous; one says 'more delicate than Syrian glass' or 'clearer than Syrian glass'.[16]

Also, there is the mosque of Damascus, one of the wonders of the world in its beauty and uniqueness; to describe it adequately would take too long. Al-Laḥḥām[17] relates from a certain elder of Damascus, who lived close by the mosque, that the latter said that he had never missed a single act of worship in it since he

[11] Here, of course, 'Syria' includes also Palestine.

[12] On the *Abdāl* (sing. *badal* 'substitute'), see Goldziher, EI² s.v.

[13] Al-Lukkām is properly the mountain chain of the hinterland of Latakia to the north of the Nahr el-Kebīr (= the modern Jebel Anṣāriyya), whereas the Lebanon mountains run southwards from the river; cf. Gaudefroy-Demombynes, *La Syrie à l'époque des Mamelouks d'après les auteurs arabes* (Paris 1932), 22.

[14] This story also appears in *Thimār al-qulūb*, 186-7, s.v. 'Abdāl al-Lukkām'.

[15] *Rikāb* also = 'stirrup', *rikābī* = 'courier, equerry'; but cf. Dozy, *Supplément*, s.v., for another explanation of *Rikābī* oil.

[16] The apples, oil and glassware of Syria, as being proverbially excellent, are also dealt with in *Thimār al-qulūb*, 421-3.

[17] Possibly the Abū'l-Ḥasan 'Alī al-Laḥḥām mentioned below, tr. p. 143.

reached the age of reason (sc. since he reached the age at which performance of the Muslim worship became legally obligatory on him), and that he had never once entered it without his eye alighting on some piece of inscriptional carving or ornamentation or some other aspect of its beauty which he had never noticed before. This one story is sufficient witness to its uniqueness.

Also, there is the Ghūṭa of Damascus, the most beautiful and healthy of the four great beauty-spots of the earth, sc. the Ghūṭa of Damascus, the waterway of Ubulla, the Bawwān defile and the region of Soghdia around Samarqand. I once heard Abū Bakr al-Khwārazmī[18] say that he had seen them all, and the Ghūṭa of Damascus was the finest and most marvellous. It was in- [158
vidious, he said, to make any distinction between its gardens adorned as they are with brilliancies and flowers, and its pools, which are covered with aquatic birds more beautiful than pheasants and peacocks; he could only compare it with paradise or with its similitude delineated on the surface of the earth.

Also amongst the special features of Syria are the cathedral church of Edessa, the lighthouse of Alexandria (*sic*)[19] and the bridge of Sanja.[20] Edessa is in the administrative district of Ḥarrān; it would take too long to enumerate the church's wonders, its paintings, its decorations, its talismans and its candelabra which give light without needing to be lit.

It is said that the two *ṭā*'s are characteristic of Syria: submissiveness (*ṭāʿa*) and plague (*ṭāʿūn*). The Syrian people are reported to be outstanding amongst the peoples of the world for their submissiveness to authority; indeed, their obedience and loyal support have become proverbial. It was only through the Syrian people that the power of Muʿāwiya became firmly established, because in them he had the backing of the most obedient of the troops, whereas ʿAlī b. Abī Ṭālib, may God be pleased with him, had on the other hand the most rebellious of the troops, those of Iraq. ʿAbd al-Malik b. Marwān once spoke about [159
Rauḥ b. Zinbāʿ,[21] saying, 'Abū Zurʿa combines in himself the legal scholarship of the Ḥijāz, the shrewdness of Iraq and the loyalty of Syria.'

Syria has always been notorious for its plagues, and the chronicles all devote considerable space to them. Many of these pestilences have spread from there to Iraq and elsewhere, although plague has never broken out in the two Holy Cities. When the Abbasids came to power, there were no more plagues till the reign of al-Muqtadir. [160

[18] Abū Bakr Muḥammad b. al-ʿAbbās al-Khwārazmī, famed poet and literary stylist and one of Thaʿālibī's friends; d. at Nīshāpūr 383/993 (cf. Ibn Khallikān, tr. III, 108-10, and *Yatīmat ad-dahr*, IV, 194-241).

[19] Apparently a confusion of the north Syrian town of Iskandarūna (=Alexandretta, Iskenderun), now in the Hatay *vilâyet* of modern Turkey, and the Egyptian Iskandariyya (= Alexandria).

[20] Sanja = a river in Ḍiyār Muḍar running between Ḥiṣn Manṣūr and Kaisūm, in the modern Turkish *vilâyet* of Adïyaman; cf. Yāqūt, *Muʿjam al-buldān*, III, 264-5, giving a description of the bridge.

[21] See above, p. 70, n. 10.

EGYPT

Its special characteristics include the abundance there of money. There used to be a saying that if anyone goes to Egypt and does not become rich, God Most High never will make him rich. According to al-Jāḥiẓ, Abū'l-Khaṭṭāb[22] asserted that at one period the taxes levied in Egypt amounted to four million dinars; but another authority puts it at two million dinars, together with the revenue exacted[23] in the form of horses and other riding-beasts and the fine, embroidered textiles of the *ṭirāz*.[24] Al-Jāḥiẓ says[25] that people have recognised cotton cloths as being special to Khurāsān and linens to Egypt; the cotton cloths and linens made by people in all other regions do not equal the quantity of the production in these two places. The taxation collected in the form of fine textiles from Egypt,[26] these being made up solely of linens,[27] often amounts to 100,000 dinars' worth. Al-Jāḥiẓ [161 also mentions that the papyrus of Egypt is to the western lands what the paper of Samarqand is to the east.

The asses of Egypt, and also its horses, are characterised by their fine appearance and spirited temperament. But whereas certain other countries have horses of equally good breeding and pedigree, no other land, in comparison with Egypt, produces such fine asses. The Caliphs would never ride anything else inside their palace precincts and gardens except Egyptian asses. Al-Mutawakkil used to ascend the minaret of Surra man ra'ā (Sāmarrā)[28] on a Marīsī ass; the steps up that minaret run round the outside, its base covers a *jarīb* of ground and it is ninety-nine *dhirā'*s high. Marīs is a village in Egypt; Bishr al-Marīsī came from there.[29] [162

Al-Jāḥiẓ relates that the poisonous serpent (*thu'bān*) is uniquely found in Egypt. It is a remarkably frequent cause of men's deaths, and the only enemy it has is the mongoose or ichneumon (*nims*). This last is one of the most wonderful creatures in existence. It is a small, very lively little animal, looking just like a piece of

[22] Cited by Mas'ūdī in *Murūj*, VI, 102, as an informant on early Abbasid affairs; and by Jāḥiẓ in *Ḥayawān*, I, 177, as an informant of Abū 'Ubaida, and in *al-Bayān wa't-tabyīn*, III, 299, with the *nisba* az-Zurārī (Zurāra = a village in the district of Kufa, according to *Murūj*, IV, 266, and Yāqūt s.v.).

[23] Reading *wūfiqat* for the *wūqifat* of J and AS. Rescher in his translation of this tenth chapter in *Orientalistische Miszellen*, I, 199, follows J's text and translates 'given in *waqf*, mortmain', but this hardly fits the context. For the technical financial term *muwāfaqa* 'agreement with a retiring tax-collector over the submission of accounts', see al-Khwārazmī, *Mafātīḥ al-'ulūm*, ed. G. van Vloten (Leiden 1895), 56; here it may refer to taxation in kind stipulated in an agreement between the tax-collector and the central government.

[24] Sc. the luxury textiles, usually having borders embroidered with inscriptions, which were produced in state factories for official use; cf. A. Grohmann, EI[1] and Suppl. s.v.

[25] Although the *dicta* of Jāḥiẓ on various aspects of economic geography are frequently cited in this tenth chapter, only on one occasion does Tha'ālibī give an exact reference; see above, Introduction, p. 30-1.

[26] *Al-ḥiml min diqq Miṣr.* I take *ḥiml* here as a technical financial term (cf. *Mafātīḥ al-'ulūm*, 62), and not, as does Rescher, *op. cit.*, 199, with the meaning 'a camel's load'; the sum of money quoted seems far too great for this interpretation.

[27] On the linens of Egypt, for which flax was grown in the Delta and especially in the Fayyūm, see Mez, *The renaissance of Islam*, 459-61.

[28] Sc. the famous helicoidal tower, the *Malwiyya* or spiral, which stands free of the Great Mosque at Sāmarrā; cf. K. A. C. Creswell, *Early Muslim architecture: Umayyads, early 'Abbāsids and Ṭūlūnids*, II, 261-5.

[29] Sc. Abū 'Abd ar-Raḥān Bishr b. Ghiyāth al-Marīsī, a famous theologian of the Murji'a sect, d. 218/833. The Muslim biographers (e.g. Sam'ānī, Yāqūt, Ibn Khallikān) connect his name with the Egyptian village of Marīs, but according to the authors of the EI[2] articles on him, Carra de Vaux, Nader and Schacht, it derives from a quarter of Baghdad with the same name.

dried-up meat. When it sees the serpent, it runs up to it, and the serpent in turn coils up round it, intending to devour it. Then the mongoose puffs itself up with air and letting out a cry, bites the serpent in two; often it bites it up into little pieces. But for the mongoose, the serpents would eat up the people of Egypt. It is more useful to the people there than the hedgehog is to the people of Sīstān.[30]

He also says that one of the drawbacks to Egypt is the fact that it hardly ever rains there, and when it does, the people abhor it intensely. God Most High has said: 'He is the one who sends the winds as bringers of good tidings in front of His mercy', meaning rain, which is an all-embracing act of mercy for all mankind.[31] Yet the people of Egypt dislike it, finding it of no particular benefit, and the crops in their fields do not utilise it.[32] [163

In his book *Shu'arā' Miṣr* 'The poets of Egypt',[33] aṣ-Ṣūlī records these verses of a certain poet (metre *Ṭawīl*):

They say that Egypt is the most fertile of all lands, but I replied to them that Baghdad is more fertile than Egypt.

Egypt is just a country like the rest of them, to which Fate brings round, alternately, prosperity and dearth.

But you heap praises on it, in accordance with your natural inclinations; no land lacks people to cherish and praise it.

If it were not so, then where is its famed prosperity for one section of the population there, who through deprivation, endure all sorts of torment?

What good can there be in a people, in whose country the earth grows sterile with the rain which spells fertility for all the rest of mankind?

Yet when they get news of rain, their hearts are gripped with fear, just as the flocks of ashen-coloured partridges take flight, panic-stricken, at dusk!

Al-Jāḥiẓ asserts that when the wind blows for thirteen days continuously from the direction of Marīs, i.e. from the south,[34] the people of Egypt buy themselves shrouds and embalming spices, being sure that a deadly plague will break out. He says that it is sufficient to point out that the Nile behaves in a fashion exactly contrary to all other rivers; it goes down when others are rising and increases when others are decreasing! [He says that] crocodiles are found in no other river but the Nile; no crocodile has ever been seen in the Tigris, Euphrates, Saiḥān, Jaiḥān or river of Balkh, i.e. the Oxus.[35] Their harmfulness [164 is well-known, and they have no beneficial aspects whatever. But

[30] Cf. Jāḥiẓ, *Ḥayawān*, IV, 120-1, on the mongoose and the serpent.

[31] Qur'ān, vii, 55/57. As Rescher notes, *op. cit.*, 200, *raḥmet* (properly 'mercy') is a common word for 'rain' in Turkish.

[32] This information from Jāḥiẓ on the rainfall and climate of Egypt also appears in Ibn al-Faqīh, *Kitāb al-buldān*, ed. de Goeje (Leiden 1885), 74-5.

[33] This book is not extant, but is mentioned in Yāqūt, *Irshād*, II, 415, and in other sources, according to Brockelmann, GAL, Suppl., I, 219.

[34] According to Mas'ūdī, *Murūj*, VI, 272-3, Marīs is the upper part of the Ṣa'īd of Egypt, extending as far as Nubia.

[35] This last, explanatory phrase appears only in the Leiden ms. of J. For smoothness and clarity in the translation, I have slightly rearranged the order of the text in this sentence and the following one.

the author of this book says: al-Jāḥiẓ alleges that crocodiles are found only in the Nile and monkeys only in the Yemen, but he is mistaken here. There are crocodiles in the Ganges of India, and monkeys are numerous in certain regions of India.[36]

I once heard the Faqīh Abū'l-Ḥasan al-Māsarjisī[37] say that amongst the special characteristics of Egypt is the fact that only rarely does one see Egyptians settling down in any country outside their own. Someone has said that the kings and great men of Egypt are hailed by the greeting 'O Mighty One!', just as one finds in the Qur'ān.[38]

Another noteworthy feature is the arrogance of the kings of Egypt and the claims of certain of them to divinity – may God curse them for this! According to Abū Ma'shar al-Munajjim ('the Astrologer'),[39] the ancient peoples living before the Flood, when they had foreknowledge that some calamity from heaven, such as an inundation or a fire, was about to overwhelm all things living on the earth and growing there, used to build massive stone pyramids in upper Egypt on the hilltops and uplands in order to be secure there from fire and water. They made two of these pyramids higher than all the rest, each of these two being 400 *dhirā'*s long, 400 *dhirā'*s wide and rising 400 *dhirā'*s into the sky. They were built of various types of marble, each separate block being a cube of between eight to ten *dhirā'*s each side, [165 and the blocks were so carefully joined together that only a person with keen eyesight could discern the joints. These blocks were engraved with inscriptions in hieroglyphic writing,[40] which only those familiar with that system of writing could read; every kind of magical incantation, healing recipe and talismanic formula could be discerned therein. The inscriptions on these two pyramids were once spelled out to one of the Caliphs, as follows: 'I have erected these two structures, and let him who claims to be a mighty ruler try to pull them down, for it is easier to destroy than to build.' The Caliph wanted to tear them down, but found that the revenue of the whole world would not suffice for it, so he left them alone.[41] There is a tradition that food used to be stored in them in the time of Joseph, peace be upon him. [166

THE SPECIALITIES OF THE YEMEN

Al-Jāḥiẓ says: these include swords, cloaks, monkeys and giraffes; these last are what are called in Persian *ushtur-gāv-palang*, i.e. they resemble to some extent camels, oxen and the panther-leopard. It is said that when a sword is made [of steel] from

[36] On the phenomenon of the crocodile, see Ibn Rusta, 80-1, tr. 88-9; Ibn al-Faqīh, 60-1; Mas'ūdī, *Murūj*, I, 235-6; Jāḥiẓ, *Ḥayawān*, Index, and cf. VII, 135, where Jāḥiẓ says that the crocodile dies if it is transported from the Nile and put into the Euphrates or Tigris.

[37] On this Shāfi'ī faqīh from Khurāsān (d. 384/994), see Ibn Khallikān, tr. II, 607. Tha'ālibī also quotes him as authority for an anecdote on Ya'qūb b. Laith's capture of Nīshāpūr, in his *Kitāb ādāb al-mulūk al-Khwārazmshāhī* (see on this, above, Introduction, p. 5), ff. 49b-50a of Istanbul ms. Es'at Efendi 1808.

[38] Cf. xii, 88.

[39] Abū Ma'shar Ja'far b. Muḥammad al-Balkhī, the Albumasar of the mediaeval Christians, famous astronomer and astrologer, d. 272/886; his *Kitāb al-aflāk wa tarkīb as-samā'* is quoted by Ibn Rusta (cf. J. M. Millás, EI[2] s.v.). The whole family, of which Abū Ma'shar was a member, was famous too for its poetic talent; cf. the *Yatīmat ad-dahr*, III, 119-22, 392-5, on the Banū'l-Munajjim.

[40] *Musnad*, a general term in early Arabia for scripts of outlandish appearance like the South Arabian and the ancient Egyptian hieroglyphs.

[41] This story about the Pyramids is resumed in Ibn Rusta, 80, tr. 87-8, and Ibn al-Faqīh, 68.

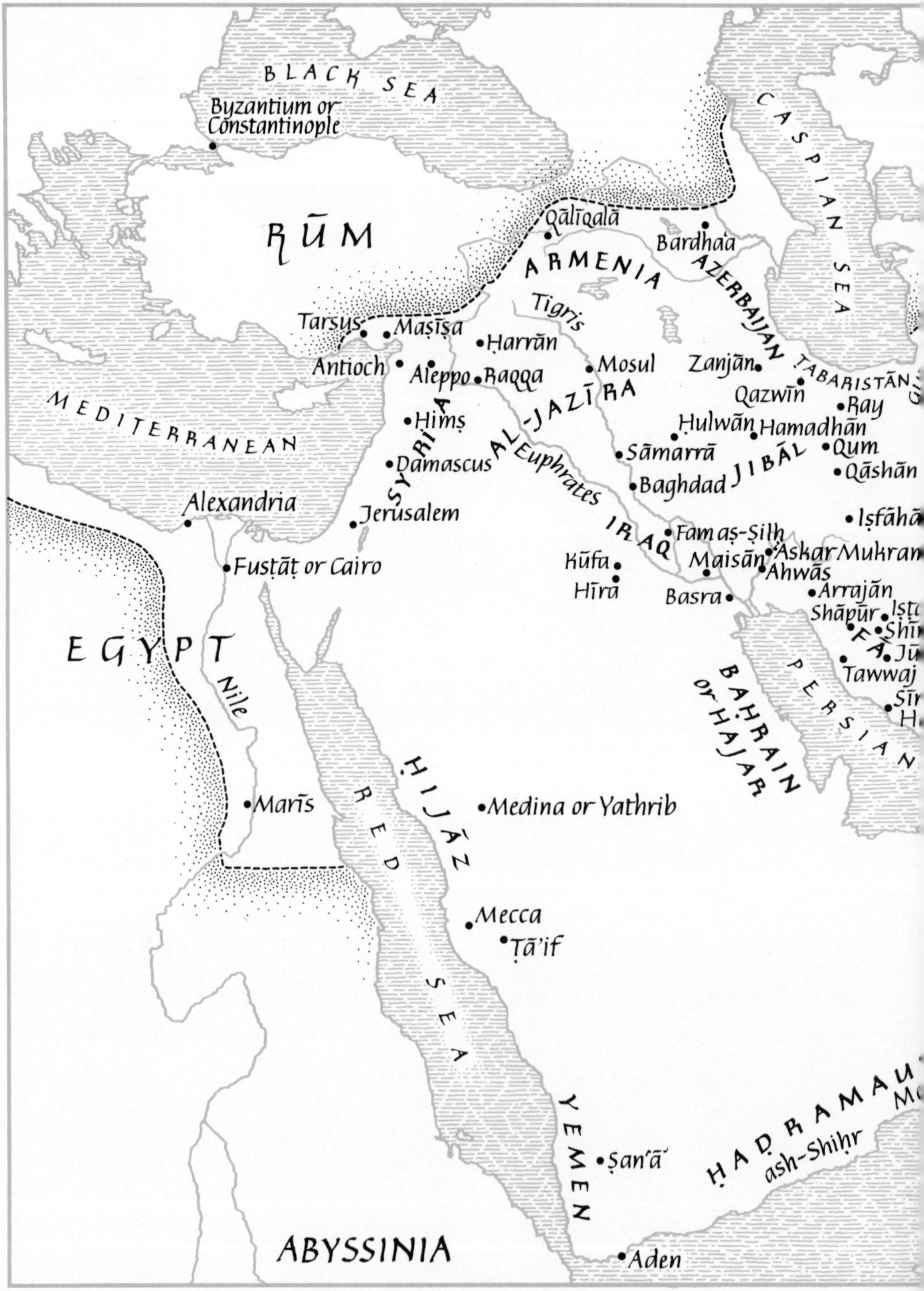
BLACK SEA
Byzantium or Constantinople
CASPIAN SEA
RŪM
Qālīqalā
Bardhaʿa
ARMENIA
AZERBAIJAN
Tigris
Tarsus
Maṣīṣa
Ḥarrān
Antioch
Aleppo
Raqqa
Mosul
Zanjān
TABARISTĀN
Qazwīn
Ray
MEDITERRANEAN
Ḥimṣ
SYRIA
AL-JAZĪRA
Ḥulwān
Hamadhān
Sāmarrā
JIBĀL
Qum
Damascus
Euphrates
Qāshān
Baghdad
Alexandria
Jerusalem
IRAQ
Fam aṣ-Ṣilḥ
Kūfa
Maisān
Ahwāz
Ḥīra
Basra
Arrajān
Shāpūr
Fusṭāṭ or Cairo
EGYPT
Nile
BAḤRAIN or HAJAR
PERSIAN
Tawwaj
Marīs
ḤIJĀZ
RED SEA
Medina or Yathrib
Mecca
Ṭā'if
YEMEN
Ṣan'ā'
ash-Shiḥr
ABYSSINIA
Aden

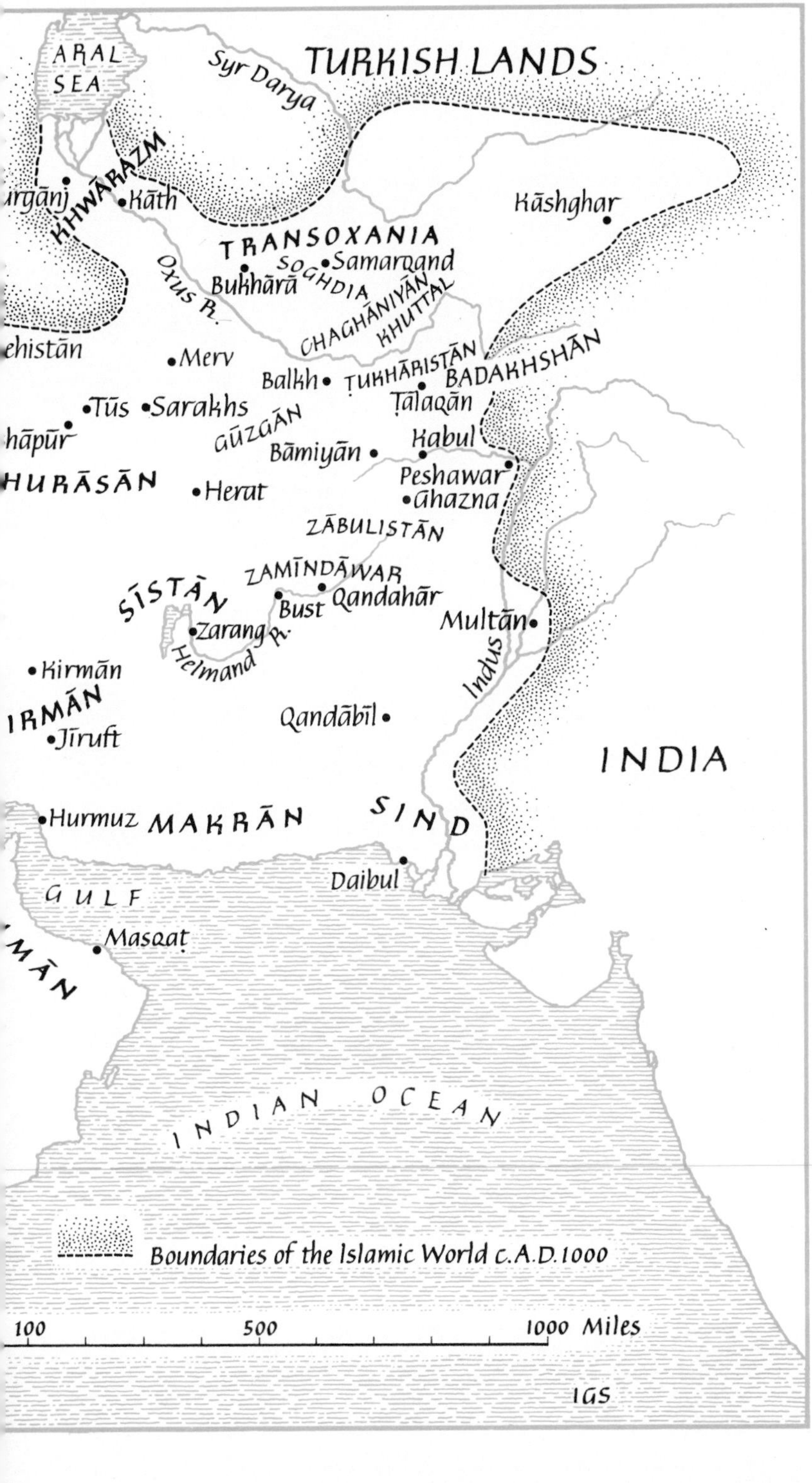
ARAL SEA
Syr Darya
TURKISH LANDS
KHWĀRAZM
Kāth
Kāshghar
TRANSOXANIA
SOGHDIA
Samarqand
Bukhārā
Oxus R.
CHAGHĀNIYĀN
KHUTTAL
Merv
Balkh
TUKHĀRISTĀN
BADAKHSHĀN
Ṭālaqān
Tūs
Sarakhs
GŪZGĀN
Kabul
Bāmiyān
Peshawar
Herat
Ghazna
ZĀBULISTĀN
ZAMĪNDĀWAR
SĪSTĀN
Bust
Qandahār
Zarang
Helmand R.
Multān
Kirmān
Indus
Qandābīl
Jīruft
INDIA
Hurmuz
MAKRĀN
SIND
Daibul
GULF
Masqat
INDIAN OCEAN
Boundaries of the Islamic World c.A.D.1000
100
500
1000 Miles
IGS

The ISLAMIC WORLD as treated by THA'ĀLIBĪ

Qala' in India[42] and tempered in the Yemen, then beware of it![43] Al-Aṣma'ī used to say that four things have become distributed all over the world, yet are only found in the Yemen: the variety of saffron called *wars*,[44] olibanum or frankincense, the dyestuff *khiṭr*[45] and the cornelian. [167

BASRA AND KUFA

It used to be said, 'Basra is the microcosm of the world, but thou art incomparable, O Baghdad!' Al-Ḥajjāj used to say, 'Kufa is a beautiful slave girl, without wealth of her own, who is sought after for her beauty, whilst Basra is an ugly old woman who is nevertheless rich and is sought after for her money.'[46] Ziyād [b. Abīhi] used to say, 'Kufa is like the uvula, which is moistened by cool and sweet water, whereas Basra is like the bladder, which only receives the water when it has become changed and nasty.' Ja'far b. Sulaimān[47] used to say, 'Iraq is the cynosure (*'ain*) of the world, Basra is cynosure of Iraq, al-Mirbad[48] is the cynosure of Basra, and my own house is the cynosure of al-Mirbad.'

Al-Jāḥiẓ has mentioned the Wādī'l-Qaṣr at Basra, and in connection with it, has repeated al-Khalīl's lines (metre *Basīṭ*)[49]:
[168

Pay a visit to the Wādī'l-Qaṣr, for what a splendid palace (qaṣr) *and river-channel* (wādī) *it is! You must certainly go there, even without a previous invitation!*

Go there, for there is no other residence remotely like it, either in the settled area or, if you will, in the desert.

Ships are grounded on the banks[50] *there, and one can find ostriches, lizards, fishes, sailors and camel-drivers.*

Then al-Jāḥiẓ explains: 'Whoever comes to this river-channel and sees the palace of Anas,[51] will see a land as white as camphor and will see lizards which can be caught, gazelles, fish and fishermen, and he will hear the sailor singing at the helm and the chant of the camel-driver urging on his beast.' Concerning the ebb and flow of the tide, he says, 'What do you think about a people who get the tide in the morning and evening, and if they wish, they let it come up, and if not, they prevent it from doing so.'[52] [169.

One of the neatest comments on the variable atmosphere of Basra has been made by Ibn Langak (metre *Ramal*)[53]:

[42] On the fine swords of Qala'/Kalah/Kalang in Malaya, where supplies of tin and iron were readily available, see S. Q. Fatimi, 'Malaysian weapons in Arabic literature: a glimpse of early trade in the Indian Ocean', *Islamic Studies*, III/2 (Karachi 1964), 199-228. On the exact meaning of al-Hind, here translated conventionally as 'India', see below, p. 139, n. 133.

[43] This saying is also cited in Nuwairī, *Nihāyat al-arab fī funūn al-adab* (Cairo 1341-74/1923-54), I, 240.

[44] On the saffron of the Yemen, see Mez, *The renaissance of Islam*, 437-8. According to the anonymous *Tuḥfat al-aḥbāb*, ed. H. P. J. Renaud and G. S. Colin (Paris 1934), 61, No. 133, *wars* = the plant *Memecylon tinctorium* L., a yellow dyestuff.

[45] According to P. Guigues, 'Les noms arabes dans Serapion, «Liber de simplicii medicina»', JA, Ser. 10, Vol. V (Jan.-June 1905), 506, 516, Nos. 117, 157, *khiṭr* = *Isatis tinctoria* L., woad.

[46] This *bon mot* also in Mas'ūdī, *Murūj*, VI, 275-6.

[47] Member of the Abbasid family, and cousin of as-Saffāḥ and al-Manṣūr; d. at Basra (Ibn Qutaiba, *Ma'ārif*, 376).

[48] On Mirbad, see Pellat, *Le milieu basrien et la formation de Ǧāḥiẓ*, 11-12, 244-5.

[49] Al-Khalīl b. Aḥmad al-Farāhīdī, grammarian, lexicographer and authority on prosody, d. 170/786-7; cf. Haywood, *Arabic lexicography*, 20ff. But these lines quoted by Tha'ālibī are attributed in several sources, e.g. *Murūj*, VI, 292, to Ibn Abī 'Uyaina.

[50] Following AS; J has *yurqā* 'are brought up'.

[51] Anas b. Mālik, the Prophet's Companion, d. *c.* 91/710; his tomb at Basra became a popular pilgrimage place (Pellat, *op. cit.*, 107).

[52] Presumably by sluices; complex hydraulic machinery was used in Lower Iraq from ancient times.

[53] On the climate of Basra, see Pellat, *op. cit.*, 15-16.

We here at Basra have a pleasant sort of life;
Whilst the north wind blows we are, as it were, amongst gardens and tillage,
But when the south wind comes along, it is like being in a privy.

It is related that ar-Rashīd said to Ja'far b. Yaḥyā [al-Barmakī] when they were once at Kufa and the night was just drawing to a close, 'Let us go out and savour the sweet air of Kufa before the mass of common people spoil it with their breaths.'

Amongst the specialities of Kufa are said to be the oils made from violets and from roses; these are exported all over the world. It is also alleged that one of the truest sayings about the people of the various regions is the one, 'the Kufan never keeps his word' (*al-Kūfī lā yūfī*).[54] [170

BAGHDAD

It is called the earthly paradise, the meeting-place of the two rivers which bring succour, i.e. the Tigris and Euphrates, the centre of the world, the city of peace, the dome of Islam; for it is the shining light of the land, the seat of the Caliphate, the place where all rare and choice things are found together, the mine of beautiful and delicate objects. Here are found the supreme exponents of every art and the unique ones of the age in every craft.[55]

Abū Isḥāq az-Zajjāj[56] used to say: 'Baghdad is the centre of world civilisation; all the rest is mere desert.' Abū'l-Faraj al-Babbaghā'[57] used to say: 'It is the city of peace (*madīnat as-salām*), nay, the city of all Islam (*madīnat al-Islām*), for the members of the house of the Prophet and the Caliphs of Islam nestled and were nurtured there, derived strength from its roots and grew up straight in the shelter of its branches. Its air is the sweetest[58] of all airs, its water the purest of all waters and its breeze the softest of all breezes.' It is in the evenly-balanced clime, in the middle of the globe, and it was always, from earliest times, the residence of the Persian emperors and then of the Islamic Caliphs.

When any person with pretensions to learning came to Abū'l-Faḍl Ibn al-'Amīd[59] and he wanted to put that person's intellect to the test, he used to ask him about Baghdad. If the alleged [171 scholar knew all about its remarkable characteristics and its beauties, and heaped praises on it, Ibn al-'Amīd took that as a pointer to his excellence and as an entitlement to his being considered intelligent. Then he would ask him about al-Jāḥiẓ, and if

[54] This accusation is doubtless a reflection of Shī'ī contempt for the people of Kufa as betrayers of the cause of al-Ḥusain b. 'Alī and various later Alids. However, in an enumeration of the characteristics of the *amṣār*, great garrison centres of the Islamic world, Jāḥiẓ attributes eloquence and correct speech to Kufa, and treachery to Ray (quoted in Maqdisī, *Aḥsan at-taqāsīm*, 33).

[55] These sayings in praise of Baghdad are also given in the *Thimār al-qulūb*, 404–6, s.v. 'Jannat al-arḍ'. The opening of Ya'qūbī's *Kitāb al-buldān*, ed. de Goeje (Leiden 1892), 233–6, tr. Wiet (Cairo 1937), 4–6, likewise contains an extended eulogy of its climate, products, civilisation and people.

[56] Abū Isḥāq was secretary to al-Qāsim b. 'Ubaidallāh, Vizier to al-Mu'taḍid and al-Muktafī, and was also an author; cf. GAL, I, 110–11, Suppl. I, 170, 507.

[57] The well-known secretary and poet, who in his youth frequented Saif ad-Daula's court, d. 398/1007–8; Tha'ālibī devotes a long section to him in the *Yatīmat ad-dahr*, I, 252–86 (cf. Blachère, EI² s.v.).

[58] J suggests *a'dhā* 'most wholesome' as an alternative reading to *a'dhabu*.

[59] Abū'l-Faḍl Muḥammad b. al-Ḥusain, celebrated as the greatest prose stylist of his day and Vizier to the Būyid Rukn ad-Daula, d. 360/969; Tha'ālibī devotes a long section to him and his son Abū'l-Fatḥ in the *Yatīmat ad-dahr*, III, 158–92.

he saw that the man was familiar with al-Jāḥiẓ's works, could quote al-Jāḥiẓ's expressions and had spent some time studying the questions raised by al-Jāḥiẓ, he pronounced him to be a shining light amongst scholars. But if he found him critical of Baghdad and not conversant with the rôle which must be imputed to it as the home of the arts and sciences of mankind, of which al-Jāḥiẓ was the supreme exponent, then no virtues which he might possess availed him after that.

When [the Ṣāḥib] Abū'l-Qāsim Ibn 'Abbād returned from Baghdad, Ibn al-'Amīd asked him about it. The former replied that Baghdad, at the side of other places, was like a master amongst slaves, and he set it up as an example of supreme excellence and perfection.[60]

Abū Naṣr Sahl b. al-Marzubān[61] once recited to me some verses which he had heard from their author, Ibn Zuraiq the secretary,[62] in praise of Baghdad (metre *Basīṭ*):

I have travelled much, and I have sought to find the equal of Baghdad and its people, but I have set myself a task which can only lead to despair;

Behold, in my opinion, Baghdad comprises the whole world, and its inhabitants are the whole human race! [172

He then recited to me the words of another poet (metre *Mutaqārib*):

May God keep moist with rain the garden which is Baghdad! It has become the refreshment of souls for all mankind,

With the proviso that it is a place of joy for the rich, but a place of sorrow for the penniless.

One of the remarkable things about Baghdad is the fact that, although the residence there of the Caliphs has made it the supreme capital, no Caliph has ever died there.[63] As 'Umāra b. 'Aqīl says (metre *Ṭawīl*)[64]:

Have you ever set eyes on a place like Baghdad in the whole length and breadth of the world? It is a veritable paradise on earth.

Its Lord has decreed that no Caliph shall ever die there; indeed, whatever He desires for His creatures, He ordains.

This has continued to be the case up to our own time, for al-Manṣūr died at Mecca; al-Mahdī at Māsapadhān; al-Hādī at 'Īsā-ābād; ar-Rashīd at Ṭūs; al-Amīn was killed; al-Ma'mūn died at Tarsus; al-Mu'taṣim and al-Wāthiq at Sāmarrā; al-Mutawakkil was killed; al-Muntaṣir died at Sāmarrā; al-Musta'īn, al-Mu'tazz and al-Muhtadī were all deposed and killed; al-Mu'tamid, al-Mu'taḍid and al-Muktafī died at al-Ḥasan- [173

[60] Tha'ālibī has also cited this episode in *ibid.*, III, 158.

[61] Prolific author and poet, resident in Nīshāpūr during Tha'ālibī's time; cf. *ibid.*, IV, 391-4.

[62] Abū'l-Ḥasan 'Alī b. Zuraiq (given by Yāqūt the *nisba* of 'al-Kūfī') lived in Baghdad as a poet and secretary in the early part of the 5th/11th century; cf. GAL, I, 82, Suppl. I, 133.

[63] Apparently the meaning is that no Caliph has ever died there a natural death or has died there whilst holding the office of Caliph.

[64] Great-grandson of the Umayyad poet Jarīr, poet and panegyrist of the Abbasids from al-Ma'mūn to al-Mutawahkil; of Bedouin origin, he acted as an informant for the Basra grammarians (cf. *Aghānī* [Beirut], XX, 436-47.

iyya; al-Muqtadir was killed; al-Qāhir was blinded; ar-Rāḍī died at al-Ḥasaniyya; al-Muttaqī and al-Mustakfī were blinded; al-Muṭī' died at Dair al-'Āqūl; and aṭ-Ṭā'i' was deposed. [174

AL-AHWĀZ

Its special characteristics include the fact that it has three towns, each celebrated for some rare and precious product which is not found in other lands of the east. These are:

[Firstly,] 'Askar Mukram, which has sugar whose excellence and extensive production are without equal in the rest of the world, even though there is much sugar-cane grown in Iraq, Gurgān and India; it is one of the most valuable products [exported from al-Ahwāz], and 50,000 *riṭls* of 'Askar Mukram sugar used to be forwarded to the central government in addition to the land tax.[65]

[Secondly,] Tustar, which produces splendidly-embroidered and costly satins, worthy to be mentioned in the same breath as those of Rūm.

[Thirdly,] as-Sūs, which produces expensive, embroidered silks of regal quality. [175

The defects of al-Ahwāz include the deadly scorpions called *jarrārāt*, although it is said that these have now decreased in numbers and left the region. Also, the people of al-Ahwāz have evolved an efficacious antidote.

Another defect is mentioned by al-Jāḥiẓ, that the chief city of al-Ahwāz is characterised by persistent, clinging fevers, which are deadly for strangers, although these fevers kill off the natives too just as quickly as they kill off the outsiders. Ibrāhīm b. al-'Abbās [aṣ-Ṣūlī][66] quoted some of the elders of al-Ahwāz about the midwives there, telling us that they often deliver babies and find that at the very moment of birth they have a fever. This fact is well-recognised amongst the midwives and often discussed by them. 'I myself', says al-Jāḥiẓ, 'have never seen there any boy or girl with rosy cheeks, with the blood-vessels visible through his skin or anything like that. Its plagues and fevers only occur when plagues and fevers have ceased to rage in all the other lands.' [176

Al-Ahwāz has the power of imprinting upon anyone who goes there many of its own peculiar characteristics and distinguishing features. Thus a Hāshimite, whether he be ugly or handsome, misshapen or well-formed, has a certain cast to his features which marks him out clearly from the rest of Quraish and from all the other Arabs. But the region comes very near to completely trans-

[65] J. Ruska, in EI[1] art. 'Sukkar', gives Bengal as the original home of the sugar-cane. The first certain mention of the product west of India is in the accounts of the conquest in 637 of the Persian town of Dastagird, when sugar purified from cane was found amongst Indian treasures. It is very probable that the cultivation of cane and the manufacture of sugar was introduced into Ahwāz and Lower Iraq at about this time; after the Muslim conquests its cultivation rapidly spread westwards, although Persia remained the main centre.

[66] See above, p. 66, n. 66.

forming and changing that; it takes away those features' distinctive aspects, gives them a sickly tinge and impresses on them its own traces. So just imagine what effect it has on other classes of people! Al-Jāḥiẓ goes on to say that the indigenous population of al-Ahwāz and those who go there do not become susceptible to all these fevers because of gastric disorders, distended bellies or over-eating; the fevers come from the very nature of the land.

In the same way, vipers abound on the mountain which comes down to and overlooks the houses in the city of al-Ahwāz, and the scorpions come into the houses and dwelling-places. If there were anything in the world worse than these vipers and scorpions, the city would not fail to generate and nurture it. The really unpleasant thing about the city is that there are lagoons and swamps of stagnant water behind it, and there are also streams fed by open
sewers from their privies and drainage channels from their [177
ablution-places and for carrying away rainwater. When the sun rises, it remains high for a long time directly facing the mountain and pouring down on the rocky place where those scorpions are. When the area becomes parched and hot, and becomes as if it were on fire,[67] it (sc. the sun?) throws off what it faces (sc. the scorpions) on to the people. The swamps and channels give off foul vapours, the air becomes foetid and everything affected by
that air becomes noisome too. [178

FĀRS

Its specialities include rosewater of an excellence unequalled in the whole world.[68] Jūrī rosewater comes from Jūr, one of the towns of Fārs, and is celebrated and proverbial for superlativeness, being exported to the most distant regions of the east and west.

As-Sarī[69] has spoken very eloquently when describing the flasks of rosewater in the following terms (metre *Rajaz*):

How many slender [flagons], like doe-eyed virgins, with their shifts wound round them, as if they were sweet-scented wallflowers!

Every maiden who has grown up in Jūr, who walks gracefully in her short, silk-lined robes,

Wafting from herself a gentle odour of perfume, like a breeze bringing with it a diffused aroma, [179

Brings a feeling of desire more intense than that of a distant one for a meeting with his loved one.

Together with the land tax, the Caliphs used to receive each year from Fārs, in accordance with the practice of requiring the specialities of each province, 30,000 flasks of Jūrī rosewater;

[67] This last phrase, *wa-'ādat jamratan wāḥidatan*, only appears in J. The Arabic of this whole paragraph is cryptic and difficult; Rescher, in *Orientalistische Miszellen*, I, 208, confesses that he may not have translated it properly.

[68] The distillation and preparation of perfumes was especially practised in Fārs; cf. Maqdisī, 443, quoted in Mez, *The renaissance of Islam*, 465-6.

[69] As-Sarī b. Aḥmad al-Kindī ar-Raffā', originally from Mosul, was a poet of Saif ad-Daula's circle, dying in 366/976-7; cf. *Yatīmat ad-dahr*, II, 117-82, and Ibn Khallikān, tr., I, 557-9.

5,000 garments made of cloth from the town of Tawwaj; 200 cloaks; 20,000 *riṭls* of black raisins; 15,000 *riṭls* of mango preserve (*anbijāt*); 10,000 *riṭls* of the edible clay of Sairāf; 1,000 *riṭls* of *julanjabīn*[70]; and a single *riṭl* of mummy (*mūmiyā*).[71] [180
This last is one of the specialities of Fārs, coming from the district of Dārābjird. They test its purity by breaking a cock's leg, and then they give it barleycorn's weight (*shā'ira*) of mummy; if the fracture heals, it appears as if there had been no break[72] there at all, but if it fails to heal, then the mummy is not pure.

According to al-Jāḥiẓ, Shīrāz, amongst all the towns of Fārs, has a remarkably sweet and perfumed atmosphere. [181

ISFAHĀN

It is famous for its wholesome atmosphere, its fertile soil and its sweet water; rarely are these qualities found together in one city.

It is related that al-Ḥajjāj appointed one of his entourage as governor over Iṣfahān and said to him, 'I have made you governor over a city whose mineral is antimony (*kuḥl*),[73] whose flying insects are bees and whose plant is saffron.' The explanation of this is that the antimony there is celebrated for its excellence, saffron grows profusely and bees abound. I once read an epistle written by 'Alī b. Ḥamza b. 'Umāra al-Iṣfahānī[74] to Abū'l-Ḥasan Ṭabāṭabā[75] in praise of these bees and their honey, in which he says that Iṣfahān honey is the best of all honey, and the very best of this is the honey which, when some of it is allowed to drip on the ground, stays in one blob like mercury, and does not become mingled with the earth. [182

Together with the land tax, 2,000 *riṭls* of honey and 20,000 *riṭls* of wax used to be taken from Iṣfahān each year to the seat of the central government.[76]

Amongst the most neatly-expressed of satires launched against Iṣfahān on account of its people are the words of the poet (metre *Khafīf*):

May God curse the town of Iṣfahān, and may He hurl upon it consumption and plague!

When I was there in summer, I had to sell my framework of canvas sheeting[77] *for keeping cool, and in one of the winter months* (kānūn), *I pawned my brazier* (kānūn). [183

THE SPECIAL FEATURES OF MOSUL

Al-Jāḥiẓ says that whoever resides in Mosul for a year, and then examines carefully his own mind, will find that it has become

[70] A preserve made from rosewater and honey (Persian *gul* + *angabīn*).

[71] Apparently the bituminous mineral variety of mummy, cf. *Tuḥfat al-aḥbāb*, 117-18, No. 263; Yāqūt, *Mu'jam al-buldān*, I, 143, s.v. Arrajān in Fārs, mentions a cave in a mountain where 'white mummy' is obtained.

[72] I read here *faṣl* for *faḍl*.

[73] *Kuḥl*, used for darkening round the eyes = antimony or antimony trisulphide, stibium; cf. Guigues, JA (Jan.-June 1905), 483-4, No. 17, under *ithmid*.

[74] Scholar and poet of Iṣfahān, and author of a book on its history and excellences; cf. Yāqūt, *Irshād*, V, 200-2.

[75] Poet and rhetorician of Iṣfahān, and of Alid descent, d. 322/934; cf. *ibid.*, VI, 284-93.

[76] According to Ibn Rusta, 157, tr. 182, the Caliphal court consumed no other honey but the pure white honey of Iṣfahān.

[77] As Rescher notes, *op. cit.*, 210, one can hardly translate *qubbat al-khaish* except with this meaning, sc. a contrivance for keeping cool.

more incisive. Someone else has commented that the curtainings of Mosul are to be mentioned in the same breath as the rugs of Qālīqalā, the mattresses of Maisān and the under-carpets of Armenia[78]; and in its excellence, the honey of Mosul must be linked with the sugar-cane of al-Ahwāz and the saffron of Qum. [184

THE SPECIALITIES OF RAY

The mantles manufactured at Ray are as famed as those of the Yemen and are, indeed, called *'Adaniyyāt* in allusion to the mantles of Aden in the Yemen. Al-Murādī[79] says, describing a peregrine falcon (metre *Kāmil*):

You would imagine that when it shakes off[80] *the dew from its wings, it was showering pearls from off one of the mantles of Ray.*

The specialities of Ray also include pieces of silk woven with a double thread through them (*munayyar*); sharp-pointed shears; good-quality combs; pomegranates of the kind known as 'fiery-coloured'[81] and those known as 'smooth-skinned' (*imlīsī*). Together with the land tax of Ray, they used to send [annually] to the central government 100,000 pomegranates and 1,000 [185
riṭls of dried peaches.

One of the cleverest of satires which have been directed against the people of Ray is that of Ismā'īl ash-Shāshī (metre *Wāfir*)[82]:

Avoid the wrath of the One [God], and do not place too much reliance on anyone;

There is no-one at Ray worthy even of the name 'No-one'![83]

It is related that Abū 'Abbād Thābit b. Yaḥyā[84] once went into al-Ma'mūn's presence, strutting in with a haughty manner, and the Caliph said (metre *Sarī'*):

The conceitedness of Khurāsān, the arrogance of the Nabataeans, the pride of the people of Khūzistān and the perfidy of the soldiers of the guard,

All meet together in you, and in addition to all that, you are a Rāzī, deeply sunk in erroneous ways.

[78] Cf. R. Ettinghausen, EI[1] Suppl. art. 'Ḳālī', citing Yāqūt that the term *qālī* 'carpet' is a shortened *nisba* from Qālīqalā = Erzerum. The first carpets generally known in the Islamic world were from Armenia, and these were renowned for their fine wool and their crimson colour; Marco Polo praises Armenian carpets as the finest in the world.

[79] Abū'l-Ḥusain Muḥammad al-Murādī, poet of Bukhārā and a member of the Sāmānid Naṣr b. Aḥmad's court circle; cf. *Yatīmat ad-dahr*, IV, 74-8 and Lazard, *Les premiers poètes persans* (Tehran-Paris 1964), I, 23.

[80] Following the *tanaffaḍa* of AS instead of the *tanaqqaḍa* of J.

[81] Following the suggested reading *hīrij/hērij* of AS; the texts have *t.h.r.j.*

[82] Būyid poet, in the circle of the Ṣāḥib Ibn al-'Abbād; cf. *Yatīmat ad-dahr*, III, 385-91.

[83] The translation of these two lines is uncertain. According to Rescher, *op. cit.*, 211, the second line as given in the text is metrically disturbed; he emends the last phrase of the second verse from *li'smi lā aḥadi* to *li'smi 'l-Aḥadi* and translates 'There is no-one at Ray who merits the name of the One [God]', sc. merits a theophoric name like 'Abd al-Aḥad. In fact, the line as it stands in the text scans perfectly as *Wāfir*, dimeter.

[84] Abū 'Abbād ar-Rāzī, Vizier to al-Ma'mūn, cf. Sourdel, *Le vizirat 'Abbāside*, I, 231-2; his character was notoriously harsh. The anecdote which follows is also given by Tha'ālibī in his *Thimār al-qulūb*, 191-2, s.v. 'Luṣūṣ ar-Rayy'.

Aṣ-Ṣūlī says that by the words 'you are a Rāzī', he means that he takes bribes, and he imputes thievery to him, because skilful thieves are especially attributed to Ray. [186

ṬABARISTĀN

It is said that the things which would adorn anywhere else, sc. trees, vegetation and streams, mar it. Its specialities include the variety of citron called *utrujj*[85], cloaks, coarse linen towels, linen undergarments and cotton head-coverings. A peculiar feature is that dirhams are brought to Ṭabaristān from all parts of the world in payment for the linen towels exported from there, but they never pass out of the country again. [187

JURJĀN (GURGĀN)

Gurgān comprises both plains and mountains, inland and coastal regions. Its people are able to enumerate over a hundred different kinds of aromatic herbs, vegetables and plants of the open plains, together with fruits and berries of the lowlands and mountains, and all these are freely available to anyone. The lowest strata of the population, and many people who have come in from outside, can live merely by picking and gathering them together and then selling them. These products of the soil include pomegranate seeds, the seeds of the *qaṭūnā*,[86] the apricot and the perfumed[87] narcissus. However, the most outstanding of the fruits of Gurgān are its figs and jujubes; the latter are one of the specialities of the province, and are of an unparalleled quality. One may find displayed in the markets of Gurgān, at one and the same time, both winter and summer, fruits and vegetables, including aubergines, cucumbers, radishes, carrots, beans and sugar-cane. All through the winter months one can always obtain kids and lambs, fresh milk, sweet-smelling herbs, flowers and fruits, like lavender, wallflowers and violets, citrons and oranges. One also finds in [188
Gurgān fish, waterfowl, partridges and pheasants.

The people of Gurgān resemble those of Iraq in their cleanliness, handsomeness, elegance, magnanimity, ease of life and liberality. It is sometimes called 'Baghdad the Lesser', except that it is fever-ridden and sultry, with its weather liable to change several times during the course of a single day, very damp and lethal for incomers.[88] Indeed, Gurgān is said to be the graveyard of the people of Khurāsān, and it is recorded in some old book that there is a place in Khurāsān called Gurgān to which people whose lives are only going to be short are driven (sc. by Fate). Abū Turāb an-

85 *Utrujj* is translated here as 'citron' (= *Citrus limonum Risso* or *Citrus medica var. β* L.), but is more properly the cedrate, *Citrus medica Risso*; cf. Guigues, JA (Jan.-June 1905), 489-90, No. 46.

86 *Bizr qaṭūnā* = the seeds of the flea-wort or flea-bane, the plantain *Plantago psyllium* L., so-called because the seeds resemble fleas; these seeds are very sticky and are used in the preparation of muslin cloths. Cf. Guigues, *op. cit.*, 494, No. 62.

87 I read with J *al-miskī* instead of the *as-sikkī* of AS.

88 See on the variableness of the climate of Māzandarān, the Hon. G. N. Curzon, *Persia and the Persian question* (London 1892), I, 360ff., and H. L. Rabino di Borgomale, *Mázandarán and Astarábád*, GMS, N.S. VII (London 1928), 9.

Nīshāpūrī[89] used to say that when the countries of the world were being divided out amongst the angels, Gurgān fell within the share of Abū Yaḥyā, the Angel of Death, because pestilence is so rife there. [189

[89] I have not been able to identify this man.

Concerning the variableness of its climate, the present author has composed these verses (metre *Ṭawīl*):

On many a debilitating day in Gurgān I have been driven to laughter, and at the same time I have marvelled at its strange nature.[90]

The changeableness of its weather has made me fearful, but there is no place of refuge from God's decree.

What can you do about a day which is fickle and variable, with cold followed by blazing heat?

In the first part of the day, you need to put on furs and kindle a fire, whereas towards the end of it, you call for snow and canvas sheeting (sc. for keeping cool).

[90] I follow the *min khulqihi* of J in preference to the *min khurqihi* of A S. These verses appear also in the *Thimār al-qulūb*, 440, s.v. 'Hawā' Jurjān', but with several variants.

Al-Ma'mūn once returned from Khurāsān to Iraq via Gurgān. It rained there continuously for nearly a month, until he became weary and disgusted, saying, 'Let's get out of this perpetual drizzle!' [190

The specialities of Gurgān include black-coloured garments, cloths made from double-threaded yarn[91] and 'poppy-coloured' cloths, which are superior to the *ḥafī* cloths of Nishapur in their fineness and delicacy. [191

[91] *Mabārim*; cf. Lane, *Lexicon*, s.v. *mubram*, 'a garment or piece of cloth, of which the thread is twisted of two yarns, or distinct twists'.

NĪSHĀPŪR

It is said that every town named after Shāpūr is outstanding and full of choice things, such as Shāpūr in Fārs, Jundīshāpūr in al-Ahwāz, Farshāpūr in India (sc. Peshawar) and above all, Nīshāpūr, which is the navel of Khurāsān and its supreme pride.[92]

[92] According to Tha'ālibī in the *Ghurar as-siyar*, 494, 529, Shāpūr b. Ardashīr founded the first two towns and a later emperor, Shāpūr b. Hurmuz Dhū'l-Aktāf, the second pair of towns.

Al-Ma'mūn used to say that the outstanding city (literally, 'eye') of Syria was Damascus; of Rūm, Constantinople; of al-Jazīra, ar-Raqqa; of Iraq, Baghdad; of Jibāl, Iṣfahān; of Khurāsān, Nīshāpūr; and of Transoxania, Samarqand. 'Amr b. al-Laith used to say, 'How should I not fight to defend a city whose [192
characteristic plant is the rhubarb (*rībās*),[93] whose soil produces *nuql* and whose ground also yields turquoises?' By *nuql* he merely

[93] *Rheum ribes*, translated by Dozy, *Supplément*, as 'rhubarbe groseille'. This variety of rhubarb seems to be indigenous to Persia; it is treated at length by the Islamic writers on *materia medica*, including Abū Manṣūr Muwaffaq and Ibn al-Baiṭar. Cf. B. Laufer, *Sino-Iranica, Chinese contributions to the history of civilisation in ancient Iran, with special reference to the history of cultivated plants and products*, Field Museum of Natural History Publications 201, Anthropological Ser. Vol. XV, No. 3 (Chicago 1919), 547-51.

TB K

meant edible earth, whose like is found nowhere else in the world.[94] It is exported from Zauzan in the district of Nīshāpūr both to adjacent countries and to the remote corners of the world, and given as a present to kings and great leaders. A *riṭl* of it is often sold in Egypt and the Maghrib for a dinar. Muḥammad b. Zakariyā' ar-Rāzī[95] extolled its virtues and composed a small book exclusively about it and on how it should be eaten after a meal. Abū Ṭālib has written concerning it (metre *Sarī'*)[96]:

Lavish upon me edible earth, that substance from which we were created and to which we return.

When first one sees it, it looks like lumps of camphor sprinkled with subtly-compounded perfume. [193

As for the turquoises,[97] they are found nowhere else but at Nīshāpūr. The price of a setting of one of these jewels often reaches 200 dinars, provided that it weighs over a *mithqāl*, combines the two qualities of being milky-white and green in colour, has been unaffected after exposure to fire and untouched by a file, and is not changed in any way by the action upon it of boiling water. Amongst the attractive qualities of the turquoise is the auspiciousness which lies in its name (*fīrūz* = in Persian, 'victorious, successful'), and the high opinion of it held by kings and great men, this last arising from the combination of its intrinsic beauty and the favourable omen which prominent leaders draw from it. It is said to have a special property whereby a man's heart becomes strengthened merely by looking at it, just as the sapphire has the property of making the soul rejoice. The turquoises of Nīshāpūr are accounted amongst the most precious of all jewels, along with the sapphires of Ceylon, the pearls of 'Umān, the chrysolites of Egypt, the cornelians of the Yemen, the garnets of Balkh and the rubies of Badakhshān. [194

When the Sāmānid Ismā'īl b. Aḥmad came to Nīshāpūr, he was greatly struck by its attractiveness and healthiness, saying, 'What a wonderful place it would be, were it not for two defects: the waters which run beneath the earth there[98] ought to be on the surface, and the learned men on the surface ought to be under the earth!'

[94] On the edible earth (= diatomaceous earth or kieselguhr, made up of the siliceous remains of minute aquatic organisms) of the Nīshāpūr district, see Ibn Ḥauqal, *Kitāb ṣūrat al-arḍ*, ed. Kramers (Leiden 1938-9), II, 446-7; he says that *aṭ-ṭīn an-najāḥī*, found in the region between Nīshāpūr and Qā'in, is exported all over the world. The whole subject of earth-eating is exhaustively treated by Laufer in his monograph *Geophagy*, Field Museum of Natural History Publications, 280, Anthropological Ser. Vol. XVIII, No. 2 (Chicago 1930), 101-98, cf. pp. 150-5 on this phenomenon amongst the Persians and Arabs.

[95] Sc. ar-Rāzī, the Rhazes of mediaeval Europe, the greatest authority of his age on medicine, active during part of his career at the court of the Sāmānid Abū Ṣāliḥ Manṣūr b. Isḥāq; d. 311/923 or 320/932 (cf. P. Kraus and S. Pines in EI[1] s.v.). The work mentioned here on edible earth is no longer extant, but Rāzī on this is quoted by Ibn al-Baiṭar in his *Jāmi' al-mufradāt al-akbar*, cf. Laufer, *op. cit.*, 150ff.

[96] Abū Ṭālib 'Abd as-Salām al-Ma'mūnī, poet and littérateur, descendant of the Caliph al-Ma'mūn. He left Baghdad and ended up at Bukhārā, where Tha'ālibī met him. According to Tha'ālibī, he never forgot his royal blood, and, until his premature death in 383/993, the constant aim of his life was to march on Baghdad with an army and seize the Caliphate (*Yatīmat ad-dahr*, IV, 161-91, cf. Barthold, *Turkestan*, 258).

[97] See Laufer, *Note on turquois in the east*, Field Museum of Natural History Publications, 169, Anthropological Ser. Vol. XIII, No. 1 (Chicago 1913), 38ff., on the antiquity of turquoises in Persia and their export thence to India.

[98] An allusion to the extensive system of *qanāts* or underground irrigation channels of Nīshāpūr, cf. Bosworth, *The Ghaznavids: their empire in Afghanistan and eastern Iran 994-1040*, 155-7.

The specialities of Nīshāpūr include finely-woven (*ḥafī*) textiles, closely-woven towels, *tākhtaj* cloth (? with a twisted thread running through it), *rākhtaj* silks and uniformly-coloured silks. As for sets of robes, *'attābī* and *saqlāṭūnī* cloths, Nīshāpūr [195
shares pre-eminence here with Baghdad and Iṣfahān. The term *sāburī* is applied to any fine and delicate cloth; it is originally a relative adjectival form from 'Nīshāpūr', arabised to *sāburī*.

A poem about Nīshāpūr composed by one of the Ṭāhirids was once recited to me (metre *Khafīf*):

Nīshāpūr has no peer in all the world: a good soil and a most merciful lord over it.[99] [196

However, al-Murādī has made complaints about the people of Nīshāpūr in his lines (metre *Basīṭ*)[100]:

Do not come to Nīshāpūr as a stranger, unless you have some bond of influence with the ruling power there;

If you have none, no social and intellectual polish will avail you, no noble lineage will profit you, nor will people show any respect for your status.

And also in his lines (metre *Basīṭ*):

Al-Murādī has pronounced a verdict which is not to be impugned, and his counsel should be received by all intelligent people:

Do not come to Nīshāpūr as a stranger, for a stranger at Nīshāpūr is duped. [197

ṬŪS

Its special features include the shrine of [the Imām] 'Alī b. Mūsā ar-Riḍā, and a certain poet has said concerning Ṭūs (metre *Basīṭ*):

O land of Ṭūs, may God refresh you with His mercy! What blessings you enfold, O Ṭūs!

Your earth is hallowed above all others, and a pure one, buried there at Sīnābād, adorns it.

O tomb, you are a tomb which encompasses learning, nobility of character, purity of soul and holiness,

A unique pride! For you are blessed through having his body, and are protected by the noble angels!

I have heard one of the elders of Ṭūs say that Hārūn ar-Rashīd is in fact buried in the tomb popularly attributed to ar-Riḍā, and ar-Riḍā in the one considered to be Hārūn's, the two tombs being adjacent to each other, and that this substitution was arranged by al-Ma'mūn; but God knows best. [198

The specialities of Ṭūs include jet, a unique product which is

[99] Allusion to Qur'ān, xxxiv, 14/15. In Yāqūt, *Mu'jam al-buldān*, v, 332, this line is attributed to Abū'l-'Abbās az-Zauzanī al-Ma'mūnī.

[100] On al-Murādī, see above, p. 129, n. 79; these verses are also quoted in *Yatīmat ad-dahr*, iv, 75.

exported to all parts of the world, and the white stone of which cooking-pots, frying-pans and censers are made; one can make from it everything which is normally made from glass, such as drinking-cups, water-jugs, etc. I have heard Abū Ja'far Muḥammad b. Mūsā al-Mūsawī aṭ-Ṭūsī[101] say, 'Abū Manṣūr Muḥammad b. 'Abd ar-Razzāq used to comment that God Most High had made stone malleable for the people of Ṭūs, just as He had made iron malleable for David.'[102] [199

HERAT

I once heard Abū Bakr al-Khwārazmī say that there were only three things that he envied the people of Herat for: that the shrine of 'Abdallāh b. Mu'āwiya b. 'Abdallāh b. Ja'far b. Abī Ṭālib is there[103]; that a beverage from the *qishmish* fruit is made there; and that Abū'l-Qāsim ad-Dā'ūdī[104] resides there.

A poet of Herat, called as-Sāmī,[105] has said (metre *Sarī'*):

Herat is a place of unbounded fertility; its characteristic plants are the mandragora and narcissus.

No-one leaves it for another place except when he has become penniless.

The specialities of Herat include currants made from the small variety of green grape called *qishmish* and *Ṭā'ifī* raisins,[106] both of which are exported far and wide. Al-Ma'mūnī[107] once [200 recited to me some lines in praise of *Ṭā'ifī* raisins (metre *Munsariḥ*):

How often do the topers enjoy a dessert of Ṭā'ifī raisins brought in with the wine!

When they are placed in a flagon, it appears like a flask of garnet filled with honey.

Other specialities of Herat are furs made from the throat and crop feathers of aquatic birds like the pelican and cormorant (*ḥawāṣil*), which are finer than those of Egypt and Ābaskūn.[108]

[101] Cited as an authority several times in the *Yatīmat ad-dahr*; see Mawlawī Abū Mūsá Aḥmadu'l-Ḥaqq, *Farīdatu'l-'aṣr* (Calcutta 1915), 169-70.

[102] Allusion to Qur'ān, xxxiv, 10. I have altered the *'Abd ar-Rāziq* of the texts to the correct *'Abd ar-Razzāq*. Abū Manṣūr was the local ruler of Ṭūs, descendant of a very old Iranian family; d. 350/962. It was for him that a translation from the Pahlavi of the Iranian national epic, the *Khwadhāy-nāmak* or 'Book of kings', was made into New Persian; it was from this translation that an older preface to Firdausī's *Shāh-nāma*, found prefixed to some manuscripts of the poem, was made in the middle years of the 4th/10th century (cf. Minorsky, 'The older preface to the *Shāh-nāma*', *Studi orientalistici in onore di G. Levi della Vida* [Rome 1956], II, 161-6).

[103] 'Abdallāh b. Mu'āwiya led an Alid rising in Kufa in 127/744, and with the help of the Khawārij, held much of southern and western Persia. Defeated by the Umayyad Caliph Marwān II's troops, he fled to Khurāsān, but was executed at Nīshāpūr on Abū Muslim's orders. He was buried at Herat, where his tomb became a place of pilgrimage (cf. *Aghānī* [Beirut], XI, 120-42 =[Dār al-Kutub] XII, 216-38; Muir, *The Caliphate*, 411-12; Zetterstéen, EI² s.v.). In the 9th/15th century the tomb was reconstructed by a Timurid governor of Herat (Mu'īn ad-Dīn Zamchī Isfizārī, *Rauḍāt al-jannāt fī auṣāf madīnat Harāt*, ed. S. M. Kāẓim Imām [Tehran 1338-9/1959-60], I, 281-2). The shrine exists today in the northern quarter of Herat, and is still venerated; it is illustrated in Plate XII accompanying A. Z. V. Togan's article 'Herat' in *Islâm Ansiklopedisi* (Istanbul 1940-).

[104] AS has erroneously *ad-Dāwarī* for the *nisba*, and I have followed J, whose reading is confirmed by *Yatīmat ad-dahr*, IV, 345, where Abū'l-Qāsim ad-Dā'ūdī is called 'the unique one of the literary men and scholars of Herat'.

[105] In *ibid.*, IV, 350, Tha'ālibī mentions this man as Abū Aḥmad as-Sāwī al-Harawī.

[106] On these, see *Ḥudūd al-'ālam*, 104-5, and Laufer, *Sino-Iranica*, 231, 241, who believes that *qishmish* is a Turkish word; according to the 17th century French traveller Tavernier, these grapes, dried into raisins, were still exported to India from Shīrāz.

[107] See above, p. 132, n. 96.

[108] Ābaskūn, in early Islamic times a flourishing port on the Caspian coast of Gurgān; cf. Minorsky, EI² s.v.

Amongst the products of Herat exported to the far corners of the earth are white cotton cloths, cloths made from double-threaded yarn, satin brocades and fine copperware. [201

MERV

It is said that it was built by Dhū'l-Qarnain (sc. Alexander the Great) and that the prophet 'Uzair, peace be upon him, prayed there. In the Islamic period, it was long the seat of the governors of Khurāsān until 'Abdallāh b. Ṭāhir transferred to Nīshāpūr and made that his capital. The Arabs used to call all thick and coarse cloths brought from Khurāsān *Marawī*,[109] and all finely-woven ones *Shāhajānī*, for they considered Merv to be the focal point of Khurāsān and the city was called Merv ash-Shāhajān; to this day, all fine garments are called *Shāhajānī*.

The specialities of Merv include cloths woven with a gold thread (*mulḥam*).[110] Abū'l-Fatḥ al-Bustī, the secretary,[111] said to me one day, 'Do you know a city beginning with the letter *mīm*, from which four products are frequently brought to other lands for giving away as presents, and each one also beginning with *mīm*?' I retorted, 'I can't think of one on the spur of the moment, but if I can think about it, I might be able to recall one to mind.' He immediately said, however, 'It's Merv. From it one [202 gets *mulḥam* cloth, *mulabban* confectionery, *murrī* brine for pickling[112] and sweeping-brushes (*makānis*).'

Some of the neatest lines I have ever heard in praise of Merv are those of a certain poet who was a secretary (metre *Khafīf*):

A healthy spot, abundant running water and earth whose sweetness surpasses even that of subtly-compounded perfume!

Whenever a man plans to depart from there, its very name prevents him from leaving (*ma-rū* = in Persian, 'do not go!').[113] [203

BALKH

Balkh is one of the focal points of Khurāsān; there are in fact four of these, Nīshāpūr, Merv, Herat and Balkh. Balkh is one of the oldest of cities and kings have especially favoured it as a capital. It is said that one may see in it elements reminiscent of Iraq, Khurāsān and India. The Oxus is connected with it too, for one calls it 'the river of Balkh'. Shahīd b. al-Ḥusain used to say, 'Life in summer at Balkh is like an altered form of its name.'[114]

I once heard a poem by the late Yaḥyā b. Mu'ādh ar-Rāzī,[115] may God have mercy on him, written when he left Balkh for Khuttal (metre *Wāfir*):

[109] Cf. Mez, *The renaissance of Islam*, 463, on the coarse flannels and cloths of Merv; Mutanabbī, *Dīwan* (Beirut 1318/1900), 16, speaks of the true Merv cloths as 'monkeys' wear', *libs al-qurūd*.

[110] On these, see Dozy, *Dictionnaire détaillé des noms des vêtements arabes* (Amsterdam 1845), 113.

[111] The famous poet and stylist, renowned for his use of paronomasia and hence called the *Ṣāḥib at-tajnīs*; d. *c.* 400/1010 after service in the chanceries of Sebüktigin and Maḥmūd of Ghazna (cf. J. W. Fück, EI² s.v.). Tha'ālibī was a great friend of Bustī; he composed for him his *Kitāb aḥsan mā sami'tu*, made a selection of his poetry (see above, Introduction, p. 10) and devoted to him a long section in the *Yatīmat ad-dahr*, IV, 303-34.

[112] *Murrī* brine prepared from the gut of anchovies was also used medicinally; cf. Guigues, JA (July-Dec. 1905), 63, No. 385. A *Risāla fī'l-murrī* by Jāḥiẓ is mentioned in Yūsuf b. 'Umar at-Turkumānī, *al-Mu'tamad fī'l-adwiya al-mufrada* (Cairo 1370/1951), 492, but is not otherwise known.

[113] These two lines are attributed in *Yatīmat ad-dahr*, IV, 80, to the poet and official Abū 'Alī as-Sājī.

[114] Sc. an altered form of the consonantal dots of *B.l.kh*; AS suggests *thalj* 'snow', but J suggests more plausibly the Persian word *talkh* 'bitter'. On Shahīd al-Balkhī, see Lazard, *Les premiers poètes persans*, I, 20-1.

[115] A famous Ṣūfī mystic, who died at Nīshāpūr in 258/872; cf. Ibn Khallikān, tr. IV, 51-4.

We departed early in the morning from the people of Balkh, may peace rest upon that city and its populace!

What happiness and kindness we enjoyed there! Its people are indeed noble and generous! [204

If you are contemplating settling down amongst any people, then you will find Balkh a most pleasant spot.

Its specialities include garnets, the nenuphar or waterlily,[116] soap and many other things I am unable to mention here. [205

BUST

Its air is said to be like that of Iraq and its water like that of the Euphrates; indeed, Bust unites within itself the best aspects of many other regions. One of my friends asked me about Bust. I replied that it is best described by putting it into the dual form, i.e. it is a garden (*bustān*). Then I went on to mention this story and this *bon mot* to the Commander-in-Chief, Amīr Abū'l-Muẓaffar Naṣr ad-Dīn[117]; he was delighted, and he often repeated it afterwards. I heard Abū'l-Fatḥ Bustī the secretary say that Abū Naṣr al-Maqdisī[118] used to say, 'In all the countries of the earth which I have travelled through, I have never seen one superior to Bust in beauty, healthiness, abundance of provisions, dates, sweet-smelling herbs and cultivated vegetables. I firmly believe that whoever dies at Bust, having the assurance of divine forgiveness, is simply transported from one garden of paradise to another.'

Its specialities include plums of a quality unmatched elsewhere; they are considered to be amongst those superlative fruits generally recognised as specialities of their regions, all of which specialities are mentioned *en bloc* at the end of the book. As for the [206
so-called figs of Sīstān, they ought more properly to be attributed to Bust, for they constitute a further speciality of Bust, one which is exported to Khurāsān and elsewhere.

But the proudest boast which Bust can make is that it has brought forth the unique figure of the age, the crown of the epoch, the outstanding figure of both this inferior world and the superior one, the Ṣāḥib Shams al-Kufāt [Aḥmad b. Ḥasan al-Maimandī].[119] It has brought into our minds the line (metre *Ṭawīl*):

When you have raised a town to such a pitch of glory (literally, *'have drawn it up by the arm'*), *there is no wonder that you should be called the heaven of its heaven.*[120]

The author of this book has written some verses in praise of this noble and exalted town, including the following (metre *Wāfir*):

[116] Nenuphar = *Nymphaea alba, N. lutea, N. caerulea,* etc., mentioned here as a speciality because the roots of the last species at least were commonly eaten as food in the Middle East and India; cf. Guigues, *op. cit.*, 65, No. 400, and *Tuḥfat al-aḥbāb*, 128-9, No. 288.

[117] See above, Introduction, p. 6.

[118] Possibly the al-Muṭahhar b. Ṭāhir al-Maqdisī al-Bustī, who in 355/966 wrote at Bust his historical compilation, the *Kitāb al-bad' wa't-ta'rīkh* 'Book of creation and history' (cf. GAL, Supp. I, 222); al-Muṭahhar's *kunya* does not seem to be recorded.

[119] Sc. the dedicatee of the book, see above, Introduction, p. 6.

[120] This is the interpretation of Defrémery in JA (July-Dec. 1867), 351, quoting Sylvestre de Sacy, *Chrestomathie arabe*², I, 397, n. 10; Rescher omits this verse from his translation in *Orientalistische Miszellen*, I, 220.

I have become a great lover of liberality, for it is your own nature, and I have kissed (bustu) *the earth of Bust, for it is your encampment-ground;*

This present age has no desire to reap and harvest me, for amongst the circles of those with the polish of polite learning, I am your seed. [207

GHAZNA

It is well-known for its pure air, fertile soil and sweet water. It is mountainous and has a septentrional climate; people there are long-lived and have few illnesses. What do you think of a region which produces gold, yet has no harmful snakes or scorpions or insects? It is the most wholesome and the cleanest of all lands.

Its specialities include the property of bringing forth bold and courageous men; Abū Muslim wrote to Abū Dā'ūd[121] for the latter to send him some of the men of Zābulistān and the horses of Ṭukhāristān.[122] But the most exalted of the merits of Ghazna and the most noble of its characteristics is that it is the birthplace of Sultan Abū'l-Qāsim Maḥmūd, son of Nāṣir ad-Dīn [Sebüktigin], may God have mercy on him.[123] Concerning Ghazna, the [208
author has written (metre *Basīṭ*):

O seat of power, we see all beauty summed up in you, and the most auspicious events of the age have arisen from you.

It is as if the garden of paradise had descended[124] *on the land of Ghazna, rushing ahead of its creator.*

I heard Abū Sa'd Muḥammad b. Manṣūr,[125] the local leader (*za'īm*) of the people of Gurgān, say that he had never seen a town pleasanter in summer than Ghazna, with a more spring-like climate, or more free from noxious reptiles and insects. Then he added, 'The scarceness of fruit there is one of its good points, because an abundance of fruits is always linked with an abundance of diseases; the less fruit grown in a place, the less sickness there.' Finally he said, 'I saw four things at Ghazna whose like I have seen nowhere else: *amīrī* apples, those contrivances [209
which they call *zhāla* (sc. inflatable skins used as pontoons for crossing rivers),[126] the rhubarb plant and the buttermilk drink *dūghbāj*,[127] and all these are specialities of the place.' The present author has written concerning *amīrī* apples (metre *Basīṭ*):

[121] Abū Dā'ūd Khālid b. Ibrāhīm adh-Dhuhlī, one of Abū Muslim's generals in eastern Khurāsān just after the Abbasid revolution, and 137-40/754-7 governor of Nīshāpūr.

[122] In the Iranian national epic Zābulistān is the land of heroes and the home of Zāl and Rustam; cf. Marquart, *Ērānsahr nach der Geographie des Ps. Moses Xorenac'i, Abhandlungen der Königl. Gesell. der Wissenschaften zu Göttingen*, Phil.-Hist. Kl., N.F. III/3 (Berlin 1901), 39-40. The valleys of the upper Oxus lands, including Ṭukhāristān, were famous for horse-breeding; see the references in Bosworth, 'Ghaznevid military organisation', *Der Islam*, XXXVI (1960), 58-9.

[123] The prayer for mercy after Maḥmūd's name is doubtless a later interpolation.

[124] Following the variant *qad nazalat* given for this line in Nuwairī, *Nihayat al-arab*, I, 365.

[125] Abū Sa'd appears in early Ghaznavid history as one of the envoys to Ghazna sent by the Ziyārid Manūchihr b. Qābūs to seek the hand in marriage of Maḥmūd's daughter; see his biography in Ḥamza b. Yūsuf as-Sahmī, *Ta'rīkh Jurjān* (Hyderabad 1369/1950), 411. Abū Sa'd is also mentioned in the biography of his son Abū'l-Maḥāsin, also *ra'īs* of Gurgān during Mas'ūd of Ghazna's time, in Tha'ālibī's *Tatimmat al-yatīma*; Tha'ālibī himself received hospitality from Abū Sa'd when in Gurgān in 403/1012-13.

[126] Thus defined in the earliest known vocabulary of New Persian, Asadī Ṭūsī's *Lughat-i Furs* (Tehran 1336/1957), 118-19.

[127] Sc. the modern Persian *dūgh* = Arabic *laban* = Turkish *ayran*, a drink made from yoghourt and water.

The apples of Ghazna are of great benefit and are sweet-smelling, as if they were made up of honeycomb, aromatic herbs and wine,

And their juice is like the saliva of a moon-faced youth, whose cheeks have always the flush of roses and apples. [210

SIJISTĀN (SISTĀN)

In certain historical accounts there is recorded that some ancient authority said of it that its water was scanty, its dates of poor quality and its brigands very audacious; and that if a small army is sent there, it is liable to perish, and if a numerous one is sent, it will die of hunger anyway.[128]

When al-Muwaffaq marched against 'Amr b. al-Laith, who was then in Fārs, the latter abandoned Fārs and made for Kirmān. Al-Muwaffaq pursued him, and 'Amr drew him on to the [211
Sīstān road. Al-Muwaffaq wanted to continue his march, but someone said to him, 'Why should you penetrate into the desert, when you will find nothing but sand and poisonous vipers?' So he turned back to Iraq, and later sent Ibn Abī'l-Aṣbagh to make peace with 'Amr on the basis of the latter paying tribute. It is related that al-Muwaffaq had taken with him on his campaign leather vessels filled with Tigris water, but when he reached the Helmand river in Sīstān, he found it extremely sweet-tasting and pleasant. He compared it with the Tigris water and found no difference between the two in regard to sweetness and agreeableness. Consequently, he ordered the Tigris water to be poured away and said, 'This local water makes it superfluous to carry the Tigris water any further.'[129]

Ḥāḍir b. Muḥammad aṭ-Ṭūsī[130] recited to me the lines of the Qāḍī Abū 'Alī al-Musabbaḥī al-Baṣrī (metre *Mutaqārib*)[131]:

My coming to Sīstān was a bad turn of fortune, and that I should stay there was almost incredible, [212

For Sīstān has no natural advantages beyond its fine narcissi and fresh dates.

Shabīb b. Shaiba[132] described the vipers of Sīstān in these terms: 'The small ones pierce like swords, but the big ones spell death.' The vipers of Sīstān are bracketed with the serpents of Egypt, the virulent scorpions of al-Ahwāz and the ordinary scorpions of Shahrazūr, whilst the snake-charmers of Sīstān are mentioned in the same breath as the philosophers of ancient Greece, the goldsmiths of Ḥarrān, the weavers of the Yemen, the secretaries of the Sawād (sc. central Iraq), the physicians of Jundīshāpūr, the

128 This saying is found in Balādhurī, *Futūḥ al-buldān*, 420-1, where the words are attributed to the general Ḥakīm b. Jabala al-'Abdī, reporting back to the Caliph 'Uthmān after a reconnaissance of the region.

129 This unsuccessful campaign of al-Muwaffaq against the Ṣaffārids took place in 274/887; cf. Nöldeke, in *Sketches from eastern history* (Edinburgh 1892), 198-9.

130 Ḥāḍir aṭ-Ṭūsī is cited in *Yatīmat ad-dahr*, IV, 126, 145, 150, as having recited verses to Tha'ālibī.

131 AS corrects the *al-Masīḥī* of J to *al-Musabbaḥī*. Abū 'Alī was in charge of the redress of grievances (*Ṣāḥib al-Maẓālim*) at Balkh and then qāḍī in Sīstān; see his biography in *Yatīmat ad-dahr*, IV, 147-9.

132 This man is known only from the parallel citation of this passage in the *Thimār al-qulūb*, 337, s.v. 'Afā'ī Sijistān', and from another mention of him at p. 22 of that work.

brigands of Tarsus, the archers of the Turks and the [213
sorcerers of India.

The specialities of Sīstān include drinking-bowls, bells for hawks, drums for ceremonial occasions and silk brocade hangings and coverings. [214

INDIA[133]

Someone has described India thus: 'Its seas are full of pearls, its mountains are full of sapphires, its trees are the aloes and its leaves give sweet-smelling perfumes.'[134] Indian aloes-wood is mentioned together with other outstandingly fragrant products attributed to specific countries, like Tibetan musk and the ambergris of ash-Shiḥr. In this connection, Ibn Maṭrān ash-Shāshī[135] has said, on the occasion of his seeking a gift of ambergris (metre *Basīṭ*):

... *In order that your two hands might present me with dazzling gifts, those marked with straight veins and those with curved markings.*

The countries where they occur are three only, India, the land of the Turks and the Arabian peninsula (referring to aloes-wood, musk and ambergris).[136]

India is richly-endowed with specialities which are not found elsewhere, including elephants, rhinoceroses, tigers, peacocks, parrots, turkeys, the two birds called *b.nāk.r.k.* (?) and [215
shārak,[137] rubies, white sandalwood, teak, aloes-wood, the ore containing zinc oxide (*tūtiyā*),[138] cloves, spikenard, nutmegs and velvet textiles, etc. Accordingly, it has many specialities not even found in Byzantium, of which the Greeks only have the following: satin brocades, gum mastic, scammony, Lemnian earth or *terra sigillata*, fine brocades of the kind called *buzyūn*[139] and various other textiles. [216

BUKHĀRĀ

Ismā'īl b. Aḥmad used to say, 'I can only compare Bukhārā, in the chaos and filth of the inner city, and the healthiness and pleasant-

133 *Al-Hind.* Since the early Arabs mainly knew of India through maritime trade, al-Hind tends to mean peninsular India and Further India, i.e. Malaysia and Indonesia; the part of north-western India known through land contact was called Sind. Cf. the discussion in S. Q. Fatimi, 'Two letters from the Mahārājā to the Khalīfah', *Islamic Studies*, II/I (Karachi 1963), 122ff.

134 Perhaps one should read here *khiṭr* 'indigo' for the '*iṭr* of the texts.

135 Abū Muḥammad al-Ḥasan b. 'Alī b. Maṭrān, poet of Bukhārā, was employed at one time in the postal service or *Barīd* of the Sāmānids. According to Tha'ālibī, *Yatīmat ad-dahr*, IV, 115-22, cf. 103, his *dīwān* of poetry was shown to the Ṣāḥib Ibn 'Abbād, who commented, 'I never imagined that Transoxania could produce a poet like this.'

136 These three aromatic products seem to have been put together into one supremely luxurious compound; Abū Bakr al-Khwārazmī speaks in one of his verses of *nadd muthallath* 'the ambergris made up of three components' (*Yatīmat ad-dahr*, IV, 319), and Tha'ālibī himself mentions it in the *Ghurar as-siyar*. 709.

137 The section on India in the *Ḥudud al-'ālam*, 86, mentions the *shārak* (tr. by Minorsky as 'Indian cuckoo') and the *k.rk.rī* bird; and in his 'Addenda to the Ḥudūd al-'ālam', BSOAS, XVII (1955), 256, Minorsky quotes H. W. Bailey that there may be a connection of the latter term with Sanskrit *kukkuṭī* 'domestic fowl' and its Prakrits derivatives. According to the *Burhān-i qāṭi'*, the *shārak* is a kind of talking bird like the parrot.

138 On tutty, and the fame of India up to modern times for the export of zinc, see Laufer, *Sino-Iranica*, 511-15.

139 *Buzyūn* brocades are included amongst the most luxurious cloths of that kind by Jāḥiẓ in his *Kitāb at-tabaṣṣur bi't-tijāra*, cf. Pellat in *Arabica*, I (1954), 158.

ness of its environs, with a man whose inside is rotten but whose outward appearance is fair.' People have disparaged it profusely. One of the neatest things said in this connection is what Abū'ṭ-Ṭayyib al-Ṭāhirī has remarked (metre *Sarī'*)[140]:

Know that the bā' *and the first* alif *of* Bukhārā *are superfluous;*

It is excrement (kharā) *pure and simple, and its people are like birds imprisoned for ever in its cage.*

And also what Abū Aḥmad b. Abī Bakr the secretary[141] has said (metre *Ramal*):

Bukhārā is the anus of the world, and we have rushed headlong into it!

Would that it would fart us forth at this minute, for we have stayed there too long! [217

SAMARQAND

When first it came into Qutaiba b. Muslim's view, he saw a sight of extraordinary beauty, enough to dazzle the eye. He said to his companions, 'Suggest to me a comparison for it', but they were impotent to do so. He therefore made something up himself, saying, 'Its verdure is like the broad span of the heavens, its palaces are like the shining stars and its streams like the Milky Way.' They recognised this comparison as extremely apt, and marvelled at the accuracy of his observation. [218

Its specialities include paper, which has driven out of use the Egyptian papyrus and the parchment which previous generations employed; this is because it looks better, is more supple, is more easily handled and is more convenient for writing on. It is only made in Samarqand and China.[142] The author of the *Kitāb al-masālik wa'l-mamālik* 'Book of roads and provinces'[143] relates that amongst the Chinese prisoners-of-war captured by Ziyād b. Ṣāliḥ and brought to Samarqand were some artisans who manufactured paper in Samarqand[144]; then it was manufactured on a wide scale and passed into general use, until it became an important export commodity for the people of Samarqand. Its value was universally recognised and people everywhere used it. [219

Further specialities of Samarqand are sal ammoniac, Wadhārī textiles,[145] mercury, hazel nuts and slaves. Ṭāhir b. 'Abdallāh b.

140 Abū'ṭ-Ṭayyib Ṭāhir b. Muḥammad was a descendant of the Ṭāhirid family which governed Khurāsān in the 3rd/9th century. According to Tha'ālibī, he lived on revenues from the former estates of the Ṭāhirids granted to him by the Sāmānids, but he never ceased to hate the Amīrs as supplanters of his own family (*Yatīmat ad-dahr*, IV, 69-73). In *ibid.*, 71, however, these two verses are attributed to Abū 'Alī as-Sājī.

141 Sc. the al-'Aṭawānī mentioned above.

142 According to Mez, *The renaissance of Islam*, 467-9, quoting Karabacek, dated papyri cease entirely in 323/935 and dated paper documents start in 300/912; cf. also, EI[1] and Suppl. arts. 'Ḳirṭās' (A. Grohmann) and EI[1] art. 'Kāghadh' (Cl. Huart), and Laufer, *Sino-Iranica*, 557-9, who points out that Chinese paper was imported into Transoxania in the 1st/7th century and was even known under the Sāsānids, although it was rare and precious. [*see also* Addenda and Corrigenda].

143 Presumably the work by the early 4th/10th century Sāmānid Vizier Abū 'Abdallāh Muḥammad b. Aḥmad al-Jaihānī, no longer extant but known from copious extracts in later writers, cf. Minorsky, *Sharaf al-Zamān Ṭāhir Marvazī on China, the Turks and India* (London 1942), 6ff.

144 Sc. in 133/751 when Ziyād decisively defeated in the region of Talas a Chinese army which had appeared in Transoxania; cf. Barthold, *Turkestan*, 195-6, and Gibb, *The Arab conquests in Central Asia*, 95-8.

145 I.e. textiles from Wadhār, a town in the Samarqand oasis settled by the Arabs and famous for its cotton fabrics; cf. Barthold, *op. cit.*, 94-5, and C. H. Becker, EI[1] art. 'Dībādj'.

Ṭāhir once issued an instruction to his agents, 'If you ever come across a Ṭukhāristān draught horse, a Bardha'a mule, an Egyptian ass or a Samarqand slave, then buy it immediately, and don't bother referring back to me for a decision.' [220

CHINA

The Arabs used to call every delicately or curiously-made vessel and such like, whatever its real origin, 'Chinese', because finely-made things are a speciality of China. The designation 'china' has remained in use till this day for the celebrated type of dishes. In the past, as at the present time, the Chinese have been famous for the skill of their hands and for their expertise in fashioning rare and beautiful objects. The Chinese themselves say, 'Except for us, the people of the world are all blind – unless one takes into account the people of Babylon, who are merely one-eyed.'[146]

They are extraordinarily skilled at shaping statues, and they excel at making carved representations and pictures.[147] [They carry this to such a pitch] that one of their artists will make a representation of a man, leaving out absolutely nothing except the man's soul; then the artist will no longer feel satisfied with it, and will turn it into a man who is laughing. Then he will be still further dissatisfied, and will differentiate between the laugh of a man laughing derisively and one laughing out of con- [221
fusion; or between a man smiling and one wondering in amazement; or between a laugh expressing pure joy and one expressing scorn. In this way, he makes one expression turn into another and so on.

They also have fine, translucent pottery, used for cooking purposes; a piece of this may be used equally for boiling things, for frying or simply as a dish for eating from. The best of these are the delicate, evenly-pigmented, clearly-resounding apricot-coloured ware, and after that, the cream-coloured ware with similar characteristics.[148]

The Chinese have excellent, particoloured silks, and silks with shapes depicted on them which only appear in certain lights; these are called *kimkhāw*.[149] They also have coats proofed with wax against the rain, which will withstand the heaviest wetting, and table-napkins for wiping away fat or grease which, when dirty, can be thrown into the fire and made clean, without getting at all burnt.[150] They make iron into steel, and from this, [222
mirrors, talismanic amulets, etc. are made; it is often bought for several times its weight in silver. They have the *fārmānī* (? *Fāry-*

[146] This saying, with a slight variation, is also attributed to the Chinese in Marvazī's *Ṭabā'i' al-ḥayawān*, and as Minorsky remarks, *op. cit.*, 14, 65, the saying must be quite old.

[147] Mas'ūdī, in *Murūj*, I, 323-4, says that in China the painters of masterpieces of verisimilitude were automatically rewarded by the Emperor himself.

[148] See Laufer, *The beginnings of porcelain in China*, Field Museum of Natural History Publication 192, Anthropological Ser., Vol. XV, No. 2 (Chicago 1917), 96-7, on the import into the Islamic lands of T'ang porcelain and the finds of it at Sāmarrā, and also P. Kahle, 'Chinese porcelain in the lands of Islam', in *Opera minora* (Leiden 1956), 326-61.

[149] AS corrects the *k.m.khār* of J. According to Laufer, *Sino-Iranica*, 539, this was a gold brocade; the word itself may be Chinese.

[150] I.e table-napkins of asbestos; according to F. Hirth, *China and the Roman Orient* (Shanghai 1885), 249-52, if the writings of the philosopher Lieh-tzŭ can be trusted, asbestos (whose name in Chinese means 'the cloth that can be cleaned by fire') was known in China *c.* 1000 B.C.

ābī, Farghānī) squirrel skins, considered one of the most precious furs there is, and felts which are more sought-after than those of the Maghrib. Al-Jāḥiẓ says in his book *At-tabaṣṣur bi't-tijāra* 'An enquiry into commercial practice'[151] that the best felts are those made in China, then – the red ones made in the Maghrib and [223 then the white ones made at Ṭālaqān. Another authority states that the best woollen cloths come from Egypt, and the next best come from Armenia, Takrīt and Rūyān in that order. [224

THE TURKISH LANDS

In the profusion of their specialities, the Turkish lands form a parallel to India: musk; furs of the sable marten, the grey squirrel, the ermine, the mink,[152] the black fox and the white mountain hare; rhinoceros horn (*khutuww*)[153]; *khadang* hardwood[154]; jade; white goshawks; horses; slaves; and yaks, from whose [225 shaggy coats and bushy tails are made fly-whisks and decorative emblems on the end of spear-shafts and flag-poles.

As for Tibet, which is to be included with the Turkish lands, it is famous for producing on the one hand a noble metal, and on the other hand, for producing an exhilarating psychological effect. The precious metal is gold, which is very plentiful there[155]; the psychological effect is that if anyone stays in Tibet, there comes over him a feeling of great joy, whose source is quite unknown, and he remains in this happy and laughing state until he leaves the country.[156] [226

KHWĀRAZM

The specialities and items of commerce of Khwārazm are as numerous as those of the adjoining Turkish lands. Its exports include slaves; sheep; pelts, especially those of the red and black foxes; good-quality bows; salted fish; and buttermilk cheese (*raḥqīn*), which is as typical of the region as *murrī* brine is of Merv. Its specialities also include the kind of melon called *bāranj*, reputedly the sweetest and nicest-tasting of all melons.[157] They were first exported to al-Ma'mūn, then to al-Wāthiq, being packed in snow inside leaden containers. A single container, if it arrived safely, was valued at 700 dirhams. Another product of Khwārazm is the cotton cloth called *āranj*.[158] The *amīrī* [227

151 See above, Introduction, p. 30-1.

152 The identification of the *fanak* with the mink is made by F. Viré in EI² s.v.

153 *Khutuww* (which perhaps in a context of the Turkish lands = fossil ivory from mammoths rather than rhinoceros horn) was ground into powder and used as a medicament in both the Far East and the Islamic lands. Amongst the considerable literature on *khutuww*, see the Excursus §74b in A. Z. V. Togan, *Ibn Faḍlāns Reisebericht*, Abh. für die Kunde des Morgenlandes, XXIV/3 (Leipzig 1939), 216-17.

154 *Khadang* hardwood was much used for carving bowls and beakers; cf. Togan, *op. it.*, 211-15, Excursus §73c, who identifies it with the birch.

155 On the fame of Tibet for gold, see W. Tomaschek, 'Kritik der ältesten Nachrichten über den Skythischen Norden', SBWAW, CXVI (1888), 752-3; Tomaschek conjectures that in classical times, the Issedones got their famous gold for export from the region of the Pamirs and northern Tibet.

156 The phenomenon of joy experienced in Tibet is remarked on by Jāḥiẓ, *Ḥayawān*, VII, 230, and is universally mentioned in the later sources describing Tibet.

157 According to the *Tāj al-'arūs*, *bāranj* = 'coconut'; perhaps here, 'a variety of melon resembling the coconut in shape or colour'. Or is it simply the Persian *bā rang* 'coloured'? The melons of Khwārazm were praised some centuries later as being 'incomparable' in flavour by Ibn Baṭṭūṭa, *Riḥla*, III, 15-16.

158 <*Arang* 'colour'? The reading of the word is confirmed by its mention in Maqdisī, 325.

cloth from there is said to be the equal of the *ḥafī* cloth of Nīshāpūr, the *munayyar* cloth of Ray, the 'poppy-coloured' cloth of Gurgān and the *Dabīqī* cloth of Egypt.

Amongst all the countries of the world, Khwārazm has the coldest climate, so that even the Oxus freezes over in winter, and elephants, caravans and armies can pass over it.[159] It remains thus frozen for a period of forty days to two months. The Khwārazm-Shāh Ma'mūn b. Ma'mūn[160] asked the author of this book to extemporise some verses about the excessive cold of Khwārazm, so I recited (metre *Basīṭ*):

How appalling is the cold of Khwārazm, when it bares its fangs and makes our bodies tremble and shake!

The sun is hidden there, and the wind makes people's skins chapped and bleeding, so that they lose all powers of endurance and strength.

The water freezes like stone, the dogs cower in holes and the biting cold wind drives on the icy weather.

If you were to steal only a fleeting kiss from your beloved, you would see your own mouth frozen fast to his. [228

Abū'l-Ḥasan al-Laḥḥām[161] has said about the people of Khwārazm (metre *Kāmil*):

The people of Khwārazm are not to be numbered amongst the progeny of Adam; by God's truth, they are in fact nothing but beasts!

Show me the like in all the world of their [misshapen] heads and foreheads,[162] their [outlandish] speech[163] and their leather boots!

If our forefather Adam acknowledges them as his own, then I refuse to recognise Adam as our ancestor.[164] [229

INTERESTING STORIES AND *Bons Mots* CONCERNING VARIOUS LANDS

When ar-Rashīd was about to establish himself at Antioch, its people disliked the prospect, and one of their elders said to him, 'O Commander of the Faithful, this is no real part of your lands!' He asked him why this was so. The elder replied, 'Because fine perfume deteriorates here until it is good for nothing, and swords become rusty, even if they are [of steel] from Qala' in India and Yemenī tempering. Often the rain begins and goes on for two months, and one never sees a clear sky for even a day during that period.'[165]

[159] Cf. Ibn Faḍlān on the cold of Gurgānj, where he spent the winter of 309/921-2: the Oxus was frozen over for three months to a thickness of seventeen spans, so that horses, mules, asses, carts, etc. could cross over it (Togan, *Ibn Faḍlāns Reisebericht*, text 7-8, tr. 13-14). However, Yāqūt accuses Ibn Faḍlān of lying and exaggeration about its thickness (*Mu'jam al-buldān*, II, 397-8).

[160] See above, Introduction, pp. 4-5.

[161] AS corrects the name from the 'al-Lajjām' of J. Abū'l-Ḥasan 'Alī al-Laḥḥām al-Ḥarrānī, a poet who settled at Bukhārā, was famed for the savagery of his satires (*Yatīmat ad-dahr*, IV, 102-15).

[162] Cf. Maqdisī, 285-6 = Yāqūt, *op. cit.*, II, 396-7, on the flattened heads of the people of Khwārazm. When Maqdisī remarked on it, he was told that mothers, in order to prevent their children from being enslaved, had adopted a custom of the Turks and tied scarves of finely-woven material over the tops of the children's heads, thereby flattening them.

[163] The geographers of the 4th/10th century all comment on the incomprehensibility of Khwārazmian speech; according to Ibn Faḍlān, 'The Khwārazmians are uncouth in both their speech and their nature, indeed, their speech is like the chattering of starlings' (Togan, *op. cit.*, text 7, tr. 12). The Khwārazmian language, an Eastern Iranian one akin to Soghdian, lasted in Lower Khwārazm till the 8th/14th century.

[164] I follow AS in supplying the last hemistich from the parallel citation of these verses in *Yatīmat ad-dahr*, IV, 111. Rescher's translation of this tenth chapter ends here.

[165] This anecdote seems to go back to Jāḥiẓ, *Hayawān*, III, 143-4, and appears also in Ibn Rusta, 59, tr. 62-3, and Ibn al-Faqīh, 116.

Ar-Rashīd asked 'Abd al-Malik b. Ṣāliḥ al-Hāshimī[166] about
Manbij; he replied that it had good air and sweet water and that
illnesses were uncommon there. Ar-Rashīd said, 'What [230
about the nights there?' 'Abd al-Malik replied, 'The whole of a
night there is as pleasant as the time around dawn.'

Al-Jāḥiẓ relates that if anyone remains long in Baḥrain, his
spleen becomes enlarged and his abdomen distended.[167] The
people there all aver that they have there a certain variety of
dates[168] which, if taken when just beginning to ripen and made
into date-wine, and then drunk by someone wearing a white
garment, has the effect of dyeing the garment until it becomes like
a crimson one. Al-Jāḥiẓ also says that if anyone keeps a protracted
fast in summertime at Maṣīṣa,[169] his mind becomes deranged, and
that indeed, many of the local people have gone mad be- [231
cause of the scorching heat. He goes on to add that if anyone
comes from the region of Iraq to the land of the Zanj (sc. to East
Africa), his skin inevitably becomes cracked and scabby whilst
he remains there. Moreover, if anyone drinks an excessive amount
of coconut milk, the intoxicating effect blots out his mind until he
becomes a near-idiot.

Abū Zunbūr al-Mādharā'ī[170] relates that on his property at
Tiberias, called the 'pleasure-ground of Hishām', there is [232
a spring which has the peculiar property of running for seven
years and then drying up for seven years; it has been celebrated
for this from time immemorial.

A certain tax official from Armenia and Azerbaijan has related that there is there a certain place where, if the local people sow 1,000 *jarībs*, the amount of rain necessary for this acreage accordingly falls and waters the sown land; and if they sow less than that, a correspondingly smaller amount of rain falls, the exact amount required. If a lot of ground has been sown, then there is a lot of rain; and vice versa. The reason for this is quite unknown, but the rain falling always corresponds to the amount of land sown.

I have read, in the Qāḍī Abū'l-Ḥasan 'Alī b. 'Abd al-'Azīz al-
Jurjānī's own hand, in his work the *Kitāb ar-ru'asā' wa'l-jilla*
'Book of prominent and outstanding men',[171] the following incident: that 'Abdallāh b. Ṭāhir wrote to al-Wāthiq that a [233
section of a vineyard in Ṭukhāristān had moved during the night
to another spot 120 *dhirā*'s away.

I once heard recited Abū'l-Fatḥ al-Bustī's poem on Samarqand (metre *Sarī'*):

[166] A member of the Abbasid family, who held various provincial governorships under al-Hādī, ar-Rashīd and al-Amīn, dying in 196/811-12. He was accused of coveting the Caliphate for himself, cf. Ṭabarī, III, 680.

[167] *Ḥayawān*, IV, 139. Most of the curiosa in this paragraph appear also in Ibn Rusta, 82-3, tr. 91, drawing directly on Ibn Khurradādhbih, 170-1.

[168] In the two latter sources mentioned in the previous note, this variety is named as the *nābijī* one.

[169] Maṣīṣa was one of the *thughūr* on the frontier with the Byzantines; it lies on the Ceyhan river of Turkey, a few miles east of Adana, and is the modern Misis.

[170] Abū Zunbūr flourished in the reign of al-Muqtadir, when he was governor of Egypt and Syria. The Mādharā'ī family were tax-farmers of Egypts and clients of the Vizier 'Alī b. 'Īsā; see on them H. L. Gottschalk, *Die Mādarā'ijjūn. Ein Beitrag zur Geschichte Ägyptens unter dem Islam* (Berlin 1931).

[171] Al-Jurjānī, author of the well-known *Wasāṭa bain al-Mutanabbī wa-khuṣūmihī*, was qāḍī of Gurgān and then of Ray in the time of the Būyid Fakhr ad-Daula, dying in 392/1002 at Nīshāpūr; cf. *Yatīmat ad-dahr*, IV, 3-26, Yāqūt, *Irshād*, V, 249-58, and Ibn Khallikān, tr. II, 221-3. The work mentioned here by Tha'ālibī is not apparently extant, but is further quoted by Tha'ālibī in his unpublished short work, the *Kitāb at-taḥsīn wa't-taqbīḥ*, Istanbul ms. Rağip Paşa 1473, f. 128b.

Man has a garden of paradise prepared for him in the next life, but the paradise of this present life is Samarqand.

O you who compare the region of Balkh with Samarqand, can there be any comparison between the colocynth and sugar-candy (qand)?

Abū Rabī' al-Balkhī has said (metre *Mujtathth*)[172]:

Shāsh is a garden (janna) *in summer, and a shield* (junna) *against the harmful effect of the heat.*

Abū'l-Ḥasan 'Alī b. Aḥmad al-Maṣīṣī,[173] known as an archer and as a poet, told me: 'Once during a convivial gathering [234 at 'Aḍud ad-Daula Fanā-Khusrau's court at Shīrāz, a light-hearted and bantering disputation took place between Abū 'Alī al-Hā'im[174] and Abū Dulaf al-Khazrajī.[175] Abū 'Alī said to Abū Dulaf, "May God rain down on your head the plagues of Syria, the fevers of Khaibar, the diseased spleens of Baḥrain, the boils of al-Jazīra and the gerfalcons (*sanāqir*)[176] of Dehistān! And may He afflict you with the guinea-worm of Medina, the inflammation of Fārs and the ulcers of Balkh!"

'Abū Dulaf riposted, "You miserable wretch! Are you reading out the maledictions of *Tabbat* (sc. of *Sūrat al-Masad*) upon Abū Lahab, or carrying dates to Hajar or putting black garments on the officers of the guard?[177] On the contrary, may God bring down on *you* the serpents of Egypt, the vipers of Sīstān, the ordinary scorpions of Shahrazūr and the virulent scorpions of al-Ahwāz, and may He bring down on *me* the mantles of the Yemen, [235 the fine linens of Egypt, the brocades of Rūm, the satins of Sūs, the silks of China, the cloaks of Fārs, the robes of Iṣfahān, the *saqlāṭūnī* cloth of Baghdad, the turbans of Ubulla, the *tawwazī* cloth of Tawwaj, the *munayyar* cloth of Ray, the *ḥafī* cloth of Nīshāpūr, the *mulḥam* cloth of Merv, the grey squirrel furs of the Kirghiz lands, the sable marten furs of Bulghār, the fox furs of the Khazar lands, the mink of Kāshghar, the ermine of [236 the Toghuz-Oghuz country, the furs made in Herat from the crop and neck feathers of birds, the trouser-cords of Armenia and the stockings of Qazwīn. Moreover, may He lay down for me the under-carpets of Armenia, the rugs of Qālīqalā, the mattresses of Maisān and the woven mats of Baghdad. May He appoint [237 to serve me Greek eunuchs, Turkish military slaves, slave girls from Bukhārā and concubines from Samarqand; and may He set me to ride on the swift mounts of the desert, the fine-bred camels of the Ḥijāz, the nags of Ṭukhāristān, the asses of Egypt and the mules of Bardha'a. May He let me eat of the apples of Syria, the fresh dates of Iraq, the bananas of the Yemen, the nuts of

172 According to the *Yatīmat ad-dahr*, IV, 350-1, Abū Rabī' was an official employed by the Sāmānid government in the investigation of *maẓālim*.

173 Tha'ālibī frequently cites him as an informant, under the name 'Alī b. Ma'mūr ad-Dulafī al-Maṣīṣī, in both the *Yatīmat ad-dahr* and the *Tatimmat al-yatīma*; cf. Mawlawī Abū Mūsá Aḥmadu'l-Ḥaqq, *Farīdatu'l-'aṣr*, 364-5.

174 Abū 'Alī Aḥmad b. 'Alī al-Hā'im al-Madā'inī was one of 'Aḍud ad-Daula's courtiers and a friend of the well-known author, the Qāḍī al-Muḥassin b. 'Alī at-Tanūkhī; cf. Rūdhrāwarī, in *Eclipse of the 'Abbasid Caliphate*, III, 19-20, tr. VI, 12-13.

175 Abū Dulaf Mis'ar b. Muhalhil al-Yanbū'ī al-Khazrajī, author and traveller in Persia and Central Asia, flourished in the middle years of the 4th/10th century, and seems to have been patronised by both the Būyids and Sāmānids; cf. *Yatīmat ad-dahr*, III, 356-77, and Minorsky, EI² s.v.

176 The text here is clearly defective; some illness or affliction alone fits the context.

177 These expressions being proverbial for carrying coals to Newcastle.

India, the beans of Kufa, the sugar-cane of al-Ahwāz, the honey of Iṣfahān, the sugar-cane syrup (*fānīdh*) of Māskān,[178] the dates of Kirmān, the date-syrup of Arrajān, the figs of Ḥulwān, the grapes of Baghdad, the jujubes of Gurgān, the plums [238
of Bust, the pomegranates of Ray, the pears of Nihāwand, the quinces of Nīshāpūr, the apricots of Ṭūs, the *mulabban* confectionery of Merv and the melons of Khwārazm; and may He let me breathe the musk of Tibet, the aloes-wood of India, the ambergris of ash-Shiḥr, the camphor of Sumatra (*Fanṣūr*), the citrons of Ṭabaristān, the oranges of Basra, the narcissi of Gurgān, the waterlilies of as-Sairawān, the roses of Jūr, the wallflowers of Baghdad, [239
the saffron of Qum and the basil of Samarqand."

'Fanā-Khusrau was delighted by this, and amazed at the excellence of his familiarity with the specialities of all lands, both east and west. He exclaimed, "O Abū Dulaf, you are a monarch frequenting the company of monarchs!", and he rewarded him with a robe of honour and a gift of money.'

The completion and end of the book *Laṭā'if al-ma'ārif*. Praise be to God, the Lord of the Worlds, and prayers be upon the best of His Creation, Muḥammad, his family and his Companions! God alone is our sufficiency, and what better helper could there be?

178 According to J. Ruska, EI^{1} art. 'Sukkar', *fānīdh* (<Sanskrit *phāṇita*) results from the second boiling of the sugar-cane. According to Yāqūt, *Mu'jam al-buldān*, v, 42, Māskān adjoined Makrān (i.e. it was in modern Baluchistan), and *fānīdh* was one of its exports.

Addenda and Corrigenda.

Chapter One, page 39, note 5

It may also be noted that Idrīs is associated or identified with Hermes Trismegistus, the founder of hermetic philosophy who, according to the *Rasā'il* or Epistles of the tenth-century Basran group of the *Ikhwān aṣ-Ṣafā'*, the 'Pure Ones', journeyed to Saturn and spent thirty years there learning the secrets of the heavens before bringing them down to mankind (cited in Seyyed Hossein Nasr, *An introduction to Islamic cosmological doctrines* [Cambridge, Mass. 1964], 75-6). I am grateful to Prof. M. E. Marmura of Toronto University for this reference.

Chapter One, page 41, line 3

Professor Marmura has also suggested to me that *qadar* may not here have its conservative, orthodox meaning of 'predestination', but the Mu'tazilī one of 'freedom of the will, ability to create one's own acts'. In view of Ibn ar-Rūmī's well-known fearful and superstitious nature, which might be expected to incline him towards a determinist and fatalistic view of human activity, might he not be referring in a derogatory fashion to the Mu'tazilī sense of *qadar*? Against this, however, we have Ibn ar-Rūmī's own words that he was himself a supporter of the Mu'tazila and their views on free will; cf. 'A.M. al-'Aqqād, *Ibn ar-Rūmī, ḥayātuhu min shi'rihi*[4] (Cairo 1373/1957), 217ff., and Guest, *Life and works of Ibn er Rûmî*, 48, 120. Perhaps it is safest to leave *qadar* translated as 'predestination', whilst bearing in mind the ambiguous meaning of the word.

Chapter Ten, page 131, note 93

The plant *rībās* ought more accurately to be translated as 'currant-fruited rhubarb' (the Arabic-Syriac term *ya'mīsā* is also found for this plant).

TB L

Chapter Ten, page 140, note 142

Professor Nabia Abbott of the Oriental Institute, University of Chicago, writes to me that 'The information in the first part of n. 142 is out of date. The Oriental Institute paper fragment of the *Arabian Nights* bears the secondary date of 266 A.H. and the *Nights* book is some half a century earlier. Paper book mss. are available from the second half of the third century. The earliest is dated 252 A.H. I have drawn attention to these in my article on the Arabian Nights fragment published in JNES, VIII (1949), esp. pp. 146-9. . . . Papyri documents and literary fragments do not "cease entirely" in 323/935; see my *Oriental Institute Papyri*, LXXV (1957) Document 8. Margoliouth, *Catalogue of Arabic papyri in the John Rylands Library*, reprints a number of papyri fragments from the second half of the 4th/10th century, none of which are illustrated and hence give no opportunity to either confirm or question the dates.'

Bibliography of the principal works consulted.

1. Primary sources: texts and translations.

anon., *Ḥudūd al-ʿālam*, tr. V. Minorsky, GMS, N.S. XI (London 1937)

anon., *Tuḥfat al-aḥbāb*, ed. and tr. H. P. J. Renaud and G. S. Colin, *Glossaire de la matière médicale marocaine* (Paris 1934)

al-Bākharzī, Abū'l-Ḥasan ʿAlī b. al-Ḥusain, *Dumyat al-qaṣr wa-ʿuṣrat ahl al-ʿaṣr* (Aleppo 1349/1930)

al-Bakrī, Abū ʿUbaid ʿAbdallāh b. ʿAbd al-ʿAzīz, *Muʿjam mā 'staʿjam min asmāʾ al-bilād waʾl-mawāḍiʿ* (Cairo 1364-71/1945-51, 4 vols.)

al-Balādhurī, Abū'l-Ḥasan Aḥmad b. Yaḥyā, *Ansāb al-ashrāf*, I, ed. M. Ḥamīdallāh (Cairo 1959), V, ed. S. D. F. Goitein (Jerusalem 1936)

idem, *Futūḥ al-buldān* (Cairo 1959)

Ibn al-Abbār, Abū ʿAbdallāh Muḥammad b. ʿAbdallāh al-Quḍāʿī, *Iʿtāb al-kuttāb*, ed. Ṣāliḥ al-Ashtar (Damascus 1380/1961)

Ibn ʿAbd Rabbihi, Shihāb ad-Dīn Aḥmad, *al-ʿIqd al-farīd*, ed. Aḥmad Amīn, etc. (Cairo 1367-9/1948-50, 6 vols.)

Ibn al-Athīr, Abū'l-Ḥasan ʿAlī b. Muḥammad, *al-Kāmil fīʾt-taʾrīkh*, ed. C. J. Tornberg, *Chronicon quod perfectissimum inscribitur* (Leiden 1851-76, 14 vols.)

Ibn Baṭṭūṭa, Abū ʿAbdallāh Muḥammad aṭ-Ṭanjī, *Riḥla* or *Tuḥfat an-nuẓẓār fī gharāʾib al-amṣār wa ʿajāʾib al-asfār*, ed. and tr. C. Defrémery and B. R. Sanguinetti, *Les voyages d'Ibn Batoutah* (Paris 1853-9, 4 vols.)

Ibn Duraid, Abū Bakr Muḥammad b. al-Ḥasan, *Kitāb al-ishtiqāq*, ed. F. Wüstenfeld (Göttingen 1850)

Ibn Faḍlān, Aḥmad, *Riḥla*, ed. and tr. A. Z. V. Togan, *Ibn Faḍlāns Reisebericht*, Abhandlungen für die Kunde des Morgenlandes, XXIV/3 (Leipzig 1939)

Ibn al-Faqīh, Abū Bakr Aḥmad b. Ibrāhīm al-Hamadhānī, *Kitāb al-buldān*, ed. M. J. de Goeje, BGA, V (Leiden 1885)

Ibn Khaldūn, Abū Zaid ʿAbd ar-Raḥmān b. Muḥammad, *al-Muqaddima*, tr. F. Rosenthal, *The Muqaddimah, an introduction to history* (New York 1958, 3 vols.)

Ibn Khallikān, Abū'l-ʿAbbās Aḥmad b. Muḥammad al-Irbilī, *Wafayāt al-aʿyān wa-anbāʾ az-zamān*, tr. Baron Mc Guckin de

Slane, *Ibn Khallikan's biographical dictionary* (Paris 1842-71, 4 vols.)

Ibn Khurradādhbih, Abū'l-Qāsim 'Ubaidallāh b. 'Abdallāh, *al-Masālik wa'l-mamālik*. ed. de Goeje, BGA, VI (Leiden 1889)

Ibn an-Nadīm, Abū'l-Faraj Muḥammad b. Isḥāq, *Kitāb al-fihrist* (Cairo 1348/1929-30)

Ibn Qutaiba, Abū Muḥammad 'Abdallāh b. Muslim, *Kitāb al-'Arab*, in *Rasā'il al-bulaghā'*[4], ed. M. Kurd 'Alī (Cairo 1374/1954)

idem, *Kitāb al-ma'ārif*, ed. Tharwat 'Ukkāsha (Cairo 1960)

idem, *Kitāb ash-shi'r wa'sh-shu'arā'*, ed. de Goeje (Leiden 1904)

Ibn Rusta, Abū 'Alī Aḥmad b. 'Umar, *Kitāb al-a'lāq an-nafīsa*, ed. de Goeje, BGA, VII (Leiden 1892), tr. G. Wiet, *Les atours précieux* (Cairo 1955)

Ibn az-Zubair, Qāḍī Abū'l-Ḥusain Aḥmad, *Kitāb adh-dhakhā'ir wa't-tuḥaf*, ed. Muḥ. Ḥamīdallāh (Kuwait 1959)

al-Iṣfahānī, Abū'l-Faraj 'Alī b. al-Ḥusain, *Kitāb al-aghānī* (Beirut 1956-7, 21 vols.; Cairo, Dār al-Kutub, 1346- /1927- , 16 vols.)

al-Jāḥiẓ, 'Amr b. Baḥr, *al-Bayān wa't-tabyīn*, ed. 'Abd as-Salām Muḥ. Hārūn (Cairo 1366/1947, 4 vols.)

idem, *Kitāb al-bukhalā'*, ed. Ṭāhā Ḥājirī (Cairo 1958), tr. Ch. Pellat, *Le livre des avares* (Paris 1951)

idem, *Kitāb al-ḥayawān*, ed 'Abd as-Salām Muḥ. Hārūn (Cairo 1356-64/1938-45, 7 vols.)

idem, *Kitāb at-tabaṣṣur bi't-tijāra*, tr. Pellat in 'Ǧāḥiẓiana I. Le *Kitāb al-tabaṣṣur bi-l-tiǧāra* attribué a Ǧāḥiẓ', *Arabica*, I (1954), 153-65

al-Jāḥiẓ, Pseudo-, *Kitāb at-tāj fī akhlāq al-mulūk*, tr. Pellat, *Le livre de la couronne* (Paris 1954)

al-Jahshiyārī, Abū 'Abdallāh Muḥammad b. 'Abdūs, *Kitāb al-wuzarā' wa'l-kuttāb* (Baghdad 1357/1938)

al-Khwārazmī, Abū 'Abdallāh Muḥammad b. Aḥmad, *Mafātīḥ al-'ulūm*, ed. G. van Vloten (Leiden 1895)

al-Maqdisī, Abū 'Abdallāh Muḥammad b. Aḥmad, *Aḥsan at-taqāsīm fī ma'rifat al-aqālīm*, ed. de Goeje, BGA, III (Leiden 1906)

Marvazī, Sharaf az-Zamān, Ṭāhir, *Ṭabā'i' al-ḥayawān*, partially ed. and tr. V. Minorsky, *Marvazī on China, the Turks and India* (London 1942)

al-Mas'ūdī, Abū'l-Ḥasan 'Alī b. al-Ḥusain, *Kitāb at-tanbīh wa'l-ishrāf*, ed. de Goeje, BGA, VIII (Leiden 1894), tr. Baron Carra de Vaux, *Le livre de l'avertissement et de la revision* (Paris 1897)

idem, *Murūj adh-dhahab wa-ma'ādin al-jauhar*, ed. and tr. C. Barbier de Meynard and Pavet de Courteille, *Les prairies d'or* (Paris 1861-77, 9 vols.)

Miskawaih, Abū 'Abdallāh Aḥmad b. Muḥammad, *Tajārib al-*

umam wa-ta'āqib al-humam, and his continuators ar-Rūdhrāwarī and Hilāl aṣ-Ṣābi', ed. and tr. H. F. Amedroz and D. S. Margoliouth, *The eclipse of the 'Abbasid Caliphate* (Oxford 1921-2, 7 vols.)
al-Mubarrad, Abū'l-'Abbās Muḥammad b. Yazīd, *al-Kāmil* (Cairo 1376/1956, 4 vols.)
Muḥammad b. Ḥabīb al-Baghdādī, *Kitāb al-muḥabbar*, ed. I. Lichtenstädter (Hyderabad 1361/1942)
Niẓām al-Mulk, Abū 'Alī Ḥasan b. 'Alī Ṭūsī, *Siyāsat-nāma*, ed. M. M. Qazwīnī and Chahārdihī (Tehran 1334/1956), tr. H. Darke, *The book of government or rules for kings* (London 1960)
Niẓāmī 'Arūḍī Samarqandī, *Chahār maqāla*, ed. Qazwīnī and M. Mu'īn (Tehran 1333/1954), tr. E. G. Browne, *Revised translation*, GMS, XI/2 (London 1921)
an-Nuwairī, Shihāb ad-Dīn Aḥmad b. 'Abd al-Wahhāb, *Nihāyat al-arab fī funūn al-adab* (Cairo 1340-74/1922-55, 18 vols.)
al-Qalqashandī, Abū'l-'Abbās Aḥmad b. 'Alī, *Ṣubḥ al-a'shā fī ṣinā'at al-inshā'* (Cairo 1331-40/1913-22, 14 vols.)
Qur'ān, Introduction and tr. R. Blachère, *Le Coran* (Paris 1947-51, 3 vols.)
aṣ-Ṣābi', Abū'l-Ḥasan Hilāl b. al-Muḥassin, *Kitāb al-wuzarā'* (Cairo 1958)
ash-Shābushtī, Abū'l-Ḥasan 'Alī b. Muḥammad, *Kitāb ad-diyārāt*, ed. G. 'Awwād (Baghdad 1370/1951), partially tr. E. Sachau, 'Vom Klosterbuch des Šâbuštî', APAW (1919), No. 10, pp. 1-43
aṭ-Ṭabarī, Abū Ja'far Muḥammad b. Jarīr, *Ta'rīkh ar-rusul wa'l-mulūk*, ed. de Goeje, etc., *Annales* (Leiden 1879-1901), tr. of one section by E. Marin, *The reign of al-Mu'taṣim* (833-42) (New Haven, Conn. 1951)
ath-Tha'ālibī, Abū Manṣūr 'Abd al-Malik b. Muḥammad, *Kitāb bard al-akbād fī'l-a'dād* in *Khams rasā'il* (Istanbul 1301/1884), tr. O. Rescher, 'Zahlensprüche in der arabischen Litteratur (das K. "berd el-akbâd" des Tha'âlibî)', in *Orientalistische Miszellen*, II (Istanbul 1926), 38-99
idem, *Laṭā'if al-ma'ārif*, ed. P. de Jong (Leiden 1867), ed. Ibrāhīm al-Abyārī and Ḥasan Kāmil aṣ-Ṣairafī (Cairo 1379/1960), tr. of tenth chapter by Rescher, 'Das Kapitel X aus eth-Tha'âlibî's Laṭâ'if el-ma'ârif: Über die Eigentumlichkeiten der Länder und Städte', in *Orientalistische Miszellen*, I (Istanbul 1925), 194-228
idem, *Ta'rīkh ghurar as-siyar*, ed. and tr. H. Zotenberg, *Histoire des rois des Perses* (Paris 1900)
idem, *Tatimmat al-yatīma*, ed. 'Abbās Iqbāl (Tehran 1353/1934, 2 vols.)
idem, *Thimār al-qulūb fi'l-muḍāf wa'l-mansūb* (Cairo 1326/1908)

idem, *Yatīmat ad-dahr fī maḥāsin ahl al-ʻaṣr* (Cairo 1375-7/1956-8, 4 vols.); indices in Mawlawī Abū Mūsá Aḥmadu'l-Ḥaqq, *Farīdatu'l-ʻaṣr: a comprehensive index of persons, places, books etc. referred to in the* Yatīmatu'l-dahr, *the famous anthology of Thaʻālibī*, Bibliotheca Indica N.S. No. 1215 (Calcutta 1915)

ath-Thaʻlabī, Abū Isḥāq Aḥmad b. Muḥammad, *ʻArā'is al-majālis fī qiṣaṣ al-anbiyā'* (Cairo 1347/1928)

al-Yaʻqūbī, Abū'l-ʻAbbās Aḥmad b. Isḥāq, called Ibn Wāḍiḥ, *Kitāb al-buldān*, ed. de Goeje, BGA, VII (Leiden 1892), tr. Wiet, *Les pays* (Cairo 1937)

idem, *Mushākalat an-nās li-zamānihim*, ed. W. Millward (Beirut 1962), tr. Millward, 'The adaptation of men to their time: an historical essay by al-Yaʻqūbī', JAOS LXXXIV (1964), 329-44

Yāqūt, Abū ʻAbdallāh Yaʻqūb b. ʻAbdallāh al-Ḥamāwī, *Irshād al-arīb li-maʻrifat al-adīb*, ed. Margoliouth, GMS VI/1-7 (London 1907-26, 7 vols.)

idem, *Muʻjam al-buldan* (Beirut 1374-6/1955-7, 5 vols.)

2. Secondary sources and reference works.

Arnold, Sir T. W., *The Caliphate* (Oxford 1924)

Barbier de Meynard, A.-C., 'Surnoms et sobriquets dans la littérature arabe', JA, Ser. 10, Vol. IX (Jan.-June 1907), 173-244, 365-428, Vol. X (July-Dec. 1907), 55-118, 193-273

Barthold, W., *Turkestan down to the Mongol invasion*², GMS, N.S. V (London 1928)

Bosworth, C. E., *The Ghaznavids: their empire in Afghanistan and eastern Iran* 994-1040 (Edinburgh 1963)

Bousquet, G.-H., *La morale de l'Islam et son ethique sexuelle* (Paris 1953)

Brockelmann, C., *Geschichte der arabischen Literatur* (Leiden 1937-49, 5 vols.)

Browne, E. G., *A literary history of Persia* (London and Cambridge 1902-24, 4 vols.)

Caetani, L. and Gabrieli, G., *Onomasticon arabicum ossia repertorio alfabetico dei nomi di persona e di luogo contenuti nelle principali opere storiche, biografiche e geografiche, stampate e monoscritte, relative all' Islam.* I *Fonti—Introduzione.* II *A* (*Aʻābil—ʻAbdallāh*) (Rome 1915, 2 vols.)

Canard, M., *Histoire de la dynastie des H'amdânides de Jazîra et de Syrie*, Publications de la Faculté des Lettres d'Alger, Ser. 2, Vols. XXI-XXII (Paris 1953)

Creswell, K. A. C., *Early Muslim architecture: Umayyads, early ʻAbbāsids and Ṭūlūnids* (Oxford 1932-40, 2 vols.)

Dozy, R. P. A., *Dictionnaire détaillé des noms de vêtements chez les Arabes* (Amsterdam 1845)

idem, *Supplément aux dictionnaires arabes* (Leiden 1881, 2 vols.)
Fleischer, H. L., *Kleinere Schriften* (Leipzig 1885-8, 3 vols.)
Gaudefroy-Demombynes, M., *Le pèlerinage à la Mekke* (Paris 1923)
Gibb, H. A. R., *The Arab conquests in Central Asia* (London 1923)
de Goeje, M. J., *Mémoire sur les Carmathes du Bahraïn et les Fatimides* (Leiden 1886)
Goldziher, I., *Muhammedanische Studien* (Halle 1888-9, 2 vols.)
idem, *Abhandlungen zur arabischen Philologie* (Leiden 1896-99, 2 vols.)
idem, 'Gesetzliche Bestimmungen über Kunja-Namen in Islam', ZDMG, LI (1897), 256-66
Guest, R., *Life and works of Ibn er Rûmî* (London 1944)
Guigues, P., 'Les noms arabes dans Sérapion, «Liber de simplicii medicina». Essai de restitution et d'identification de noms arabes de médicaments usités au moyen âge', JA, Ser. 10, Vol. v (Jan.-June 1905), 473-546, Vol. vi (July-Dec. 1905), 49-112
Haywood, J. A., *Arabic lexicography, its history and its place in the general history of lexicography* (Leiden 1960)
Lammens, H., *Études sur le règne du Calife Omaiyade Mo'âwia Ier* (Paris 1908)
idem, *Fāṭima et les filles de Mahomet* (Rome 1912)
idem, *Le berceau de l'Islam, l'Arabie occidentale à la veille de l'Hégire. I Le climat – les Bédouins* (Rome 1914)
idem, *Le Califat de Yazîd Ier* (Beirut 1921)
idem, *La cité arabe de Ṭāif à la veille de l'Hégire* (Beirut 1922)
idem, *L'Arabie occidentale avant l'Hégire* (Beirut 1928)
idem, *Études sur le siècle des Omayyades* (Beirut 1930)
Lane, E. W., *An Arabic-English lexicon* (London 1863-93, 8 vols.)
Laufer, B., *Sino-Iranica, Chinese contributions to the history of civilisation in ancient Iran, with special reference to the history of cultivated plants and products*, Field Museum of Natural History Publication No. 201, Anthropological Series, Vol. xv, No. 3 (Chicago 1919), 185-630.
idem, *Geophagy*, Field Museum of Natural History Publication No. 280, Anthropological Series, Vol. xviii, No. 2. (Chicago 1930), 101-98
Lazard, G., *Les premiers poètes persans IXe-Xe siècles* (Tehran-Paris, 2 vols. 1964)
Le Strange, G., *The lands of the eastern Caliphate* (Cambridge 1905)
idem, *Baghdad during the Abbasid Caliphate* (Oxford 1924)
Levy, R., *The social structure of Islam*² (Cambridge 1957)
Margoliouth, D. S., *Lectures on Arabic historians* (Calcutta 1930)
Marquart, J., *Ērānšahr nach der Geographie des Ps. Moses Xorenac'i*,

Abhandlungen der Königl. Gesell. der Wissenschaften zu Göttingen, Phil.-Hist. Kl., N.F. III/3 (Berlin 1901)
Mez, A., *The renaissance of Islam*, Eng. tr. (Patna 1937)
Mubārak, Zakī, *La prose arabe au IVe siècle de l'Hégire (Xe siècle)* (Paris 1931)
Muir, Sir W., *The Caliphate, its rise, decline and fall*[4] (Edinburgh 1915)
Nicholson, R. A., *A literary history of the Arabs* (Cambridge 1930)
Pellat, Ch., *Le milieu basrien et la formation de Ǧāḥiẓ* (Paris 1953)
idem, 'Ǧāḥiẓiana III. Essai d'inventaire de l'œuvre ǧāḥiẓienne', *Arabica*, III (1956), 147-80
Sachau, E., 'Zur Geschichte und Chronologie von Khwârazm', SBWAW, LXXIII (1873), 471-506, LXXXIV (1873), 285-330
Sourdel, D., *Le vizirat 'Abbāside de 749 à 936 (132 à 324 de l'Hégire)* (Damascus 1959-60, 2 vols.)
Sprengling, M., 'From Persian to Arabic', AJSL, LVI (1939), 175-224, 325-36
Spuler, B., *Iran in früh-islamischer Zeit* (Wiesbaden 1952)
van Vloten, G., *Recherches sur la domination arabe, le chiitisme et les croyances messianiques sous le califat des Omeyyades* (Amsterdam 1894)
Walker, J., *A catalogue of the Muhammadan coins in the British Museum*. I *A catalogue of the Arab-Sassanian coins* (London 1941), II *Arab-Byzantine and post-reform Umaiyad coins* (London 1956)
Watt, W. Montgomery, *Muhammad at Mecca* (Oxford 1953)
idem, *Muhammad at Medina* (Oxford 1956)
Wellhausen, J., *Reste arabischen Heidentums*[2] (Berlin 1897)
idem, *The Arab kingdom and its fall*, Eng. tr. (Calcutta 1927)
Zambaur, E. de, *Manuel de généalogie et de chronologie pour l'histoire de l'Islam* (Hanover 1927)

1

Persons, dynasties, tribes

Abān b. al-Ḥakam 108
Abān b. 'Uthmān 80
Abāna b. Sa'īd 68
al-'Abbās
b. 'Abd al-Muṭṭalib 42, 76, 80, 95-6, 107
b. 'Amr al-Ghanawī 113
b. al-Faḍl 74
b. al-Hādī 105
b. al-Ḥasan al-Jarjarā'ī 62, 95-6, 106
b. al-Ma'mūn 110
b. Mirdās 90
b. Muḥammad 105
al-'Abbāsa 49
'Abbāsids 21-4, 26-7, 29, 48, 50, 77, 81, 97-9, 101-2, 119
'Abdallāh
b. al-'Abbās 50, 70, 73, 95-6, 107
b. Abī Sarḥ 68-9
b. 'Alī 86, 112
b. al-Amīn 105
b. 'Āmir b. Kuraiz 45, 70, 88, 91
b. 'Amr b. al-'Āṣ 108
b. 'Amr b. 'Uthmān 80
b. 'Anbasa 91
b. al-Arqam 69
b. Aus 69
b. Budail 92
b. al-Ḥārith 58
b. al-Ḥasan 91
b. Ja'far 50, 70
b. Jud'ān 102
b. Khalaf 70
b. Khālid 57-8
b. Marwān 108
b. Mas'ūd 80, 95
b. Mu'āwiya b. 'Abdallāh 134
b. Mu'āwiya b. Abī Sufyān 92
'Abdallāh (*contd.*)
b. Muslim 59
b. al-Muṭī' 70
b. Ṭāhir 108, 110, 135, 144
b. 'Ubaida 108
b. Ubayy 91
b. 'Umair 109
b. 'Umar b. 'Abd al-'Azīz 86
b. 'Utba 70
b. Yazīd 70
b. az-Zubair 43, 57-8, 70, 81, 86-7, 93, 109, 113
'Abd al-'Azīz
b. al-Ḥārith 108
b. Marwān 108
'Abd al-Jabbār b. 'Abd ar-Raḥmān 86
'Abd al-Malik
b. al-Ḥārith 108
al-Hāshimī 144
b. Marwān 47-8, 56-7, 69-70, 74, 81, 86, 93, 96, 108-10, 113, 119
b. 'Umair 110
b. 'Umar b. 'Abd al-'Azīz 101
'Abd Manāf 85
'Abd al-Muṭṭalib 43, 85
'Abd ar-Raḥmān
b. Abī Bakr 91
b. 'Auf 107
b. al-Ḥakam 91, 108
b. Ḥasan b. Thābit 91
b. Muḥammad b. al-Ash'ath 59, 74-5, 86
b. Salib 89
b. Ṣāliḥ 89
b. Yarbū' 90
'Abd aṣ-Ṣamad b. 'Alī 105
'Abd as-Samī' b. Muḥammad 62
'Abd al-'Uzzā b. 'Abd al-Muṭṭalib 87, 91
'Abd al-Wāḥid b. al-Ḥārith 108
'Abd al-Wārith b. Sa'īd 94
'Abda bint 'Abdallāh 80
Abdāl 118
Abel 38
Abū 'Abbād ar-Rāzī 129
Abū 'Abdallāh, Khwārazm-Shāh 104, 114
Abū Aḥmad
b. Abī Bakr 140
b. ar-Rashīd 105
Abū'l-'Ainā' 82
Abū 'Alī
al-Hā'im 145
al-Musabbaḥī 138
b. al-Qāsim 107
aṣ-Ṣaghānī 87
as-Sīmjūrī 87, 114
Abū 'Amr b. al-'Alā' 92
Abū'l-Aswad ad-Du'alī 109
Abū Ayyūb al-Mūryānī, 49
Abū Bakr 22, 43-4, 69, 80, 91, 102, 108, 113
Abū Bakr b. 'Abd ar-Raḥmān 95
Abū Burda b. Abī Mūsā 71, 74
Abū Dā'ūd adh-Dhu'lī 137
Abū'dh-Dhibbān 56
Abū Dulaf al-Khazrajī 31, 145-6
Abū'l-Faraj al-Babbaghā' 124
Abū Ḥafṣa family 23, 75-8
Abū Ḥanīfa 74, 102
Abū'l-Ḥasan
al-Jurjānī 144
al-Laḥḥām 118, 143
al-Māsarjisī 122
al-Maṣīṣī 145
Ṭabāṭabā 128

Abū Hudhaifa b. 'Utba 68
Abū Huraira 45-6
Abū'l-Ḥusain al-Murādī 129, 133
Abū Isḥāq az-Zajjāj 124
Abū Ja'far
al-Mūsawī 134
b. al-Qāsim 106
Abū Jahl 91-3, 102
Abū'l-Janūb b. Marwān 76, 78, 81
Abū Karib As'ad 42
Abū'l-Khair b. al-Khammār 4
Abū'l-Khaṭṭāb 120
Abū Lahab 57, 88, 91, 93, 145
Abū Manṣūr
b. 'Abd ar-Razzāq 134
al-'Abdūnī 65-6
Abū Ma'shar al-Munajjim 122
Abū Mūsā al-Ash'arī 70, 74
Abū Muslim 43, 86, 110, 137
Abū'l-Muthannā, Qāḍī 51
Abū Naṣr al-Marzubān 125
Abū Nuwās 63, 74, 99
Abū'l-Qāsim ad-Dā'ūdī 134
Abū Quḥāfa 94
Abū Sa'd Muḥammad 137
Abū Salama
b. 'Abd al-Asad 68
al-Khallāl 103
Abū Shaḥma b. 'Umar 91
Abū's-Simṭ Marwān 77-8
Abū Sufyān
b. Ḥarb 45, 68, 88, 90-2, 94, 102
b. al-Ḥārith 94
Abū Taghlib 24, 82
Abū Ṭālib 85, 93, 102
Abū Ṭālib al-Ma'mūnī 132, 134
Abū Ṭayyib aṭ-Ṭāhirī 140
Abū Turāb 56
Abū Turāb an-Nīshāpūrī 130-1
Abū 'Ubaida 25, 89, 91
Abū Umayya b. al-Mughīra 91
Abū Yaḥyā, the Angel of Death 131
Abū Zunbūr al-Mādharā'ī 144
al-Abyārī, Ibrāhīm vi-vii, 8, 18
Adam 38, 64, 143
'Adī
b. Ḥātim 94-5
b. Zaid 93
'Aḍud ad-Daula 24, 31, 82-4, 145-6
'Affān b. Abī'l-'Āṣ 9
al-Afshīn 111
Ahl al-Jizya 44
Aḥmad
b. 'Abdallāh 66
b. Abī Bakr 65-6
b. Abī Du'ād 112
b. Ja'far 64
b. Muḥammad 62
b. al-Mu'taṣim 105
as-Suhailī 4
al-Aḥnaf b. Qais 93-4
'Ā'id al-Kalb 54
Aiman b. Khuraim 94
'Ā'isha
bint 'Abdallāh 80
bint Ṭalḥa 79-81
Aitākh 111
al-'Ajjāj 54
'Ajūz al-Yaman 57
al-Akhḍar 54
al-Akhnas b. Sharīq 91
al-'Alā'
b. al-Ḥaḍramī 68
b. al-Ḥārith 90
b. 'Uqba 69
Alexander the Great or al-Iskandar or Dhū'l-Qarnain 41, 93, 135
'Alī
b. 'Abdallāh b. al-'Abbās 86, 95
b. 'Abdallāh b. Ja'far 86
b. Abī Ṭālib 43, 56, 68-9, 76-7, 79-80, 85, 93-4, 96, 108, 113, 119
b. Ḥamza 128
b. al-Ḥusain 86, 101
b. 'Īsā b. Māhān 50
b. al-Junaid 105
ar-Riḍā 101, 133
Zain al-'Ābidīn 101
'Alqama b. Qais 94
Amat al-Ḥamīd bint 'Abdallāh 81
al-Amīn 26, 74, 82, 98, 102, 106-7, 113, 125
Āmina
bint Sa'īd 81
bint Wahb 89
'Āmir
b. Kuraiz 92, 102
ash-Sha'bī 70, 96
b. aṭ-Ṭufail 92
Amlaḥ an-Nās 102
'Ammār b. Yāsir 94
'Amr
b. 'Abdallāh 74
'Amr (*contd.*)
b. 'Abd Manāf or Hāshim 42, 85
b. al-'Āṣ 89, 92, 102, 108
b. Laith 94, 113, 131, 138
b. Sa'īd 57, 70, 86
b. aṭ-Ṭulāṭila 88
b. az-Zubair 46
Anas b. Mālik 70, 93-4, 109, 123
Andrae, T. 25
Anṣār 69
'Antara b. Shaddād 93
Anūs or Enos 38
Anūshirwān 93
Aparwīz 72
'Aqīl b. Abī Ṭālib 94-5, 108
Aqra' b. Ḥābis 93
'Araq al-Maut 62
al-'Arrāq, Abū Naṣr 4
al-'Āṣ
b. Hishām 92, 102
b. Sa'īd 92
b. Wā'il 89, 92, 102
Asad, B. 69
Asad b. 'Abdallāh 60
Āṣaf b. Barakhyā 68
Aṣbagh b. 'Abd al-'Azīz 59
al-Ash'ath b. Qais 46-7, 75, 94
'Āshiq Banī Marwān 60
al-Ashtar an-Nakha'ī 94
'Āṣim b. 'Ubaidallāh 91
al-'Askarī, Abū Hilāl 19
Asmā' bint Abī Bakr 43
al-Aṣma'ī 123
A'ṣur 53
al-Aswad
b. 'Abd al-Yaghūth 89-90
b. al-Muṭṭalib 89
'Aṭā' b. Abī Rabāḥ 94
al-'Aṭawānī 65-6
al-'Aṭawī 65
'Ātika bint Yazīd 81
Aus b. al-Ḥakam 108
al-Auzā' 40
al-'Awwām 102
Ayyūb
b. Marwān 108
b. Salama 91
as-Sikhtiyānī 102

Bābak 110
Babba 58
Bādhinjānat al-Kātib 67
Bahrām
b. Bahrām 85
Gūr 41
Baihaqī, Abū'l-Faḍl 1, 13
al-Ba'īth 53

Bākharzī 1, 7, 9-11
Bakkār b. 'Abd al-Malik 92
al-Bal'amī 65
al-Barā' b. 'Āzib 94
al-Barīdī, Abū Manṣūr 24, 83
Barmakīs 111
Bashshār b. Burd 95
Bilāl b. Abī Burda 74
Bilqīs or the Queen of Sheba 40, 68
al-Bīrūnī, Abū'r-Raiḥān 3-4
Bishr
al-Marīsī 120
b. Marwān 108
Blachère, R. viii
Brockelmann, C. vi, 1, 8, 10
al-Buḥturī 66
Būrān 26, 99
al-Burqu'ī 110
Buṣr al-Ijjās 67
al-Bustī, Abū'l-Fatḥ viii, 10, 135-6, 144
Būyids 13, 18

Caetani, L. 1
Cain 38

aḍ-Ḍaḥḥāk b. Muzāḥim 96
ad-Dajjāl 91-2
Dā'ūd or David 40, 68, 134
Dā'ūd
b. 'Īsā 62
b. Marwān 108
Daulat Shāh 6
Defrémery, Ch. vi
Dhū'l-Kifl 85
Dhū'n-Nūn or Jonah 85
Dhū'r-Rumma 54, 95
Dhū Yazan 42
Dimna 102
Ḍirār 102
Dozy, R. vi, viii
Duhn ar-Rībās 67

Eve 64

al-Faḍl
b. al-'Abbās 96
b. ar-Rabī' 50, 74
b. Sahl 51
al-Fahmī, Thābit b. Jābir 20
Fā'iq Khāṣṣa 114
Fakhr ad-Daula 18
al-Faqīr 59
al-Fārābī 17
al-Farazdaq 58
Farda 102
Farīghūnids 114
Farqadān 41
Fāṭima 76-7, 79, 88
Fāṭimids 13-14, 27, 114
Firdausī 11
Flügel, G. v
Fück, J. viii
Furātīs 111

Gabrieli, G. 13
Gardīzī 1
Ghālib 106
Ghaznavids 1-2, 5-7, 13, 18
Ghubār al-'Askar 55
de Goeje, M. ix

Ḥabāba 60
Ḥabashiyya 102
Habbār b. al-Aswad 90-1
Ḥabīb
b. al-Ḥakam 108
b. Yaḥyā 108
al-Hādī 63, 76, 81, 102, 104-5, 107, 110, 113, 125
Ḥāḍir aṭ-Ṭūsī 138
Hagar 101
al-Hā'im, Abū 'Alī 31, 145
al-Haitham b. 'Adī 91, 96
al-Ḥajjāj 22, 47, 59, 70, 75, 110, 123
Ḥājjī Khalīfa 12
al-Ḥakam b. Abī'l-'Āṣ 88-9, 91, 102, 107
Ḥakīm b. Ḥizām 90
al-Hamadhānī, Badī' az-Zamān viii
Hamdān, B. 69
Ḥamdānids 13, 24
Ḥamdūna 99
Ḥamdūnī or Ḥamdawī, Abū Sahl 7
Ḥammād b. Abī Ḥanīfa 74
Ḥamza
b. 'Abd al-Muṭṭalib 44, 80
b. Muṣ'ab 74
Ḥarb b. 'Abd ar-Raḥmān 108
Harim b. Ḥayyān 96
Harīsat al-Hāshimī 67
al-Ḥārith
b. 'Abdallāh 58
al-Aṣghar 93
b. al-Ḥakam 108
b. al-Ḥārith 85
b. Ḥilliza 94
b. Hishām 90
b. Ka'b, B. 75
b. Qais 89
Hārūn or Aaron 68
Hārūn
b. al-Mu'taṣim 105
Hārūn (*contd.*)
ar-Rashīd 49-51, 55, 74, 76, 81-2, 87, 96, 98-9 102, 104-5, 107, 110, 113, 124-5, 133, 143-4
al-Ḥasan
b. 'Alī 47, 50, 77, 79-80, 88, 112-13
al-Baṣrī 70, 94-5
b. Qaḥṭaba 94
b. Rajā' 99
b. Sahl 26, 51, 99-100
Hāshim 87
Ḥassān b. Thābit 75, 94
Ḥāṭib b. 'Amr 68, 91
Ḥātim 42
Hazār 102
Hermes Trismegistus 147
Hibatallāh b. Ibrāhīm b. al-Mahdī 105
Hilāl aṣ-Ṣābi' 13
Ḥimyar 43
Hind
bint Abī Sufyān 58
bint Ḥamāṭa 80
Hishām
b. 'Abd al-Malik 80-1, 91, 93, 97, 113, 144
b. al-Kalbī 85
b. Shu'ba 91
b. al-Walīd 91
Ḥudhaifa
b. Badr 92
b. al-Yaman 69
Hurmuz b. Anūshirwān 95
al-Ḥusain
b. 'Alī b. Abī Ṭālib 50, 79-80, 110
b. 'Alī b. 'Īsā b. Māhān 106
b. al-Qāsim 73
b. Ṭāhir 108
b. Yaḥyā 110
al-Ḥuṭai'a 95
Ḥuwaiṭib b. 'Abd al-'Uzzā 68, 90

Ibāḍiyya 74
Iblīs or Satan 38, 40, 57
Ibn Abī'l-Aṣbagh 138
Ibn Aḥmar 94
Ibn al-'Amīd 27, 64, 124-5
Ibn 'Ayyāsh 91
Ibn Bassānı or al-Bassāmī 7, 62, 64-6
Ibn Duraid 6, 20
Ibn al-Faqīh 26
Ibn Farīghūn 17
Ibn Fāris 8
Ibn Fūrak 14
Ibn al-Jauzī 21
Ibn Khallikān 1, 7-8

Ibn Khurradādhbih 28
Ibn Langak al-Baṣrī 64, 123
Ibn Maṭrān ash-Shāshī 139
Ibn al-Muqaffa' 11
Ibn Muqbil 94
Ibn Muqla 98
Ibn al-Mu'tazz 9, 51, 78, 107, 113
Ibn Qutaiba viii, 12, 17, 19, 24-5
Ibn ar-Rūmī 41, 65-6, 147
Ibn Rusta 17, 19, 25-6
Ibn Sīnā or Avicenna 4
Ibn Zuraiq 125
Ibrāhīm or Abraham 39-40, 101, 116
Ibrāhīm
  b. al-'Abbās aṣ-Ṣūlī 66, 127
  b. 'Abdallāh b. Muṭī' 91
  b. 'Abd ar-Raḥmān b. 'Auf 95
  b. al-Mahdī 105-6
  b. Muḥammad 91
  an-Nakha'ī 94
  b. Nūḥ 98
  b. Ṣāliḥ 50
  b. al-Walīd 81
Idrīs or Enoch 22, 39, 68, 147
Ikhwān aṣ-Ṣafā' 147
Ilig Khan Naṣr 2
Ilyasa' or Elisha 85
'Imād ad-Daula b. Būya 83
'Imād ad-Dīn al-Iṣfahānī 11
Imru'ul-Qais 66
Iqbal, 'Abbās 5-6
'Īsā or Jesus or al-Masīḥ 85
'Īsā b. Mūsā 51
Isḥāq or Isaac 39
Ismā'īl or Ishmael 40, 101, 116
Ismā'īl
  b. 'Abbād, aṣ-Ṣāḥib 18, 125
  b. Aḥmad 65, 113, 132, 139
  b. Bulbul 108
  b. Ḥammād 74
  ash-Shāshī 129
  b. Ṣubaiḥ 51
Ismā'īlīs 14
Isrā'īl 85
Iṣṭakhrī 28

Jabala b. Aiham 95
Jābir b. 'Abdallāh 94
al-Ja'd b. Dirham 61
Jadhīma al-Abrash 41, 93
al-Ja'dī 61
Ja'far
  b. Abī Ṭālib aṭ-Ṭayyār 79-80, 88, 108
  b. Sulaimān al-Hāshimī 109, 123
  b. Yaḥyā al-Barmakī 124
al-Jaḥḥāf 96
al-Jāḥiẓ viii, 27, 30-1, 57, 77, 85-6, 101, 120-3, 125, 127-8, 142, 146
al-Jahshiyārī 22, 71
Jaḥẓa 64-5
al-Jaihānī 3 n. 7, 28, 30, 65, 140
Jamīla bint Nāṣir ad-Daula 24, 82-3
al-Jannābī, Abū Sa'īd 113
Jarīr
  b. 'Abdallāh 94-5
  b. 'Aṭiyya 96
Jarāda (= Aḥmad b. Muḥammad) 62
Jarāda (= Maslama b. 'Abd al-Malik) 60
al-Jazzār 59
Jibrīl or Gabriel 90
Jījak 102
Jirān al-'Aud 54
Jong, P. de v-vi, 17-18
Juml 77
Jurash, B. 80
al-Juwainī
  Abū'l-Ma'ālī 13
  Abū Muḥammad 13

Ka'b al-Baqar 62
Kābis b. Rabī'a 88
Kalb, B. 61
Karrāmiyya 13-14
Karb ad-Dawā' 62
Khadīja 43, 79-80
Khaiṭ Bāṭil 56
al-Khaizurān 81, 102
Khalī' Banī Marwān 60
Khālid
  b. 'Abdallāh 60
  b. Barmak 49
  b. Sa'īd 68
  b. Yazīd 81
Khalīfa b. Baww 109
al-Khalīl b. Aḥmad 94
Khāqān of the Turks 22, 73
Khārija b. Zaid 70
Kharrā' Nakhl 66
Khawārij 61, 74, 84
Khazars 145
Khudhaina 60
Khumār 49
Khuwailid 74
Khuzā'a, B. 74, 89
al-Khwārazmī
  Abū 'Abdallāh 17
  Abū Bakr viii, 119, 134
Kināna, B. 90
Kirghiz 145
al-Kisā'ī 19
Kulaib 92
Kulyat al-Jamal 67
al-Kumait 94
Kuraiz b. Rabī'a 91
Kusb al-Fujl 67
Kuthayyir 95
al-Kutubī, Ibn Shākir 13

Lail ash-Shitā' 67
Laṭīm al-Ḥimār 59
Laṭīm ash-Shaiṭān 57
Lecomte, G. viii, 17
Liḥyat at-Tais 66
Lijām ash-Shaiṭān 67
Lubāba
  bint 'Abdallāh 79
  bint al-Ḥārith 80
Luqmān 40-1

Ma'bad b. al-'Abbās 96
Mabramān 64
al-Madā'inī 102
Ma'dīkarib 75
Madnūn 52
Mahd al-Baqara 67
al-Mahdī 49, 62, 74, 76-7, 81-2, 98, 101-2, 104-5, 107, 113, 125
Maḥmūd
  of Ghazna 2, 4-6, 137
  b. Marwān 77-8
Maimandī, Aḥmad 6, 18, 35, 136
Maimūn b. Mihrān 70
Maimūna bint al-Ḥārith 80
Mālik 42
Mālik, B. 90
Mālik
  b. Anas 96
  b. Dīnār 102-3
  Shāh 14
al-Ma'mūn 26, 29, 51, 76, 82, 96, 98-100, 102, 107-8, 110, 112-13, 125, 129, 131, 133, 142
Ma'mūn
  b. Ma'mūn, Khwārazm-Shāh 4-5, 86, 143
  b. Muḥammad, Khwārazm-Shāh 114
Ma'mūnids 4-5
Manārat al-Khādim 67
al-Manṣūr 48-51, 61-2, 74, 82, 86, 98, 102, 105-8, 113, 125
Manṣūr
  b. al-Mahdī 105
  b. Nūḥ 95, 114

al-Maqdisī, Abū 'Abdallāh 3, 30
al-Maqdisī al-Bustī, al-Muṭahhar 3, 136
Marājil 102
Mārida 102
Marwān
b. Abī'l-Janūb 76, 78
b. al-Ḥakam 22, 46, 56, 69, 76, 81, 96, 107-8, 113
al-Ḥimār 61, 86-7, 93, 112
b. Sulaimān 76, 78
Maryam, Byzantine princess 73
Marzbān of Merv 102
Mash'ala 102
al-Masīḥī, Abū Sahl 4
Maslama b. 'Abd al-Malik 60, 101
Masrūq b. Ajda' 94
Mas'ūd of Ghazna 6-7
al-Mas'ūdī 27, 30
Mez, A. 10
Mīkālī, Abū'l-Faḍl 6
Miskawaih 64
Mu'ādh b. Muslim 50
Mu'aiqib b. Abī Fāṭima 69
al-Mu'allafa qulūbuhum 90
al-mu'ammarūn 109
Mu'āwiya
b. Abī Sufyān 45-8, 50, 68-70, 77, 81, 88, 92, 101, 104, 107-8, 113, 119
b. Yazīd 81, 113
b. Marwān 92, 108
al-Mu'ayyad b. al-Mutawakkil 110
Mubārak 49
Mubārak, Z. 9
al-Mubarrad 62-3, 75, 99
Mudrik b. al-Muhallab 108
al-Mughīra, B. 58
al-Mughīra b. Shu'ba 44-5, 70, 91-2, 94
Muhājirūn 43
al-Muhallab b. Abī Ṣufra 94, 108-9
Muḥammad the Prophet 18-19, 22-5, 42-5, 56, 68-9, 77, 79-80, 85, 88ff., 109, 113, 116-17, 146
Muḥammad
b. 'Abd ar-Raḥmān 73
b. Aḥmad 62
b. 'Ajlān 96
b. 'Alī b. 'Abdallāh b. al-'Abbās 86
b. 'Alī b. 'Abdallāh b. Ja'far 86
Muḥammad (*contd.*)
b. 'Alī b. al-Ḥusain al-Bāqir 86, 101
b. al-Ash'ath 75
b. al-Faḍl 80
b. Ḥabīb 16, 19, 23, 25
b. Ḥāṭib 43
b. Ilyās 83
al-Jawād 101
of Ghazna 7
b. Marwān 108
b. al-Qāsim 73, 95
b. Sa'd 59
b. Sallām 50, 80
b. Sīrīn 70, 94, 102
b. Sulaimān 49
b. Ṭāhir 108
b. al-Wāthiq 105
b. Zakariyā' 132
al-Muhtadī 73, 98, 102, 111, 113, 125
Muḥtājids 17
Mu'izz ad-Daula b. Būya 83
Mujammi' az-Zāhid 102
Mukhāriq 102
al-Mukhtār b. Abī 'Ubaid 94, 110
al-Muktafī 62, 73, 98, 102, 112-13, 125
al-Mumazziq 52
Munabbih b. al-Ḥajjāj 91-2
al-Muntaṣir 72, 77, 98, 102, 113, 125
Muqabbil ar-Rīḥ 55
Muqawwim an-Nāqa 60-1
al-Muqtadir 51, 62, 73, 87, 98-9, 102, 106-7, 111-13, 119, 126
Murād, B. 75
al-Muraqqish the Elder 94
al-Muraqqish the Younger 52
Murra, B. 48
Mūsā or Moses 40, 43, 68, 80
Mūsā Aṭbiq 62
Mūsā al-Kāẓim 101
Mūsā b. al-Ma'mūn 105
Mūsā Shahawāt 54
Mūsā b. 'Ubaida 108
Muṣ'ab b. az-Zubair 58-9, 74, 79-81, 110
Musawwida 61
al-Musayyab, Zuhair b. 'Alas 53
al-Musayyib 102
Muslim b. Mu'attib 88
al-Musta'īn 63, 102, 110, 113, 125
al-Mustakfī 95, 102, 113, 126
al-Mustaughir 53
al-Mu'taḍid 73, 98, 102, 108, 113, 125
al-Mutalammis 52
al-Mu'tamid 67, 73, 98, 102, 111, 113, 125
al-Mutanabbī viii
al-Mu'taṣim 76, 82, 98, 102, 105-8, 110-13, 125
al-Mutawakkil 26, 63, 66, 72, 77, 87, 98, 100, 102, 105, 109, 113, 120, 125
Mutawwaj b. Maḥmūd 78
Mu'tazila 147
al-Mu'tazz 26, 62-3, 72, 98, 100, 102, 110-11, 113, 125
al-Muṭī' 102, 113, 126
al-Muttaqī 95, 102, 113, 126
al-Muwaffaq 108, 138
al-Muzarrid 53

Nabataeans 129
an-Nābigha adh-Dhubyānī 52
an-Naḍr b. al-Ḥārith 91-2, 102
Naṣr, B. 90
Naṣr
b. Aḥmad the Elder, 104
b. Aḥmad b. Ismā'īl 65, 104
b. Sebüktigin 6, 136
Nāṣir ad-Daula b. Ḥamdān 83
an-Na'thal 56
Nicholson, R. A. 25
Nifṭawaih 63-4
Niqāb al-'Anz 67
Niẓām al-Mulk 13-14
Nubaih b. al-Ḥajjaj 92
an-Nu'mān b. al-Mundhir 73, 93
Nūḥ
b. Manṣūr 2, 87, 114
b. Naṣr 87
Nutaila bint Janūb 42

Pellat, Ch. viii, 31
Pharaoh 95

Qabīḥa 63, 102
al-Qādir 102
al-Qāhir 73, 95, 102, 113, 126
Qain b. Jasr, B. 52
Qaina 102
Qainān 102
Qais
b. 'Adī 90
b. Ma'dīkarib 75
b. Sa'd b. 'Ubāda 92, 94

al-Qalqashandī 19
Qarakhanids 2
Qarāmiṭa 83, 113
Qarāṭīs 102
Qārūn or Korah 41
al-Qāsim
  b. Muḥammad b. Abī Bakr 95, 101
  b. 'Ubaidallāh 73, 106
Qatāda b. Du'āma 94
Qaṭarī b. al-Fujā'a 87
al-Qubā' 58
Qudāma b. Ja'far 9, 26
al-Qufl al-'Aṣīr 67
Qulāba bint Rayyān 81
Qutham b. al-'Abbās 88, 96
Quraish 16, 24-5, 42, 44, 54, 56-7, 58, 88ff., 126
Quṣayy 85
al-Qushairī 13
Qutaiba b. Muslim 59, 102, 140
al-Quṭāmī 54

ar-Rabī' 74
ar-Rabī' b. Ziyād 70, 94
ar-Rāḍī 102, 113, 126
ar-Rāghib al-Iṣfahānī v
Raiḥān al-Kanīf 67
Raiṭa bint al-Ḥārith 101
Ramla bint az-Zubair 81
Rashḥ al-Ḥajar 56-7
Rauḥ b. Zinbā' 70, 119
Rescher (Reşer), O. vii-viii
Rijl aṭ-Ṭā'ūs 67
Rosenthal, F. 2
Rukn ad-Daula b. Būya 83
Ruqayya
  bint 'Abdallāh 80
  bint Muḥammad 79
ar-Ruqayyāt, Ibn Qais 54

Sa'd
  b. Abī Waqqāṣ 43, 95, 102
  b. Hishām 91
  b. Mālik, B. 53
Sadhāb 63
aṣ-Ṣafadī 7-9, 12
as-Saffāh 86, 98, 101, 113
Ṣafūrā 80
Ṣafwān b. Umayya 90
Sahl b. 'Amr 92
Sahm, B. 92
aṣ-Ṣairafī, Ḥasan Kāmil vi-vii, 8, 18
Ṣakhr b. Ḥarb 87
Salāma 102
Ṣāliḥ b. al-Ḥakam 108
Sālim b. 'Abdallāh 101
Sallāma 60
Salm b. 'Amr 105
Salmā bint 'Umais 80
Sāmānids 1-4, 13, 17, 65
Samij 63
Ṣamṣām ad-Daula 95, 114
Sarāwīl al-Ba'īr 67
Ṣarī' al-Ghawānī 55
Sāsānids 11, 21-2, 27
Sawwār
  b. 'Abdallāh 74
  b. Qudāma 74
Sa'īd
  b. 'Abd al-'Azīz 60
  b. al-'Āṣ 91
  b. al-Ḥārith 108
  b. Jubair 70
  b. al-Musayyib 102
  b. Nimrān 69
  b. 'Uthmān 45
Sebüktigin 2, 18
Seljuqs 2, 7, 14
Shabīb b. Shaiba 138
ash-Shābushtī 26
Shaghib 102
Shāh-Āfrīd 73, 81
Shahīd al-Balkhī 135
Shaḥm al-Ḥazīn 62
Shaiba b. Rabī'a 91
ash-Shammākh 53
Shāpūr Dhū'l-Aktāf 104
ash-Sharqī al-Quṭāmī 85
Shī'a, Shī'ism 13-14, 101, 109
Shīrūya b. Aparwīz 72-3
Shu'ba b. al-Ḥajjāj 96
Shujā' 102
Shūrā 101
Shuraiḥ b. al-Ḥārith 70, 94, 109
Shu'ūbiyya 12, 25
Sībawaih 8, 63-4
as-Sijistānī, Abū Ḥātim 20
Ṣūf al-Kalb 67
Sufyān b. 'Uyaina 38
Suhail b. 'Amr 90, 92
Sukaina bint al-Ḥusain 80-1, 95
Sulaim, B. 90
Sulaimān or Solomon 40, 68, 105
Sulaimān
  b. 'Abd al-Malik 80-1, 97, 113
  b. al-Manṣūr 105
  b. Mihrān 94
  b. Wahb 73
  b. Yaḥyā b. Abī Ḥafṣa 76
  b. Yaḥyā b. al-Ḥakam 108
aṣ-Ṣūlī
  Abū Bakr Muḥammad 22, 26, 71, 78, 106, 110, 113, 121, 130
  Ibrāhīm 66, 127
Sumayya Umm 'Ammār 44

Ta'abbaṭa Sharran 20, 53
aṭ-Ṭabarī, Abū Ja'far 12
Tābi'ūn 109
Ṭāhir
  b. 'Abdallāh 108, 140-1
  b. al-Ḥusain 94, 108
Ṭāhirids 133
aṭ-Ṭā'i' 102, 113, 126
Ṭalḥa b. 'Ubaidallāh 68, 70, 102
Ṭālib b. Abī Ṭālib 108
Tamīm, freedman of al-Manṣūr 106
T'ang dynasty 30, 141
Ṭarafa 53
ath-Tha'labī, Abū Isḥāq Aḥmad 19
Thābit b. Sinān 13, 95
Thaqīf 40, 90-1
Ṭimās 66
Toghuz-Oghuz 145

'Ubaida as-Salmānī 94
'Ubaidallāh
  b. al-'Abbās 47, 96
  b. 'Abdallāh b. Ṭāhir 113
  b. Abī Rāfi' 70
  b. Marwān 108
  b. Sulaimān 73
  b. Ziyād 48, 75, 94-5, 110, 112
Ubayy
  b. Ka'b 68
  b. Khalaf 92
Ufnūn 52
'Ujaif b. 'Anbasa 111
Umaima 53
'Umair b. al-Ḥubāb 43
'Umar
  b. al-Khaṭṭāb 22, 44-5, 59, 68, 70, 74, 80, 95-6, 108-9, 113
  b. 'Abd al-'Azīz 59-60, 70, 96-7, 113
  b. 'Abd ar-Raḥmān 108
  b. al-Ḥakam 108
  b. Marwān 108
  b. Nūḥ 110
'Umāra
  b. 'Aqīl 125
  b. Ḥamza 73-4
Umayya b. Khalaf 91, 102
Umayyads 21-2, 24, 26, 56, 59, 61, 77, 96-7
Umm 'Āṣim 59
Umm Jamīl 57
Umm Kulthūm bint 'Abdallāh 81
Umm Mūsā bint Manṣūr 102

Umm Sa'īd bint 'Abdallāh 80
'Uqail 42
'Uqba b. Abī Mu'aiṭ 88, 91-2, 102
'Utba
b. Abī Sufyān 91-2, 94
b. Abī Waqqāṣ 102
b. Rabī'a 93
al-'Utbī
Muḥammad b. 'Abdallāh 20
Muḥammad b. 'Abd al-Jabbār 1, 6, 9
Utrujja 62
'Uthmān
b. 'Abd ar-Raḥmān 108
b. 'Affān 21, 23, 45, 56, 68-70, 75, 79, 87, 94, 96, 102, 113
b. 'Anbasa 70
b. al-Ḥakam the Elder 108
b. al-Ḥakam the Younger 108
'Uwaif al-Qawāfī 53
'Uyaina b. Ḥiṣn 90, 93
'Uzair or Ezra 41, 61, 135

Valeton, J. P. v

Wahb b. Munabbih 57
Wajīhids 83 n.
al-Walīd
b. 'Abd al-Malik 48, 80-1, 97, 113
b. al-Mughīra 43, 89, 92, 102
b. 'Utba 79
b. Yazīd 60, 81, 97, 113
Wallāda bint al-'Abbās 81
al-Wāqidī 96
al-Warrāq 63
Wāṣil b. 'Aṭā' 94, 103
al-Wāthiq 29, 98, 102, 111-13, 125
Wushmagīr b. Ziyār 83

Yaḥyā
b. Abī Ḥafṣa 76
b. al-Ḥakam 108
b. Marwān 77-8
b. Mu'ādh ar-Rāzī 135
b. Sa'īd 94
Ya'qūb or Jacob 85
al-Ya'qūbī 27
Yarfā 45
Yazdajird 93
Yazīd
b. 'Abd al-Malik 60, 80-1, 93, 97, 113
b. Abī Muslim 70
b. Abī Sufyān 68
Yazīd (*contd.*)
b. Mu'āwiya 48, 50, 54, 101, 113
b. al-Muhallab 60, 102, 108
b. al-Walīd 22, 73, 81
Yūnus or Jonas 85
Yūsha' or Joshua 68
Yūsuf or Joseph 9, 21, 40, 45, 68, 72, 80, 122
Yūsuf
b. al-Wajīh 83
b. Yaḥyā 108

az-Zāgh 60
Zaid
b. Ḥāritha 43
b. al-Khaṭṭāb 96
b. Thābit 21, 68-9
Zainab bint Sulaimān 50
Ẓalūm 102
Zam'a 89-90
Zanj 144
Ẓill ash-Shaiṭān 59
Ziyād
b. Abīhi 45-6, 70, 92-3, 123
b. al-Muhallab 108
b. Ṣāliḥ 140
Zotenberg, H. 8, 11, 17-18
Zubaida 49, 81-2, 99, 102
az-Zubair
b. al-'Awwām 74, 102
b. Bakkār 80
Zuhra 102

2

Places, rivers, battles

Ābaskūn 135
Abhar 83
Abyssinia 43
al-Aḥsā' 83
Ahwāz 29, 83, 117, 126-7, 129, 131, 138, 145-6
Alexandria 28, 119
Āmul 66
Antioch 117, 143
al-'Aqr 108
Armenia 29, 129, 142, 144-5
Arrajān 146
'Askar Mukram 126
Azerbaijan 144
al-Azhar 14
Babylon 141
Badakhshān 132
Badr 44
Baghdad or Madīnat as-Salām 16, 21, 27, 29, 48, 66-7, 87, 105-6, 121, 123-5, 131, 133, 145-6
Baḥrain 45, 144-5
Balkh 87, 132, 135-6, 145
Bāmiyān 87
Bardha'a 141, 145
Basra 29, 45-6, 48-9, 58, 70, 94, 123-4
Bawwān defile 119
Bukhārā 3, 17, 27, 139-40, 145
Bulghār 145
Bust 18, 27, 114, 136-7, 146
Buzurgvār 99-100

Cairo 14
Camel, Battle of the 74, 76, 94
Ceylon 29, 132
Chaghāniyān 17
China 27, 29-31, 140-2, 145
Constantinople 131

Dair al-'Āqūl 126
Dair al-Jāthalīq 74
Damascus 28, 118-19, 131
Dārābjird 128
Dehistān 145
Diyār Bakr 83
Diyār Rabī'a 83

Edessa 28, 119
Egypt 29, 87, 114, 120-2, 132, 135, 138, 143, 145
Euphrates 35, 121, 124, 136

Fam aṣ-Ṣilḥ 26, 99-100
Fārs 28, 49, 70, 83, 127-8, 138, 145
Fijār, War of 74
al-Fusṭāṭ 87

Ganges 122
Ghazna 4, 6, 27, 137-8
Ghūṭa 119
Gurgān 29, 83, 104, 126, 130-1, 137, 143, 146
Gurgānj 4, 114
Gūzgān 114

Ḥaḍramaut 29, 40
Hajar 113, 145
Hamadhān 94

Ḥarrān 119, 138
al-Ḥasaniyya 125-6
Helmand 138
Herat 29, 134-5, 145
Ḥijāz 101, 119, 145
Ḥimṣ 118
al-Ḥīra 92, 112
Ḥulwān 146
Hurmuz 104
Huzū 84

Ifriqiyya 96
India 27, 29, 122, 126, 135, 139, 146
Iraq 27, 30, 60, 83, 101, 117, 119, 126, 130-1, 135-6, 144-5
al-'Irḍ 52
'Īsā-ābād 125
Iṣfahān or Jayy 17, 29, 83, 87, 128, 131, 133, 145-6

al-Jazīra 131, 145
Jerusalem or al-Bait al-Maqdis or Īlyā' 39, 87
Jibāl 18, 83, 110, 114, 131
Jibāl ash-Shurāt 84
Jundīshāpūr 131, 138
Jūr 29, 127, 146

Ka'ba, the 38, 42-3, 82, 116-17
Kāshghar 145
Kāth 87
Khaibar 145
Khurāsān 2-7, 12-13, 27, 45, 59-60, 87, 104, 120, 129-31, 135
Khuttal 135
Khwārazm 2-5, 27-9, 87, 104, 142-3
Kirmān 83, 98, 138, 146
Kūfa 103, 109-10, 123-4, 146

Lebanon Mts. 118
al-Lukkām 118

Maghrib 31, 132, 142
Maimand 18
Mahra 75
Maisān 129, 145
Manbij 144
Marghāb 88
Marīs 120-1
Māsapadhān 104, 125
Maṣīṣa 144
Māskān 146
al-Mirbad 123
Mecca 20, 24, 27, 43, 69, 87, 89-90, 109, 116-17, 119, 125
Medina or Ṭaiba 27, 29, 46, 69-70, 87, 96, 101, 109, 117-19, 145
Merv or Merv ash-Shāhajān 12, 28-9, 102, 135, 142, 145-6
Mosul 83, 128-9

Nile 122-3
Nīshāpūr 1-3, 7, 13-14, 21, 28-9, 66-7, 87, 131-3, 135, 143, 145
Niẓāmiyyas 14

Oxus or River of Balkh 45, 121, 135

Peshawar or Farshāpūr 131
Pyramids 122

al-Qaddūm 39
Qala' 123, 143
Qālīqalā 129, 145
Qandābīl 108
Qandahār 18
Qāshān 83
Qazwīn 145
al-Qubba al-Khaḍrā' 106
Qudaid 74
Qum 83, 129, 146

ar-Raqqa 131
Ray or al-Muḥammadiyya 18, 28-9, 83, 87, 129-30, 143, 145-6
Rūm or Byzantium, Greeks 29, 131, 138-9, 145
Rūyān 142

as-Sairawān 146
Samarqand 27-9, 59-60, 88, 96, 119-20, 131, 140-1, 144-6
Sāmarrā 30, 120, 125
Ṣanja 119
Sarakhs 114
Sawād 138
Shahrazūr 138, 145
Shāpūr 131
ash-Shiḥr 29, 139, 146
Shīrāz 31, 128, 145
Ṣiffīn 46
Sīstān 6, 86-7, 136, 138-9, 145
Soghdia 119
Sumatra 146
as-Sūs 126, 145
Syria 29, 42, 89-90, 96, 117-19, 131, 145

Ṭabaristān 75, 83, 130
Ṭā'if 96
Takrīt 142
Ṭālaqān 31, 142
Tarsus 96, 125, 139
Tawwaj 145
Tiberias 144
Tibet 29-30, 139, 142, 146
Tigris 84, 121, 124, 138
Transoxania 104, 131
Ṭukhāristān 137, 141, 144-5
Turks, Turkish lands 139, 142, 145
Ṭūs 29, 96, 125, 133-4, 146
Tustar 126
Ṭuwā 43

Ubulla 119, 145
'Umān 83, 132

Wādī'l-Qaṣr 29, 123
Wadī's-Sibā' 74

Yamāma 61
Yarmūk, Battle of the 94
Yathrib 87
Yemen 27, 29, 43, 57, 59, 122-3, 132, 138, 143, 145

Zābulistān 137
Zamīndāwar 18
Zanjān 83
Zarang 87
Zauzan 29

3

Products, specialities, etc.

adab 15-16, 28
aloes-wood 29, 139, 146
ambergris 29, 139, 146
amīrī apples 137-8
amīrī cloth 142-3
'ammāriyya 82
anbijāt, mango preserve 128
apples 29, 118, 145
apricots 130
āranj cloth 142
'aṣabāt 76 n.
asbestos table-napkins 141
ashdaq 57 n.
'attābī cloth 28, 133
awā'il 19
azraq 93 n.

bāranj melons 29, 142
Barīd 28, 104–5
binn, binnī fish 65
black fox 142
b.nāk.r.k bird 139
bows 142
buzyūn brocades 139

camphor 145
carpets 29, 129, 145
Chinese porcelain 141
chrysolites 132
cloaks 29, 128-9, 145
cloves 139
combs 129
cornelians 123, 132
curtainings 129

Dabīqī cloth 46, 143
dhawū'l-arḥām 76 n.
dūghbāj 137
durrā'a 3

elephants 139
ermine 142, 145

fanak, mink 142, 145
fānīdh, sugar-cane syrup 146
farmānī squirrel skins 141-2
faṣl al-khiṭāb 40
felts 31, 142
figs 130, 136, 146
frankincense 123

garnets 132, 136
glass 29, 118
gold 142
goshawks 142
grey squirrels 142, 145
gum mastic 139

ḥafī textiles 28, 131, 133, 143, 145
ḥaram 116-17
harīsa 67 n.
hawāṣil 134–5, 145
al-Ḥimār 61
honey 29, 128-9

'Īd al-Jiṭr 47
al-īlāf 42

jade 142
jammāzāt 49
jet 29, 133-4
jujubes 130, 146
Jūrī rosewater 29, 127

kāmakh pickles 65
khadang hardwood 142
khaish, canvas sheeting 48
khallālūn 103
khiṭr dyestuff 123
khudhain 60
Khurāsānī garments 98
khutuww, ?fossil ivory 142
kimkhāw silks 141
kuḥl, antimony 128
kunya 20

laqab 19-21
laṭaf 79 n.
linens 120, 145

madīra 46
malāḥim 24
Malwiya 120
maqṣūra 45
Marawī, Marvazī cloths 98, 135
Marīsī asses 29, 120, 141, 145
Marvazī turbans 98
mathālib 91
mercury 140
mihmān 41
miswāk 39
mongoose 120-1
mubram cloth 131
mulabban confectionery 135, 146
mulḥam cloth 28, 145
mūmiyā, mummy 128
munayyar cloth 28, 129, 143, 145
murrī brine 135, 142
musk 139, 142, 146
musnad 122

nadd muthallath 139 n.
narcissus 130
nisba 20
nuql, edible earth 29, 128, 131-2
nutmegs 139

paper 29, 120, 140, 147-8
papyrus 29, 120, 140, 148
parchment 140
parrots 139
peacocks 139
pearls 132
plums 136, 146
pomegranates 129-30, 146
'poppy-coloured' cloths 131, 143

qadar 41, 147
qadūm 39
Qaṣab fārisī, Giant reed 98
qaṭūnā seeds 130
qishmish raisins 29, 134

raḥqīn cheese 142
raisins 128
rākhtaj silks 133
rhinocerus 139
rībās, rhubarb 131, 137
rikābī olive oil 29, 118
rubies 132, 139

sable martens 142, 145
sāburī cloth 28, 133
saffron 123, 128-9, 146
salted fish 142
sandalwood 130
sapphires 132
saqlaṭūnī cloth 133, 145
satin brocades 126, 135, 139, 145
sawīq 41, 82
scammony 139
scorpions 126-7, 138, 145
Shāhajānī cloths 135
shārak bird 139
shears 129
Shu'aibī garments 98
silks 126, 145
sipāya, tripod 49
slaves 49, 101, 140-2, 145
spikenard 139
sweeping-brushes 135
swords 29, 122-3
sugar, sugar-cane 29, 127, 129, 146

ṭā'a, obedience 119
Ṭā'fī raisins 134
ṭailasān 3
tākhtaj cloth 133
ṭā'ūn, plague 119
Tawwajī cloth 128, 145
terra sigillata or Lemnian earth 139
tharīd 42
thu'bān, poisonous serpent 120, 138, 145
tigers 139
ṭirāz 120
towels 130
turkeys 139
turquoises 131-2
tūtiyā, zinc oxide 139

ushtur-gāv-palang, giraffe 122
utrujj citrons 130

velvets 139
vipers 127, 138, 145

Wadhārī cloth 28, 140
walī al-'ahd 45
white mountain hare 142
woollens 142

yaks 142
Yazanī lances 42

zhāla, inflatable pontoons 137
zinā 91 n.
zindīq, *zandaqa* 92

4

Book titles

K. Ādāb al-mulūk al-Khwārazmshāhī 5
Aḥāsin kalim an-nabī wa'ṣ-ṣaḥāba v, 16
Aḥsan at-taqāsīm 30
al-A'lāq an-nafīsa 17, 19
K. al-Amṣār 30
Arabian nights 148
K. al-Aurāq 26, 98

K. al-Bad' wa't-ta'rīkh 3
Bard al-akbād 4, 28

K. adh-Dhakhīra 7
K. ad-Diyārāt 26
Dumyat al-qaṣr 1, 11

Faḍl al-'Arab 'alā'l-'Ajam 12
Fiqh al-lugha 9
al-Fuṣūl al-fārisiyya 12

Ghurar al-maḍāḥik 16

Ḥilyat al-muḥāḍara 16

Iḥṣā' al-'ulūm 17
K. al-Iqtibās 9
K. al-Ishtiqāq 20

al-Jawāhir al-ḥisān 12
Jawāmi' al-'ulūm 17

Kanz al-kuttāb 15
Kashf an-niqāb 21
Kharīdat al-qaṣr 11
Khāṣṣ al-khāṣṣ 15
Khudāy-nāma 11
K. al-Kināya wa't-ta'rīḍ 5, 9

K. al-Laṭā'if wa'ẓ-ẓarā'if 5, 16

K. al-Ma'ārif 17, 19, 24-5
Mafātīḥ al-'ulūm 17
Mā jarā bain al-Mutanabbī wa-Saif ad-Daula 8
Makārim al-akhlāq 12
K. al-Masālik wa'l-mamālik 28, 30, 140
Miftāḥ al-faṣāḥa 9
K. al-Muḥabbar 16-17, 19, 23, 25
Muḥāḍarāt al-udabā' v
K. al-Munammaq 25
Mu'nis al-udabā' 5
Mu'nis al-waḥīd v
Murūj adh-dhahab 30
K. al-Mutashābih 6

Nashr an-naẓm 5
Naẓm fiqh al-lugha 9

Qiṣaṣ al-anbiyā' 19
Qur'ān 20-1, 25, 122

K. ar-Ru'asā' wa'l-jilla 144

Shāh-nāma 11
K. Siḥr al-bayān 9
K. aṣ-Ṣinā'atain 19
Sirāj al-mulūk 5, 16
Sirr al-wizāra 16
K. as-Siyāsa 16
Ṣubḥ al-a'shā 19
Sūrat al-masad 145

K. at-Tabaṣṣur bi't-tijāra 30-1, 142
K. at-Tajnīs 9
at-Tamthīl wa'l-muḥāḍarāt 9
K. at-Tanbīh 30
Ta'rīkh ghurar as-siyar 1-3, 6, 10-13
Ta'rīkh ar-rusul wa'l-mulūk 12
Ta'rīkh Thābit b. Sinān aṣ-Ṣābi' 95
Tatimmat al-yatīma 5, 10
Thimār al-qulūb v, 6, 8-9, 28

'Uyūn at-tawārīkh 13

al-Wāfī bi'l-wafayāt 7
K. al-Wuzarā' (of Jahshiyārī) 22, 71
K. al-Wuzarā' (of Ṣūlī) 22, 71

Yatīmat ad-dahr v, viii, 1, 3-5, 8, 10, 12, 22, 71

K. aẓ-Ẓarf min shi'r al-Bustī 10